COLD
PEACE

COLD
PEACE

Avoiding the New Cold War

MICHAEL DOYLE

Liveright Publishing Corporation

A Division of W. W. Norton & Company
Celebrating a Century of Independent Publishing

For information about permission to reproduce selections from this book, write to
Permissions, Liveright Publishing Corporation, a division of W. W. Norton & Company, Inc.,
500 Fifth Avenue, New York, NY 10110

For information about special discounts for bulk purchases, please contact
W. W. Norton Special Sales at specialsales@wwnorton.com or 800-233-4830

Manufacturing by Lake Book Manufacturing
Book design by Chris Welch
Production manager: Anna Oler

ISBN 978-1-63149-606-6

Liveright Publishing Corporation, 500 Fifth Avenue, New York, N.Y. 10110
www.wwnorton.com

W. W. Norton & Company Ltd., 15 Carlisle Street, London W1D 3BS

1 2 3 4 5 6 7 8 9 0

For
Leah Maeve Jurek
in hope that her generation will
live in peace

Contents

COLD
PEACE

Introduction

From Cold War
to Cold Peace

It is now increasingly clear that the post–Cold War era is over. This makes me remember with nostalgia that wonderful day in 1988 at the UN General Assembly when the Cold War began to end, the day when Mikhail Gorbachev declared human rights were not just Western (as they were seen to be during the Cold War) but human and global.[1] The Berlin Wall fell, the Warsaw Pact crumbled, and then the USSR collapsed and Russia began to democratize. And, in 1989, young Chinese erected a statue of liberty in Tiananmen Square,[2] heralding the possibility of a liberal "spring" spreading to the other Communist great power.

The early 1990s were hopeful times but also times of missed opportunity. I share some of the sad irony expressed by the great Cold War novelist, David Cornwell (pen name John le Carré), who said in 2001 that the right power lost the Cold War, but the wrong one won it.[3] In 2020, le Carré elaborated through a 1990 comment of the character he identified with, George Smiley: "One day, history may tell us who really won. If a democratic Russia emerges—why, then Russia will have been the winner. And if the West chokes on its own materialism, then the West may still turn out to be the loser."[4] Le Carré hoped for a peace without victors in a newly constructed international order. Unfortunately, we entered an era of US unipolarity mixed with much arrogance.

Russia descended into populist and, later, autocratic kleptocracy, and Eastern Europe fled west into dependency on NATO and the European Union. China succeeded in borrowing the market while holding democracy at bay.

Today, in the emerging new cold war, we are paying the price for a failure of creativity in the 1990s. And, it is more serious than it appeared just a few years ago; it is more dangerous than just traded insults. Ukrainians today are bearing the costs as they valiantly attempt to defend their national independence.

Instead of marking the end to strife over ideology and the start of an ever-growing international liberal order of peace and cooperation or a return to a classical multipolar balance of power, the post–Cold War era is being followed by a new cold war. This is a war—so far, cold—among great powers and between clashing systems of government. It is characterized by industrial competition, information subversion, and cyber warfare.

None of this has escaped the politicians. President Biden concluded his first news conference of 2021 with these words: "I predict to you," he told reporters, "your children or grandchildren are going to be doing their doctoral thesis on the issue of who succeeded: autocracy or democracy? Because that is what is at stake."[5]

This new geopolitical world has grave implications for the curbing of climate change, the promotion of human rights, and the protection of national security. Citizens around the world need a more concerted effort to manage global security tensions and a more careful but determined human rights strategy, both adapted to these times and designed to ensure that the post–Cold War era transcends the war in Ukraine and turns into, at least, a cold peace.

For the United States, such an effort must include much more careful and coherent diplomacy with both Russia and China, aimed at establishing a détente that is based on a mutual nonsubversion understanding. It must also instigate substantial reforms in domestic policy aimed at establishing resilience and reinforcing a more egalitarian order. Enhancing liberal security, promoting prosperity, and supporting human rights calls for reasserting international rule-of-law principles, reaffirming existing alliances, addressing domestic inequalities in some liberal democracies, and improving trade regimes—all are necessary to foster conditions for better times in international relations.

Fortunately, while there is a danger of *a* cold war, there is no danger of replaying *the* Cold War. Cold War II is unlikely to be as extreme as Cold War I. Three factors weigh against escalation. The first is a rational appreciation of the likely costs of a cold war between the United States and China. One need only recall that China has had an economic growth rate more than twice that of the United States, a GNP close to that of the United States, and a population three times that of the United States. The second is an unprecedentedly large global common interest in mutually dependent prosperity and protecting the planet from environmental deterioration. The third is that Russia and China are authoritarian, not totalitarian. Putinism is not Stalinist Communism, Xi-ism is not Maoism, and no one is a Nazi.

Yet the United States, Russia, and China are unlikely to establish a "warm" peace, such as that enjoyed within Western Europe or between Europe and the United States and its other allies.

None of the powers are unusually aggressive. In recent years, the United States did invade Afghanistan and Iraq (the latter on the basis of very faulty intelligence) and intervened with allies in Libya and Syria. Russia invaded Georgia and Ukraine (twice). China asserts territorial claims over the South China Sea and demands sovereignty over self-ruling Taiwan.

The deeper source of global conflict is defensive. The United States and its allies do not want to impose democracy by force.[6] They want to make "a world safe for democracy" in which national security is affordable, elections are secure, markets are free, and in which human rights remain an ideal. China and Russia do not seek to impose autocracy for its own sake. They, correspondingly, seek "a world safe for autocracy" in which governments are free to have or not have elections and human rights, markets and information are subject to state direction, and no one outside the government questions state policy. Both sides are threatened because those two visions (both systemic, so-called *milieu* goals) are incompatible, unless both sides agree to difficult compromises.

Restoring the prospect of diplomatic accommodation will be difficult after the shock, war crimes, and severe retaliatory sanctions generated by the invasion of Ukraine. But even the worst wars end. Cold War détente followed the war in Vietnam and the Soviet invasion of Czechoslovakia.

Cold war strife can develop into a compromise, a cold peace détente, if a nonsubversion pact can be implemented; that is, if neither side attempts to attack the political independence or territorial integrity of the other. Critical debates over promoting national interests and human rights should remain permissible, but they need to be accompanied by negotiations over cyber conflict, industrial competition, Ukraine, Taiwan, and the South China Sea. The United States needs to develop a defense in depth: protecting the democratic process against cyberattack and launching a New Deal to address the domestic inequalities that fuel subversion in contemporary democracies (like the attempted putsch on January 6, 2021, in Washington, DC).

In this book, I will paint a picture of the dangers of a new cold war that we are approaching. Although the tensions between the United States and China and Russia are dominating world politics, we should not assume that they are the only source of insecurities, and I will identify them as well.

I will outline the definitions and contours of the emerging new cold war in Part One of this book. In Part Two, I will argue that like the original Cold War, this is a deeply structured conflict, both internationally and transnationally. Inspired by the logic of bipolarity and of hegemonic transition internationally, some (most notably Graham Allison) have warned of a new "Thucydides Trap," wherein a rising power challenges slipping powers, and war resolves the rivalry. Transnationally, the conflict is a domestically driven political rivalry between social and political systems, with each having supported subversive domestic transformation. The new technologies of cyber warfare and information war are enabling conditions, but what is important today is the weaponization of those technologies in a deadly rivalry.

The conflict reinforces itself. Some notable American statesmen, the late Senator John McCain prominent among them, have identified a new cold war in Russian subversive threats. They have called for an alliance of democracies to confront those threats. What the McCain analysis misses are the ways in which the United States has threatened Russia and China with the advance of NATO eastward and a post-Cold War declared military strategy of global predominance. I am not unsympathetic to the value of better coordinating the democracies. In the later 1930s, eloquent (but ineffective) pleas were made to unite them, but today, the threat from the autocracies is neither sufficiently extreme nor appreciated enough to sustain a fully united response. And the policy differences among the democracies preclude tight coordination across the broad spectrum of issues that would be needed for a formal, institutionalized alliance.

Others cite just the factors McCain neglects and describe an aggressive Western campaign against Russia and China that the Russians and Chinese have simply been defending themselves against by creating buffer zones in Ukraine and Georgia and the South China Sea. These strategists underplay the internal drivers of nationalism, corporatism, and autocracy—and the connection among the three—that drive foreign campaigns for prestige and resources by those powers. The new autocracies employ state power in international corporate competition and cultivate external enemies to validate the need for internal oppression.

In considering these domestic drivers of conflict, I will make distinctions among forms of corporatism (including the kinds imposed by the state through planning and those arising from below in various forms of cronyism) and among forms of nationalism and autocracy. I will also explore how these interrelate and make, in varying ways, stable relations between them and the varieties of capitalism, liberalism, and democracy immensely difficult.

The new cold war that I describe would be clear were it not for the US 2016 election. Donald Trump was not the root cause but an anomaly in this conflict. Indeed, the new cold war would be clearer and more confrontational had Hillary Clinton become president with her commitments to human rights, democracy, and global markets. Although Trump's style, personality, and preferences resembled no contemporary leader as much as they did Vladimir Putin, the Trump-Putin bromance was no guarantee of cooperative US-Russia relations. Trump is an exacerbating force in this new cold war because of his militarism, instability, and unpredictability. Now with President Joe Biden in office, these global divides between democracy and autocracy have become clearer, and President Biden has not de-escalated the new cold war but instead driven it forward.

In Part Three, I explore the new cold war's important historical analogues. Contrary to some pundits, I explain that Putin is not Stalin, Xi is not Mao, and no one today is Hitler. Yet I will also highlight that there are important links between twentieth-century Fascism and twenty-first-century "corporatist, nationalist autocracy." There are fascinating links between the ideology and policies of Putinism and the ideas and policies of Mussolini in his attacks on Ethiopia and intervention in the Spanish Republic. As MacGregor Knox has argued, Mussolini tried to seize military glory and expand his foreign control in order to support his campaign to build a domestic Fascist state. There are even important links between the strategic environment and choices made by the Japanese military regime of the 1930s and the environment confronted and policies chosen by President Xi Jinping in China today. I do not say that we are about to replay World War II. Nuclear deterrence, geoeconomics, and other differences are vitally significant. But we have much to learn from the circumstances the statesmen of the Interwar period faced and the mistakes they made.

In Part Four, I will provide evidence that another cold war is not inevitable and outline vital compromises that can make a cold peace viable. However, the domestic structural roots of the conflict make it unlikely that the United States, Russia, and China will establish a "warm" peace, such as that enjoyed within Western Europe or among Europe and the United States, Canada, Australia, and Japan.

The Cold War cost $11 trillion (1990 dollars) in US defense spending alone. Though "cold" by and large between the superpowers, it helped produce 14 million casualties in proxy wars and stimulated conflicts.[7] Our concern today is what the new cold war means not only for global security but also for a more humane world in which human rights and the planet can be protected. My claim clearly is that these are not good times for global security, world prosperity, environmental resilience, or human rights.

I will thus conclude by suggesting that we need a more concerted effort to manage global security tensions by developing compromises and common ground on climate, cyber relations, Ukraine, and Taiwan. The United States and its allies need new thinking in order to design a more careful but determined human rights strategy adapted to these times, in hopes of fostering the conditions for better times in which competition is waged if not in entente at least in détente, in a cold peace, replacing a looming cold war. In a cold peace, no great power attempts to subvert the political independence or territorial integrity of another. That is not the world we are in today, where both are challenged. Basic security is at risk, and human rights are on defense.

The world can evolve from a cold war confrontation to a cold peace détente if the major powers implement a nonsubversion pact. Critical debates over promoting national interests and human rights should remain permissible, but they need to be accompanied by negotiations over Crimea and the South China Sea. Détente may encourage a more moderate policy from Russia and China, but expectations there need to be limited. In the meantime, the United States needs to protect the democratic process against cyberattack. It also needs to cultivate a more centrist and responsible leadership. But because the rise of white nationalism backing President Trump is associated with the erosion of the middle class, the United States and other liberal countries will need to launch something like a New Deal to address the domestic inequalities that fuel populism in contemporary democracies.

In the end, we must understand the threat of a new cold war and take measures to curb it, lest we burden a new generation with a long twilight struggle of arms races and missed opportunities to address global challenges. Above all, we must strive for a détente in which covert operations directed against domestic political institutions and vital infrastructure are taken off the table in the name of mutual survival and global prosperity. This book is an invitation to begin that project.

Part One

◆

A NEW
COLD WAR?

■ **IN 2021, AS US TIES WITH RUSSIA**
and China came under increasing strain after the surge in Russia-based cybercrimes and in human rights violations by the Chinese Communist Party (CCP), a NATO summit adopted a more united stance against the "systemic threats" to the "rules-based international order" posed by Russia and China. NATO merged the two states as a dual threat to the NATO alliance once focused almost exclusively on the USSR/Russia. The G7 nations, including the United States, United Kingdom, France, Canada, Japan, Italy, and Germany, met days later and similarly criticized China for abuses relating to Xinjiang, Hong Kong, and Taiwan. After the NATO and G7 summits, Chinese Foreign Ministry spokesperson Zhao Lijian responded that the Western nations were "deliberately slandering China" and added: "It is fair to say that the China-Russia comprehensive strategic partnership of coordination for the new era is all-dimensional and all-weather. . . . Sky is the limit for down-to-earth China-Russia cooperation." When the G7 discussed the US evacuation of Afghanistan, China and Russia provocatively called for accountability for the harms inflicted by the US military on Afghan civilians. When China perceived increased coordination between India and the United States, it called them "enemies."[1]

CHAPTER ONE

Defining Cold War

The possibility of an emerging new cold war is grabbing the attention of statespersons and scholars. Former US secretary of state Henry Kissinger said the United States and China were in the "foothills of a Cold War" and warned that the conflict could be worse than World War I if left to run unconstrained. "That makes it, in my view, especially important that a period of relative tension be followed by an explicit effort to understand what the political causes are and a commitment by both sides to try to overcome those," Kissinger told a session of the New Economy Forum. "It is far from being too late for that, because we are still in the foothills of a cold war." Kissinger also noted: "Everybody knows that trade negotiations, which I hope will succeed and whose success I support, can only be a small beginning to a political discussion that I hope will take place."[1]

"The Cold War is back with a vengeance, but with a difference," UN secretary-general António Guterres declared, explaining: "The mechanisms and the safeguards to manage the risks of escalation that existed in the past no longer seem to be present."[2] H. R. McMaster, the second strategic guru of the early days of the Trump administration, heralded an emerging geopolitical struggle. In a speech previewing the Trump administration's new National Security Strategy (discussed later), he invoked warlike images of the current order with "threats to liberty and freedom" from terrorist groups, the "revisionist powers" of China and Russia, and the "rogue regimes" of Iran and North Korea as akin to the threats that the United States and its allies previously encountered from "fascism, imperialism, and communist totalitarianism."[3] And eminent scholars of international history, such as Lawrence Freedman, describe a "New Cold War" characterized by "[a]ssassination attempts, cyber-attacks, military interventions—Russia is once again playing a deadly game with the West. Yet beneath the bravado is a nation riddled with insecurities."[4] Voices from the Progressive Left have added their perspective, as did Michael Klare in a clarion piece in *The Nation* in which he highlighted the mutually provocative nuclear use doctrines of Trump and Putin, their return to Cold War–style nuclear technological racing, and the declaration by Xi that he has no term limit.[5]

Cold War Sovietologist Robert Legvold reluctantly came to the view that the rising tensions between Russia and the United States following the crisis in Ukraine amounted to a *Return to Cold War*. He added that both elements of his thesis "that the deterioration in relations amounts to a cold war and that each bears responsibility . . . will stir strong dissent."[6] But in a well-argued study, he nonetheless declared that the evidence bore his conclusion out. He then traced how the deterioration in relations came about. This book agrees with him but finds a broader realm of tension, including with China, and explores the deeper political, economic, and social roots of the new cold war divide.[7]

Others, of course, have disagreed. The president of the right-wing Hudson Institute (Kenneth Weinstein) rejects the label of "cold war" as applied to US-China relations, noting the good personal chemistry between Trump and Xi and the immense economic costs of such a conflict.[8] Others imaginatively formulate new labels, including "Hot Peace" (Michael McFaul, former US ambassador to Russia) and "Cool War" (Noah Feldman, international legal scholar), both evoking the genuine ambiguities that shape the emerging rivalry.[9]

Secretary of State Antony Blinken also rejected the label "new Cold War," but his subsequent remarks sounded like a rallying cry for another long struggle. He said he saw the relations between the United States and China as "complex"—reflecting a mix of aspects. He noted "adversarial aspects . . . competitive aspects . . . cooperative aspects—all three."[10] But of course, the US-Soviet Cold War was also complex: adversarial, competitive, and also cooperative (as extensive arms control treaties and nonproliferation treaties attested). Blinken continued his remarks by assuring the public that America will engage China "from a position of strength," will mobilize allies, and will sustain the rivalry between democracies and autocracies highlighted by President Biden in his April 2021 address to Congress. He reaffirmed US policy in an important address at George Washington University in May 2022, following the Russian invasion of Ukraine: "Even as President Putin's war continues, we will remain focused on the most serious long-term challenge to the international order—and that's posed by the People's Republic of China. China is the only country with both the intent to reshape the international order and, increasingly, the economic, diplomatic, military, and technological power to do it. Beijing's vision would move us away from the universal values that have sustained so much of the world's progress over the past seventy-five years."[11]

Importantly, as will be developed in later chapters, the conflict is deeply rooted. It is not a temporary detour in the march to an "end of history" characterized by global liberal peace. It is not simply a matter of competing presidential egos pitting Putin against Trump or Biden, and both against Xi. Most significantly, it does not just reflect a reemerging diplomatic adjustment of a classical multipolar great power rivalry, a new geopolitical bipolarity between the United States and China or the travails of a unipolar world dominated by the United States.

Instead, like the original Cold War, this is a deep conflict between social and political systems, not just a rivalry over regional military predominance in Eastern Europe, the Middle East, or the South China

Sea. The new cold war is a transnational political rivalry, with both the United States and Russia-China supporting domestic disruption or transformation. The new technologies of cyber warfare and information war are enabling conditions, but what is important today is the weaponization of those technologies in a deadly rivalry. But that then raises the question of how it differs, to the extent it does, from other forms of international relations.

We need new labels for the world we are entering. The traditional options are illustrated in Table 1. If "war" is an effort to undermine political independence and territorial integrity, "peace" is the mutual acceptance of each other's political independence and territorial sovereignty sometimes associated with a "security community," "cold" is non-armed conflict, and "hot" is armed, kinetic conflict, then the possibilities given in Table 1 arise.[12]

"Hot wars" are kinetic, armed international conflicts as occurred in both the World Wars of the twentieth century and in the many wars among states before and since. One or more parties challenge the territorial integrity or political independence of another and use force to achieve their aims.

"Cold wars" are conflicts between nations that do not involve direct military action but are "pursued primarily through economic and political actions, propaganda, acts of espionage or proxy wars waged by surrogates." As memorably defined by Walter Lippman in his classic critique of containment (Cold War),[13] these are conflicts not directly using armed force[14] and in which at least one power contests the legitimacy of the other, whether by seeking to undermine its political independence or territorial integrity. This can involve rival claims to territory, even, as was traditional in Europe, based on dynastic inheritance, such as the rivalry between France and England over who rightly ruled France and England during the Hundred Years' War.[15] It also concerns contests between capitalism and Communism, whether human rights are universal or national, and battles between religions and claims over whether autocracy or democracy is the legitimate form of rule. Apartheid was rejected by South Africa's African neighbors on the basis of lack of legitimacy of its treatment of

Table 1. States of War and Peace

	Warm Peace	Cold Peace	Cold War	Hot War
Ideological	Liberal peace, security, community	US vs. Russia-China, 2023?–	US vs. Russia-China, 2012–2022	Total war, World War II
	US-Japan, 1922-1931	US-Italy, 1925–1939	Cold War I, 1948–1990	Revolutionary wars[16]; Israel-Arab neighbors; South Korea–North Korea, 1950-1953
		US-Japan, 1931-1941	US-Cuba, 1961–	
			USSR–People's Republic of China, 1960–1989	
			Nasser Egypt–Saudi Arabia, 1958-1967	
			South Korea–North Korea	
			US-Iran, 1989–	
			Saudi Arabia-Iran, 1989–	
			Israel-Arab Neighbors	
			China-Japan, 2010–	
Less-ideological	European Concert, 1815-1830	US-UK, 1789-1812, 1815–1865	Russia-Ukraine, 2014-2022	Russia-Ukraine, 2022–
		US-France, 1793-1803		World War I
		France-UK, 1885-1898		19th-c. Balance of Power wars: US-UK, 1812-1815
		Germany-France, 1871-1914		
		Russia-UK, 1856-1918		

its African subjects. Iran and Saudi Arabia are divided by religious differences over variants of Islam, and not just commercial rivalry over oil and regional power status.

"Warm peaces" are nearly the opposite of the above. Here peaceful relations reflect the legitimacy of states because boundaries are recognized, and ideologies are seen as compatible or irrelevant. Famous examples include the Congress of Vienna settlement after the Napoleonic Wars and the Concert of Europe diplomacy that followed it. Absolutist Russia and Austria (and France with the restoration of the Bourbon monarchy) differed from the parliamentary aristocracy that ruled the United Kingdom, but the shared foundations of aristocratic landowner–dominated politics, together with the shared interest in containing the resurgence of France, made relations cooperative. The modern classic example is the liberal peace among fellow liberal democracies that gradually emerged in the nineteenth century and flourished after World War II in NATO and the European Union. Unlike the Concert of Europe's peace among legitimate states, the liberal or "democratic peace" has proved remarkably resilient, lasting among (and only among) liberal representative governments as long as democracy continued to govern the respective polities.[17]

"Cold peaces" are the most difficult to define. The idea is to establish a system barring the use of force and in which the basic legitimacy of each side is secured, even though substantial differences in legitimacy persist. The elusive détente of the US-Soviet Cold War was an attempt in that direction. It can be made more deeply institutionalized with formal guarantees and institutions of formal cooperation along the lines this book will propose for the US relationship with China and Russia.[18] Another related conceptualization highlights that a cold peace often follows a treaty establishing a formal peace but not reconciliation, as when the government or people "of at least one of the parties to the treaty continues to treat the treaty with vocal disgust domestically." Unlike cold wars, cold peaces do not include proxy wars, covert sabotage, or attempts to destabilize the political independence of rival states. Relations between Israel and Egypt after the Camp David Accords and between India and Pakistan (less successfully) before and after the Kargil conflict have been said to be cold peaces.[19]

"Great Power Competition"? Classical Concert

The Trump administration's own description in its first National Security Strategy (NSS) of the new international order was a second vision: "great power competition." What might this mean?

The NSS issued by the Trump administration trumpeted an "America First" commitment (as if previous US administrations had not sought to promote US interests) and a view that the world, far from being an "international community" (the polite nostrum-without-content employed by some previous administrations), was in fact an arena of "great power competition," in particular between the United States, on the one hand, and China and Russia, on the other.[20]

> China and Russia challenge American power, influence, and interests, attempting to erode American security and prosperity. They are determined to make economies less free and less fair, to grow their militaries, and to control information and data to repress their societies and expand their influence. At the same time, the dictatorships of the Democratic People's Republic of Korea and the Islamic Republic of Iran are determined to destabilize regions, threaten Americans and our allies, and brutalize their own people. Transnational threat groups, from jihadist terrorists to transnational criminal organizations, are actively trying to harm Americans. While these challenges differ in nature and magnitude, they are fundamentally contests between those who value human dignity and freedom and those who oppress individuals and enforce uniformity.[21]

Tough as the doctrine may have seemed, it was, in fact, deeply ambiguous. "Great power competition" could mean many things, including either a classical balance of power or a new cold war. For some, the idea of a return to great power conflict signaled a return to traditional balance-of-power realpolitik, a system manageable by external (alliance shifting) and internal (arms building) competition.[22] It evoked an image of billiard balls ricocheting over a table or the more comforting image of the eighteenth-century minuets of alliances flexibly adjusting and moderating world politics. The eighteenth-century balance in Europe was a period of moderated conflict among legitimate governments in which allies could become enemies and vice versa, all the while engaging in armed conflicts "beyond the line" in the Americas, Africa, or Asia. Strategists could be comforted by Kissingerian visions of a nineteenth-century Congress of Vienna or Concert System in which aggression would be deterred by countervailing coalitions. But the key to such a system was "alliance flexibility"—as memorably phrased by nineteenth-century British foreign secretary Palmerston: "We have no eternal allies, and we have no perpetual enemies. Our interests are eternal and perpetual, and those interests it is our duty to follow."[23]

This classic perspective has been echoed by a Trump administration "senior official," quoted by Jeffrey Goldberg, as the "No Friends, No Enemies" doctrine.[24] It also resonates with one description of Trump's former national security advisor John Bolton as a Hobbesian: "life is nasty brutish and short.... The U.S. has values domestically, but he doesn't give a shit about the values of others. If it advances your interests to work with another country, then do it," stated a colleague of Bolton's.[25]

A much more cooperative version, a revival of European "Concert of Powers," has been advanced by Richard Haass and Charles Kupchan.[26] Indeed, the 1815 Congress of Vienna was another striking example of successful international cooperation. While treating small states as pawns to be redistributed as the great powers saw fit, it overcame a diversity of ideologies, formed a Concert of Europe to negotiate differences among the European powers, and created a remarkably stable international order in Europe that lasted a full century without another world war. The most significant accomplishment was the latter, establishing a Europe-wide balance of power that both restored France and balanced it with the creation of stronger neighbors in the united Netherlands and confederated

Germany.[27] The cooperation was more challenging than the presence of a common enemy in French imperialism might lead one to suspect, and the parties to the Congress of Vienna were much more diverse than commonly noted. The Holy Alliance—a coalition consisting of Russia, Austria, and Prussia—proposed to enforce a monarchical, autocratic system of government across Europe, while Great Britain remained committed to a parliamentary system of government. Many in Great Britain were thus sympathetic to the liberal revolutions that emerged in Italy, Greece, Spain, Portugal, and elsewhere in Europe. Nonetheless, the states involved were able to establish a Concert System because, while Castlereagh—its key proponent—led the British Parliament, the powers accepted one another's legitimacy, thereby creating the conditions for diplomatic negotiations. "It is enough," Henry Kissinger has noted, as a condition of concert diplomacy, "that there exists no power which claims both exclusiveness and universality for its notion of justice."[28] States must be mindful of the often-competing conceptions of justice held by other states and be able to compromise these conceptions with their own in order to achieve effective cooperation.

The Concert System's spirit of general cooperation was, unfortunately, short-lived. It is commonly thought that the "concert" of diplomatic cooperation resulting from the 1815 Congress of Vienna lasted for a century, only to be disrupted by the start of World War I. However, as Nicolson has pointed out, balance-of-power coalitions tend to come apart as soon as the common threat against which they were originally united is eliminated. Once France, with the Bourbon monarchy restored, was no longer perceived as a threat to the peace of Europe, diverse political ideologies of the states in the congress began to break the alliance apart.[29] The revolutions of the 1820s, with the objective of attaining constitutional monarchies, split the European Concert. Austria, for example, wanted to intervene in Naples to restore autocratic monarchical rule, but Britain rejected this proposal.[30] The Congress of Vienna lost the power to implement the agenda that the Holy Alliance proposed for it, which was to enforce aristocracy and to dismantle democracy.[31] The wars of Italian and German unification in the 1860s revealed the full limitations of concert cooperation, culminating in the crisis that led to Bismarck's invasion of France in 1870. A similar international war today between two great powers would hardly qualify as successful cooperation or moderation.[32]

The central contemporary implication of classical balancing logic is that either Russia or China would realign with the United States if its interests so indicated or, correspondingly, the United States would align with Russia and China against Europe if the power balance tilted that way. But clearly, no such flexibility was implied in the Trump administration's doctrinal pronouncement between those "who value human dignity" and those "who oppress individuals and enforce uniformity." Nor does it fit the line President Biden draws between "democracies" and "autocracies." And none of those traditional balances fits the modern world of popular politics and complex economic interdependence. Global norms reflect and small states insist upon equal sovereignty, and small states reject being treated as pawns in great power games. Foreign policy is no longer the exclusive realm of landed aristocrats insulated from accountability to a democratic public or unaffected by commercial and industrial competition.

Great Power Competition as "Cold War"

A second form of "great power competition," one much more reflective of such an ideological division, is "cold war." Here the competition is between semi-fixed coalitions representing more fundamental interests and values, often rooted in domestic ideologies, such as the Cold War between the Soviet Union and the United States.

The *Merriam-Webster* dictionary offers two meanings for "cold war." The first is "a conflict over ideological differences carried on by methods short of sustained overt military action and usually without breaking off diplomatic relations." Its example for this is the Cold War ideological conflict between the United States and the USSR during the second half of the twentieth century. The second is much less extreme: "a condition of rivalry, mistrust, and often open hostility short of violence especially between power groups (such as labor and management)."

The first meaning better captures what we mean by an international cold war. A cold war in this sense is a fundamental conflict that aims at defeat (warlike) but eschews military (forceful or kinetic) means. It is hence "cold," not "hot." But while "cold," it is "warlike"—a refusal to accept and a concerted attempt to undermine the territorial integrity or political independence of another state that are the heart of sovereign rights in the modern international legal order. Moreover, "cold war" has signified a revolutionary ideological or religious conflict, not simply a conflict of material interests. It contests what constitutes a legitimate domestic order. It has extended beyond specific disputes to include comprehensive rivalries, both geographic and functional, over ways of life. The Cold War, 1948–1990, was bipolar between the United States and the USSR, between capitalist and Communist economic systems, and between democratic liberal and totalitarian dictatorial political regimes.

In the age of the classical balance of power, to seize territory one needed armed force, and to control a people's political independence (sovereignty) one needed to seize their territory. However, as international interdependence grew, trade, finance, and transnational ideology offered avenues of influence that might in the right circumstances amount to controlling political independence without territorial conquest through "hot" war. In the age of democracy and transnational communication, such pathways are deep and wide. Foreign governments can fund and manipulate political parties directly and indirectly as the United States did repeatedly during the Cold War (Italy's first postwar election, the intervention in Iran in 1953, and the list goes on) and as Putin did in the United States in 2016.

President Biden drew just this distinction in an op-ed he published on June 5, 2021, in preparation for his first presidential trip to Europe. "I have also imposed meaningful consequences for behaviors that violate U.S. sovereignty, including interference in our democratic elections. And President Putin knows that I will not hesitate to respond to future harmful activities. When we meet, I will again underscore the commitment of the United States, Europe and like-minded democracies to stand up for human rights and dignity."[33]

Another way to see the point is to note that cold wars are contests over legitimacy, not just interests. Frederick the Great, Maria Theresa, Louis XV, and George III presided over arms races, armed rivalries, and a proto-world war (the Seven Years' War). Neither they nor their aristocratic governments doubted the legitimacy of the other.[34] They fought for trade, territory, prestige, and hegemony (and survival): for whose government should rule over how much. They did not fight for what kind of government should rule according to what principles and laws and in the name of what class or ideology.[35]

When we think of cold war, we naturally think of *the* Cold War, 1948–1990, a bipolar global contest. But in the sense I am employing, cold wars can be fought between just two states, such as the United States and Iran since 1989 or India and Pakistan at various times, and even between two small states such as North Korea and South Korea or two states of enormously different capabilities such as the United States and Cuba, Russia and Ukraine, or even Taiwan and China. (And some cold wars have become "hot" as the strife between Russia and Ukraine did in 2014 and 2022.)

This does not mean that two states of a similar ideology cannot get into a cold or hot war. States of similar ideologies can dispute who is the more pure or more legitimate (think of Soviet-Chinese rivalries during the Cold War or French and English claims during the Hundred Years' War to the throne of France based on rival but still monarchical principles of dynastic inheritance).[36] Moreover, and equally obvious, two states of dissimilar ideologies can cooperate. Famously, Britain and the United States cooperated with Soviet Russia against Hitler's Germany in World War II.[37]

Still, cold wars, like total wars, tend to be revolutionary contests over legitimacy. The clear example of a "hot" total war contest was World War II. President Franklin Delano Roosevelt declared that the war was not just about protecting or freeing occupied territory from Fascism. Instead, he announced in a message to Congress on September 17, 1943 (while Allied forces were landing in Italy): "We shall not be able to claim that we have gained total victory in the war if any vestige of Fascism in any of its malignant forms is permitted to survive anywhere in the world."[38] Analogously, a cold war is a total war without the use of force.

The Soviet perspective rested on an ideological divide between Communism and capitalism, one well-reflected in this passage from the Declaration of the Soviet Constitution of 1924:

> Since the foundation of the Soviet Republics, the States of the world have been divided into two camps: the camp of Capitalism and the camp of Socialism. There, in the camp of Capitalism: national hate and inequality, colonial slavery and chauvinism, national oppression and massacres, brutalities and imperialistic wars. Here, in the camp of Socialism: reciprocal confidence and peace, national liberty and equality, the pacific co-existence and fraternal collaboration of peoples.[39]

After World War II, the USSR was a global power, and it showed it had the capability of threatening the United States and Western Europe. The US counterset of assumptions evolved intermittently from the famous "Long Telegram" and "X Article" of George Kennan,[40] to "The Iron Curtain Speech" of Winston Churchill, to its governmental articulation in the foundational strategic doctrine enunciated in the US government's National Security Council Paper NSC 68 of 1950:

> Two complex sets of factors have now basically altered this historic distribution of power [the multipolar system before World War II]. First, the defeat of Germany and Japan and the decline of the British and French Empires have interacted with the development of the United States and the Soviet Union in such a way that power increasingly gravitated to these two centres. Second, the Soviet Union, unlike previous aspirants to hegemony, is animated by a new fanatic faith, antithetical to our own, and seeks to impose its absolute authority over the rest of the world. Conflict has, therefore, become endemic and is waged, on the part of the Soviet Union, by violent or non-violent methods in accordance with the dictates of expediency. With the development of increasingly terrifying weapons of mass destruction, every individual faces the

ever-present possibility of annihilation should the conflict enter the phase of total war.[41]

The spirit carried over into the conduct of the Cold War. The US government portrayed the contest as genuinely warlike, and a conflict for survival, as the Department of Justice opined during the Bay of Pigs crisis:

> In waging a world wide contest to strengthen the free nations and contain the Communist nations, *and thereby to preserve the existence of the United States* [emphasis added], the President should be deemed to have comparable authority to meet covert activities with covert activities if he deems such action necessary and consistent with our national objectives.[42]

The leading characteristics of the Cold War were thus:

- The Cold War was a warlike conflict with extreme aims focused on defeat, illustrated by Khrushchev's famous threat of "burial" (but not by military conquest).
- Hot war between the US-led West and Soviet-led East was deterred first by the power of conventional arsenals and subsequently by the weight of nuclear deterrence.
- Instead, the United States and USSR competed with each other through proxy wars in East Asia, the Middle East, Africa, and Latin America such that the Cold War extended geographically to cover the entire world.
- They also competed across many dimensions, including through industrial rivalry, covert action, propaganda campaigns, and cultural contests (athletics, piano, chess, etc.).
- The Cold War was composed of a threefold, multidimensional, mutually reinforcing rivalry:
  - first, a bipolar international system;
  - second, competition between capitalist and Communist economic systems;

- third, contestation between two political ideologies—liberal
  democracy and Communist dictatorship.

Ideological rivalries were not and could not be absolute. Churchill once said; "If Hitler invaded Hell I would make at least a favorable reference to the devil in the House of Commons." He meant that in extreme circumstances, national security will overcome ideological opposition, as it did during World War II when Stalin became "Uncle Joe" of the United Nations wartime alliance. But absent overwhelming necessity, the cold war engenders hostility and dominates world politics.

CHAPTER TWO

Cold War II?

Today we see many of the same cold war features in the US and allied confrontation with China and Russia. These are rivalries involving more than contests over prestige, influence, power, and prosperity. They are non-armed ("cold") conflicts that significantly affect political independence and territorial integrity (hence "war"-like). Each power has experienced them differently in differing forms and degrees.

While Cold War I was "fought" in proxy wars in Vietnam, Angola, and Afghanistan and through arms racing and various forms of espionage, today (apart from the proxy war in Ukraine) the conflict mostly involves a mix of cyber espionage, technology theft, ransomware, sabotage, political interference, and arms competition. The distinguishing characteristic is cyber, which has made the competition utterly pervasive, exceptionally inexpensive, and yet potentially very destructive (although very few actual casualties can be attributed to cyber to date).[1]

Cyber Cold War

Cyber conflict has a variety of forms.[2] The first is regular state-based espionage for information. For example, as documented in a Center for Strategic and International Studies (CSIS) report, in 2013 Chinese hackers stole US weapon designs and targeted civilian and military maritime operations in the South China Sea.[3] In the same year, as Edward Snowden revealed, the United States conducted cyber espionage against Chinese targets.[4] The 2020 SolarWinds attack by a branch of Russian military intelligence penetrated the US Departments of the Treasury and Homeland Security and multiple private entities.[5]

A second is espionage for industrial technology, done by both private and public actors and combinations of the two. As one of many examples, as early as 2011, the FBI reported $11 million in losses of US businesses to Chinese trade companies. In 2021, Russian and Chinese intelligence services targeted the European Medicines Agency and stole documents related to COVID-19 vaccines and medicines. In 2022, the cybersecurity firm Cyberreason reported a "massive Chinese hacking of trade secrets" by Winnti APT Group, "which specializes in cyber espionage and intellectual property theft and is believed to work for Chinese state interests."[6]

A third is ransomware attacks for profit, a major growth sector for the cyberworld. In 2021 alone, Colonial Pipeline was the target of a ransomware attack by DarkSide, a Russian hacking group, and JBS, the world's largest meat-processing company, was the victim of a ransomware attack by the Russian group REvil. The Colonial Pipeline is the largest pipeline of refined oil products in the United States—stretching from Texas to New York and carrying 3 million barrels of fuel each day. The DarkSide attack consisted of a very ordinary password breach of security—even though Colonial Pipeline had invested $200 million into IT systems, which included cybersecurity—and resulted in an extreme gas shortage in the southeastern United States. The CEO of Colonial Pipeline made the decision to pay the $5 million/75 bitcoin ransom and then notify the authorities. The US Department of Justice was later able to recover at least $2.3

million (60 bitcoin) in cryptocurrency.[7] REvil's attack on JBS resulted in a cyberbreach that shut down operations in the United States, Canada, and Australia. JBS quickly paid the $11 million ransom in bitcoin to the hackers in order to restore operations. Its significance is reflected in the fact that JBS provides one-fifth of all the beef and pork consumed in the United States.[8] All these hacks are complicated by the fact that the US government has little contact with the private actors who are attacked, and the Russian government, among others, profits from and provides cover for hackers who agree not to attack it.[9]

A fourth is state-sponsored sabotage of industrial firms, public utilities, and banks. The US-Israeli Stuxnet attack on Iran and the Russian attacks on Ukraine are leading examples. On June 17, 2010, Iranians began to report a machine stuck rebooting itself over and over again, designed to sabotage centrifuges (critical industrial control systems integral to the purification of radioactive uranium). This "Stuxnet" was the first case of cyber sabotage (the use of digital code developed to destroy something physical) and was believed to have then been part of a sustained US campaign of cyber operations against the Iranian nuclear program known as the Olympic Games, which began during George W. Bush's presidency and continued through Barack Obama's.[10] In the past few years, Ukraine has experienced a plethora of cyberattacks from Russia that have targeted and harmed Ukrainian media, finance, transportation, military, politics, electricity, and energy. These attacks have been calculated and conducted in an attempt to sabotage and control Ukraine.[11]

A fifth is cyber political campaigns designed to influence or disrupt political processes or support separatist movements. These directly target "political independence" and "territorial integrity" and thus trigger powerful norms against aggression and in favor of self-defense responses. In 2016, in a famous instance of this, Russia was found to have influenced the 2016 US election via Facebook. The primary effects were that thirty-nine state voter databases, the Clinton campaign, the Democratic National Committee, and the Democratic Congressional Campaign Committee were hacked. Politically damaging information was released and spread as propaganda on social media outlets, and some regions' polling stations halted because of tampering on the day of the election. The FBI became aware of these Russian overseas cyberattacks months prior to the election but was unable to halt and prevent the pervasive attacks coming from many different hackers. In early 2018, twelve Russian intelligence officers were charged with hacking by the US Department of Justice, although the Kremlin denied any involvement.[12]

These attacks continued. In 2018, Microsoft found out that Russian hackers targeted the campaigns of three Democratic candidates running for the 2018 midterm elections, and, in 2019, Russian hackers targeted a number of European government agencies in the two months ahead of EU elections. But attacks were not reputedly all one-sided. Russia, for example, has accused the United States of fomenting domestic dissent during the election of Putin, and China blames the United States for dissent in Hong Kong that led to the crackdown.

For the United States, the most direct attack on political independence came in the election of 2016. The NSA, CIA, and FBI offered testimony in the US Congress in February 2018 that outlined genuine confrontation. According to their testimony, Russia was preparing a concerted cyberattack on Ukrainian industry and planned to continue a long campaign to undermine US democracy by fueling polarization with fake news. The campaign appears to have been targeted to maximize fault lines in the American body politic, including attempts to deepen the distrust of African Americans in the US criminal justice system.[13]

Moreover, there are credible allegations that Russia directly planned to tilt the US 2016 election in favor of Donald Trump, an egregious interference in US political independence. A remarkable story in *The Guardian* newspaper in 2021 outlined a clear 2016 plan by Putin to put Trump in the US presidency. A Moscow secret report to Putin—labeled "No 32–04 \ vd"—said Trump is the "most promising candidate" for the Kremlin. Trump is described as an "impulsive, mentally unstable and unbalanced individual who suffers from an inferiority complex." Moreover, the Kremlin allegedly possesses *kompromat* (potentially compromising material) from Trump's earlier visits to Russia. The Moscow report that

Putin endorsed and ordered implemented concludes: "It is acutely necessary to use all possible force to facilitate his [Trump's] election to the
post of US president."[14]

Russian efforts apparently succeeded in having a significant effect.[15]
Its attacks have extended to US election infrastructure, the state voting
systems on which the US national election relies.[16] The Mueller Report
(2019) affirmed that Russia had "penetrated computers of a county government in Florida and implanted malware in the systems of a manufac-
turer of election equipment."[17] The United States and United Kingdom
jointly soon afterward issued an assessment that Russia is engaged in
a systematic attack on network infrastructure such as routers, switch-
ers, and firewalls.[18] The British Parliament confirmed in a long delayed
2020 report that Russia has been interfering in the British political system. Beyond the assassinations of former Russian agents, Russia has
attempted to destabilize the British votes on Brexit and Scottish independence.[19] And in one of the best studies to date, the French government
identified a concerted strategy of information warfare designed to undermine democratic elections, directed specifically against France and other
European states.[20]

While the 2020 election of Joe Biden appears to have been less affected
by Russian cyber-destabilization, President Trump's lawyer Rudolph
Giuliani appeared to have cultivated close links to Ukrainian businessmen supplying questionable information about former vice president
Biden's son, Hunter Biden. This led Senate Intelligence Committee
chairman Richard Burr to warn Senators Ron Johnson of Wisconsin
and Chuck Grassley of Iowa that their probe targeting Biden lent unwar-
ranted credence to statements by the Ukrainian parliamentarian, Andrii
Derkach (whom the Treasury Department sanctioned and dubbed a Russian asset), and "could aid Russian efforts to sow chaos and distrust in the
U.S. political system."[21]

Kirstjen Nielsen, the former US secretary of homeland security,
affirmed in 2019 that cyber warfare is the top threat facing the United
States. Straying from President Trump's obsession with the "national
emergency" posed by immigrants, she condemned President Putin in par-

ticular for "a concerted effort to undermine our elections and our democratic process using cyber-enabled means."[22]

The CSIS has documented major cyberattacks in the past fifteen years.[23] They range from 2005 Chinese hacks of the US Department of Defense (Titan Rain operation), incidents targeting the naval and army strategic centers, and infiltrations of NASA networks for information on the Space Shuttle. The record runs through the 2006–2008 Russian hacking and identity theft of more than 130 million credit and debit cards to the 2021 Colonial Pipeline ransomware attack by DarkSide and the JBS ransomware attack by REvil.

Intelligence officials have even identified the unit at the spear point of Putin's "hybrid warfare." It is "Unit 29155" of the Russian military intelligence directorate (GRU). It blends propaganda, hacking attacks, and disinformation campaigns with subversion, sabotage, and assassination. It was involved in Moldova's destabilization, the poisoning of an arms dealer in Bulgaria, the assassination of a former spy in the United Kingdom, and a thwarted coup in Montenegro. Increasingly its targets appear to range across Europe.[24]

SVR-Nobelium, the Russian spy agency behind the SolarWinds hack of the US government in 2020, mounted a new cyber-espionage offensive targeting US government agencies and civil society organizations in May 2021. The hackers breached a marketing email account belonging to the US Agency for International Development (USAID)—targeting 3,000 people connected to international development and humanitarian groups in addition to government and human rights organizations. Many of the targets have been strong critics of Putin.[25]

Illustrating the bipartisan understanding of the potential threat, then former vice president and 2020 Democratic presidential candidate Biden stated: "The Russians are still engaged in trying to delegitimize our electoral process. Fact. China and others are engaged as well in activities that are designed for us to lose confidence in the outcome."[26]

China has also been identified as a cyber aggressor. In summer 2021, President Biden mobilized the European Union and NATO for a joint condemnation of China for the Microsoft hack, which allowed China to penetrate numerous governmental and private computer networks through their email systems. NATO issued an especially strong condemnation:

> We stand in solidarity with all those who have been affected by recent malicious cyber activities including the Microsoft Exchange Server compromise. Such malicious cyber activities undermine security, confidence and stability in cyberspace. We acknowledge national statements by Allies, such as Canada, the United Kingdom, and the United States, attributing responsibility for the Microsoft Exchange Server compromise to the People's Republic of China. In line with our recent Brussels Summit Communiqué, we call on all States, including China, to uphold their international commitments and obligations and to act responsibly in the international system, including in cyberspace.[27]

The United States and its allies thus accused China of coordinating private hackers and identified Chinese intelligence agents responsible for directing the attacks.[28] At nearly the same time, the United States identified China as having penetrated computer networks belonging to numerous pipeline companies, demonstrating the capacity to either hold them up to ransom (as occurred in the Russia-based hack of Colonial Pipeline in 2021) or, more ominously, disrupt them as part of a state-led sabotage.[29] China is employing a strategy of cyber espionage such that the US government considers that just about all Chinese high-tech products are considered dangerously compromised.[30]

The Strategic Technology Program of the CSIS identified 160 publicly reported instances of Chinese espionage directed at the United States since 2000. (The list of 160 does not include espionage against other countries, against US firms or persons located in China, nor more than 50 additional cases involving attempts to smuggle munitions or controlled technologies from the United States to China. They also did not include the more than 1,200 cases of intellectual property theft litigation brought by US companies against Chinese entities in either the US or Chinese legal systems.) Of the 160 incidents, 24 percent occurred between

2000 and 2009, and 76 percent occurred between 2010 and 2021. The list is impressive in its scope and consequences. The CSIS summarizes:

> For those cases where we could identify actor and intent, we found:
>
> 42% of actors were Chinese military or government employees.
> 32% were private Chinese citizens.
> 26% were non-Chinese actors (usually U.S. persons recruited by Chinese officials).
> 34% of incidents sought to acquire military technology.
> 51% of incidents sought to acquire commercial technologies.
> 16% of incidents sought to acquire information on U.S. civilian agencies or politicians.
> 41% of incidents involved cyber espionage, usually by State-affiliated actors.[31]

Other Channels of a Widening Cold War

A striking example of the new cold war's politically charged economics is the International Investment Bank. A Cold War relic once used to finance Soviet bloc foreign trade, it is a public investment bank governed by its member countries, including Russia, Cuba, Bulgaria, and Hungary. Russia controls 40 percent of its assets. Directed by a former member of Russian intelligence, the Hungarian branch recently received diplomatic immunity from Hungarian prime minister Viktor Orbán. Western officials regard it as a staging operation for Russian intelligence in the European Union, mitigating the restrictions imposed after the alleged Russian poisonings in Britain.[32]

Another example is US chipmakers' fear that their long-run interests would be undermined when the Trump administration sought to cure the US-China bilateral trade deficit. They worried that the proposed increase in Chinese imports of US chips would later require domestic production in China and hence a loss of control over proprietary technology.[33]

Trade and technology tensions between the United States and China

escalated in 2020 with the US imposition of sanctions against Huawei prohibiting the sale of US technology to it or purchases of Chinese technology from it (seeing Huawei as a source of Chinese government–controlled,
compromised technology). Washington delisted Chinese media firms
from the US stock market in response to their arrangement with the Chinese military to provide surveillance facilities to the Chinese government
to be used against the Uighurs and for spying on democratic dissidents in
Hong Kong. China responded with an order that permits Chinese companies or foreign companies in China to sue for any damages incurred from
the actions of companies that comply with the US regulations.[34]

Further driving home the breadth of the US view of China as a hostile
threat, a bipartisan report of the House Intelligence Committee affirmed
in September 2020: "The People's Republic of China (PRC) has increasingly
sought to revise the international order and global norms in a way that
furthers its own strategic interests and undermines those of the United
States specifically, and the West generally," the report declares. "Militarily,
China has embarked on a massive modernization drive—creating a 'blue
water' navy capable of operating across the oceans, investing heavily in
hypersonic weapons, developing its own fifth-generation fighter, milita-
rizing a series of atolls and islets in the South China Sea to strengthen its
claims in the region, and building its first overseas military base in Djibouti." Furthermore, China is using technology to create "a post-modern
authoritarian state in which the country's population is monitored
around the clock through their phones and an ever-growing network of
surveillance cameras equipped with facial-recognition technology. This
'digital authoritarianism' has not only been deployed at home, but has
been increasingly marketed to aspiring authoritarians abroad."[35]

As other signs of increasing tension, we can see clashes at the UN Security Council over accusations that Russia was attacking medical facilities in Syria, and, in 2020, charges by US intelligence that Russians in
the same assassination unit active in the United Kingdom, Moldova, and
elsewhere were paying Taliban forces to assassinate Coalition (including
US) troops in Afghanistan.[36]

National Security Advisor H. R. McMaster, known as a moderate in the Trump administration, summarized Washington's view in a podcast: "What China and Russia are trying to do is collapse the international political, economic order and replace it in a new order that's more consistent with their objectives. Russia wants to regain national greatness. China wants to achieve national rejuvenation. And they, in large measure, want to do it at our expense."[37] In a carefully reasoned article, former Australian prime minister Kevin Rudd identified genuine 2020 hot spots in US-China relations that might well, barring good diplomacy, escalate to war. He highlighted Hong Kong, Taiwan, and the South China Sea as particularly prone to miscalculation and escalation.[38] US senators have drawn special attention to hybrid, information-influence operations.[39]

China has reaffirmed ties to autocratic Russia, and together they are cultivating relationships with states that oppose the liberal international order supported by the United States. Russia has proposed a gas pipeline to China, and China has become Russia's leading trade partner (absorbing 16 percent of its exports, while accounting for only 1 percent of China's exports). China has also signed similar energy agreements with Iran.

In a phone call in June 2021 on the eve of the BRICS summit, Chinese foreign minister Wang Yi called his Russian counterpart Sergei Lavrov asserting that: "The US has formed small groups under the guise of democracy, used human rights as an excuse to interfere in countries' domestic politics, and exercised unilateralism under the banner of multilateralism." He added, "China and Russia, as responsible big powers and permanent members of the United Nations' Security Council, should jointly expose and stand against these perverse acts. [We should] strongly defend the United Nations-centric and law-based international order and system, preserve fairness and justice and defend multilateralism. . . . We will also give Russia full political support to its defence of legitimate rights."[40]

In 2022 on the eve of the Beijing Winter Olympics and before the Russian invasion of Ukraine, China and Russia announced a "no limits partnership" that included space, climate change, artificial intelligence, and the Internet.[41] Each affirmed its support for the other's position on Taiwan and against NATO. The Russian energy firms Gazprom and

Rosneft signed deals worth tens of billions of dollars with China, and China pledged support for currency arrangements with Russia that circumvented the dominance of the dollar in world finance. In 2022, in the wake of the Russian invasion of Ukraine, Myanmar and Iran and North Korea (autocracies all) deepened their ties to Russia and China. Iran supplies Russia with drones, North Korea supplies missiles, Iran is joining the Shanghai Cooperation Council, and the head of Myanmar's military coup has hailed Putin as "a leader of the world."[42]

President Biden has responded by mobilizing the United Kingdom, Canada, and the Europeans to condemn Chinese human rights abuses against the Uighurs, leading to the first EU human rights sanctions on China since Tiananmen Square. President Biden then convened a "Summit for Democracy" in December 2021, which brought together 275 leaders from 100 countries in order to spur collective action that addresses "sustained and alarming challenges to democracy and universal human rights." The leaders vowed to work together to confront authoritarianism, fight corruption, and promote human rights and electoral integrity.[43] The event was seen by Beijing and Moscow as another effort to draw up sides.

Heating up the rhetorical exchanges, at the Alaska Summit between China and the United States at the outset of the Biden administration, China declared its ideological "equality" with the United States. No longer deferential toward US-style liberal capitalism, the Chinese diplomats denounced US racial mistreatment (echoing the Black Lives Matter theme) and instability (the January 6 Trump-inspired insurrection against the US Capitol). The Biden team joined Trump in condemning the genocide against the Uighurs and destruction of Hong Kong's promised autonomy. All this of course raised the deeper question of Taiwan. Hong Kong's protected pluralism was long seen as the promised dream held out for the future of a reunited Taiwan. With the crushing of the Hong Kong democracy movement, that promise appeared now to be a nightmare. At the same time, Xi Jinping reasserted the "China Dream" of a unified greater China with the implicit threat of force.[44] While the United States acknowledged "One China," it also reaffirmed defense sales to Taiwan.

Russia, entrenched in Africa during the Cold War's violent East-West rivalry, largely retreated from the continent after the collapse of the Soviet Union. But in the past few years, Moscow has rekindled relations with Soviet-era clients such as Mozambique and Angola and forged new ties with other countries.[45] President Putin of Russia then launched a concerted effort to win over African countries in 2022 in the wake of the invasion of Ukraine, which severely affected food supplies on the continent.[46]

In a related intrusion in Africa, Yevgeny Prigozhin, a confidant of Putin, headed a mission to the Central African Republic that combines military assistance and advisors with commercial interests in diamonds. The Russian mercenaries are enabling the government to overawe the local warlords, and Russian diamond and gold mines in the Central African Republic are spearheading an expanding political role that Russia can export to other vulnerable countries.[47]

John J. Sullivan, then the deputy secretary of state, warned that "Russia often utilizes coercive, corrupt, and covert means to attempt to influence sovereign states, including their security and economic partnerships." The United States is responding. About 6,000 US troops and 1,000 Department of Defense civilians or contractors work on a variety of missions throughout Africa, mainly training and conducting exercises with local armies. The Kremlin, Mr. Bolton added, "continues to sell arms and energy in exchange for votes at the United Nations—votes that keep strongmen in power, undermine peace and security and run counter to the best interests of the African people."

In a 2022 example of competitive democratic versus autocratic globalization, the Solomon Islands prime minister, Manasseh Sogavare, signed an agreement with China that offers a broad mandate for China to potentially intervene when its foreign investments and diaspora are under threat as it stretches its projection of military power into the South Pacific. The security agreement is designed to ensure stability after several days of violent unrest aimed at both Chinese interests and the Sogavare government. In the secret draft agreement, "almost anything tied to China, from its citizens to small businesses to infrastructure to stadiums—like the one a Chinese contractor is building in the capital, Honiara—could be enough to spur a request for Chinese troops."[48] The real change is that the

Solomons, having previously recognized Taiwan, no longer does so and, having previously relied on Australia for security assistance, now relies on China. Unlike Australia and international financial institutions like the World Bank, China offers security to Sogavare without human rights, environmental, or other troublesome conditions.

Even the most apolitical of global harms, the COVID-19 pandemic, became geopolitically polarized in some quarters. Zhao Lijian, the spokesperson of the Chinese Foreign Ministry, has accused the United States of spreading the virus in October 2019 to Wuhan, China, through a visiting US military delegation. *Global Times*, a Chinese government outlet, later suggested that the virus originated in a US bioweapons lab in Fort Detrick, Maryland. On the other side, US senator Tom Cotton, in a Fox TV interview on February 19, 2020, implied that the "Wuhan virus" was not an accidental evolution but a conscious project of unspecified Chinese authorities.[49] Chinese commentators, reflecting official views, then claimed the virus originated elsewhere—in Italy, for example—and that China has proved the superiority of is political system by managing the response much better than its liberal rivals in the West.[50]

The Biden administration thus began to describe relations with both Russia and China as a new "gray zone" form of warfare—neither peace nor war—but constant coercive competition akin to the conflicts among intelligence agencies during the Cold War. Biden summarized the perceived global threat at the outset of his administration:

> We must also contend with the reality that the distribution of power across the world is changing, creating new threats. China, in particular, has rapidly become more assertive. It is the only competitor potentially capable of combining its economic, diplomatic, military, and technological power to mount a sustained challenge to a stable and open international system. Russia remains determined to enhance its global influence and play a disruptive role on the world stage. Both Beijing and Moscow have invested heavily in efforts meant to check U.S. strengths and prevent us from defending our interests and allies around the world.[51]

In pursuit of a strengthened stance against China, in June 2021 the US Senate overwhelmingly voted to approve the United States Innovation and Competition Act of 2021 (USICA), a sweeping package of legislation designed to enhance the ability of the United States to outcompete Chinese technology. The bill authorized about $190 billion to invest in US technology and research, including $54 billion for research into semiconductors and telecommunications equipment.[52] The bill adds China-related provisions such as prohibiting the social media app TikTok from being downloaded on government devices and blocking the purchase of drones manufactured and sold by companies backed by the Chinese government. Provocatively, it would also allow Taiwanese diplomats and military members to display their flag and wear their uniforms while in the United States on official business. Additionally, it would establish new sanctions on Chinese entities engaged in cyberattacks on the United States or theft of intellectual property from US firms. It would mandate a review of export controls on items that could be used to support human rights abuses. In many ways, ironically, it mirrored China's high-tech industrial development push, called "Made in China 2025." Not surprisingly, China soon criticized the bill as "full of Cold War mentality and ideological prejudice."[53]

In what was the most provocative Biden administration initiative in the looming new cold war, US Department of Commerce secretary Gina Raimondo said that the United States will rally allies in order to mount pressure on the world's second-largest economy. "If we really want to slow down China's rate of innovation, we need to work with Europe. . . . They're ripping off our IP, they are not playing by the rules. It's not a level playing field." She elaborated: "We don't want autocratic governments like China, writing the rules of the road. We together with our allies, who care about privacy, freedom, individual rights, individual protection, we need to write the rules of the road," and, noting the importance of export controls, "We have to work with our European allies to deny China the most advanced technology so that they can't catch up in critical areas like semiconductors. . . . We want to work with Europe, to write the rules of the road for technology, whether it's TikTok or artificial intelligence or cyber."[54]

The February 2022 invasion of Ukraine marked a new stage in the emerging cold war and has become the first proxy war of the new cold war. Invaded by Russia (with the diplomatic support of China and other autocracies), Ukraine has valiantly defended itself with the support of NATO and its wide coalition, mostly consisting of democracies. Many are rightly absorbed in the survival of Ukraine, but an equally pressing question is whether the looming new cold war that fuels the Ukraine war can be contained? Sweden and Finland upended generations of foreign policy neutrality by applying to join NATO.

Like the Cold War proxy conflicts of the Korean War (1950–1953), the Vietnam War (1955–1975), and the Afghan War (1979–1989), there have been no significant direct armed clashes between the principal patrons of the Ukraine War. The USSR and the United States never fought in Korea (though China directly participated). The USSR, China, and the United States avoided direct military clashes in Vietnam and so did the United States and USSR in Afghanistan.[55] In 2022, US and NATO aid to Ukraine was massive, both that of humanitarian and of military kind, but there were no reported direct armed conflicts between Russian forces and NATO forces.

President Biden summed up the US view of the emerging cold war conflict in his March 1, 2022, "State of the Union Address": "While it shouldn't have taken something so terrible for people around the world to see what's at stake, now everyone sees it clearly. . . . In the battle between democracy and autocracy, democracies are rising to the moment, and the world is clearly choosing the side of peace and security."[56]

The EU Gloss on Cold War

The European Union, too, has weighed in on new global tensions: "Russia can no longer be considered a strategic partner and the European Union must be prepared to impose further sanctions on it if it continues to violate international law."[57] Furthermore, the resolution condemns presidential elections in Russia, calling them "non-democratic." Russia is accused of "violating the territorial integrity of Ukraine and Georgia," "intervening in Syria and interfering in countries like Libya," and "interfering in order to influence elections and increase tensions" in Europe. It further accuses Russia of "violation of arms control agreements," including the Intermediate-Range Nuclear Forces (INF) Treaty, and "extensive violations of human rights within Russia, including torture and extrajudicial killings" and "murder by its agents using chemical weapons on European soil."

The European Parliament added to the indictment by declaring that Nord Stream 2, which doubled the supply of Russian gas to Germany through the Baltic Sea, "must be stopped because it increases the EU's dependence on Russian gas supplies, threatening its internal market and its strategic interests." Germany, however, decided to go ahead with the pipeline, until the famous *Zeitenwende* in which Chancellor Scholz reversed course. The biggest effect of Nord Stream 2, however, was to allow Russia to coerce Ukraine (cutting off gas supplies) without simultaneously cutting off gas supplies to all of Western Europe, provoking a Europe-wide counterreaction.

The European Commission warned that China is a partner but also "a systemic rival that promotes alternative models of governance," and it cautioned that the European Union must "safeguard critical digital infrastructures from potentially serious security threats" stemming from 5G networks provided by Chinese companies such as Huawei, which were banned in the United States. Elaborating on similar themes, EU commissioner Paolo Gentiloni commented on the need for the European Union to develop "geopolitical" power to match its economic clout (particularly in light of the calamitous US withdrawal from Afghanistan). He noted that the European Union would complement US and NATO measures, and with regard to China: "There is an economic cooperation [with China], trade cooperation, but we are different systems. It is inevitable that the model of a different capitalism, capitalism that is not connected with democracy, with liberty, is an alternative to the European model," he said. "And so forcefully we will be partners with [the] U.S. in this kind of confrontation, but [it's] also in the U.S. interest if this European partner is also geopolitically stronger and [has] more influence.... We always describe Europe as a quiet superpower, Venus and Mars. Okay, [the] time is now to give also Venus some geopolitical power."[58]

In an influential study published in 2021 by the French Ministry of the Army, researchers warn about the global growth of Chinese information warfare while warning that these operations will also be directed at the European Union. The authors highlighted an event in Australia as a harbinger: In Australia, journalists with Chinese-language media outlets reportedly experienced intimidation and even physical assault for publishing material critical of the CCP. China has also sought to manipulate politics among neighboring democracies. In the most high-profile case, a CCP-linked donor allegedly persuaded Australian senator Sam Dastyari to adopt the CCP's position on the South China Sea by threatening to withdraw a $400,000 donation.[59]

But while China is a subject of European concern, it is seen as a less directly threatening one than Russia. Simply put, the Europeans believe that while Putin seeks to trash the international order, China wants to compete within it and then replace it with its own. Thus French president Emmanuel Macron was prepared to criticize China over human rights abuses, but argued that the European Union needed to work with China, particularly when it came to climate change. And he rejected Biden's efforts to build a democratic coalition: "A situation to join all together against China, this is a scenario of the highest possible conflictuality" while adding, "This one, for me, is counterproductive."[60]

Russia and China Weigh In

Reciprocal and similar fears of the United States are articulated in Russia. General Valery Gerasimov, said to be Russia's leading military strategist, explained that America's "goal is liquidation of inconvenient countries, the undermining of sovereignty."[61] He was referring to the US sanctions campaign against Nicolás Maduro's government in Venezuela in 2018, but clearly Gerasimov sought to generalize the charge. And with regard to Venezuela, the charge has a real basis in US policy, as a US State Department official promised: "We will continue to hold the Maduro regime accountable until democracy and freedom are fully restored in Venezuela."[62] The United States having recognized the opposition leader Juan Guaidó as the legitimate head of state, imposed crippling economic sanctions, and repeatedly stated that "all options remained on the table," the US threats of regime change had to be taken seriously.

Major escalations, allegedly provoked by the Russian cyberattack on the United States in 2016, followed. As early as 2016, the Obama administration penetrated Russian electric utilities to send a signal as to what might follow if Russia pursued its hack of the US election.[63] The Trump administration, while dismissing allegations that Putin hacked the election for Trump, then escalated cyber warfare in general, authorizing the Central Intelligence Agency to conduct covert cyber operations against Iran and other targets. The new "presidential finding" (previously refused by both the George W. Bush and Obama administrations) gives the CIA "very specific authorities to really take the fight offensively to a handful of adversarial countries," a former US government official revealed. Russia, China, Iran, and North Korea are mentioned directly in the document, but the finding is open-ended as to cyber means and targets. The finding opened the way for the agency to launch offensive cyber operations with the aim of "producing disruption—like cutting off electricity or compromising an intelligence operation by dumping documents online—as well as destruction, similar to the US-Israeli 2009 Stuxnet attack against Iranian nuclear facilities." It permitted cyberattacks on banks and other financial institutions and even on "critical infrastructure, such as petrochemical plants, and to engage in the kind of hack-and-dump operations that Russian hackers and WikiLeaks popularized, in which tranches of stolen documents or data are leaked to journalists or posted on the internet."[64] It also lessened the standards of evidence needed to authorize covert cyber operations against entities such as media organizations, charities, religious institutions, or businesses believed to be working on behalf of adversaries' foreign intelligence services, as well as individuals affiliated with these organizations, according to former officials. In short, the Trump administration authorized the CIA to conduct just the sort of cyberwar that the United States has accused Russia and China of waging.

Masha Lipman, a noted commentator in Moscow, in October 2020 observed that the prospects for better relations between Russia and the United States were bleak no matter whether Biden or Trump won the 2020 election. Biden would consolidate European allies against Moscow: Trump was not able to protect Russia from sanctions imposed by the US Congress. The only thing that helps the Kremlin, Lipman said, was more polarization and turmoil in the United States. "Turmoil means the United States weakened," she said. "This is what the Kremlin can actually benefit from, not an improvement in relations. This is the only thing that Russia may hope for."[65]

China has also expressed its anger at the threats and disrespect it sees emanating from the United States. The Chinese Foreign Ministry, as just one example, decried US assaults on China's political independence, referencing the US sanctions employed to condemn the takeover of Hong Kong and the genocide of the Uighurs as assaults on its territorial sovereignty, highlighting depictions of a map of China used by US media in broadcasting the 2021 Olympics. The map failed to include Taiwan and the South China Sea.[66] (The United States regards Taiwan as self-governing and the South China Sea as an international body of water.)

In 2021, Beijing listed 102 ways in which the United States has interfered in Hong Kong since the mass antigovernment protests roiled the city in 2019. The Foreign Ministry published a document titled "List of Facts About U.S. Interference in Hong Kong Affairs and Support of Anti-China Forces in Hong Kong" and called it a "criminal record" of "gross interference in Hong Kong affairs." It further accused the United States, an "evil backstage manipulator," of having damaged the city's prosperity and stability. The document cited as examples: US senators meeting with Hong Kong protesters, statements by former US secretary of state Michael Pompeo condemning the arrests of activists under the security law, and the US consulate general's decision to light 400 electric candles in the building's windows to mark Beijing's 1989 crackdown in Tiananmen Square.[67] The United States regards all those acts as legitimate free speech.

These differences with China will not be overcome easily, as illustrated by President Biden in a speech to the United Nations in which he announced that support for human rights and human dignity, including giving a voice to "democratic values," was part of "our DNA as a nation."[68]

Cold War II Is Not Cold War I

When these trends are summed up, we can see that while Cold War I was predominantly "fought" through arms races and through proxy wars, such as in Vietnam, Angola, and Afghanistan, the emerging Cold War II is being "fought" mostly directly, transnationally, through industrial competition and cyber warfare. That said, proxy warfare is not off the table. The United States and Russia supported opposite sides in the Syrian civil war.[69] And the Russians directed and supported the Donbas opposition in Ukraine, while the United States and Europeans supplied weapons and finance to the Ukrainian government, until the full-scale Russian invasion of 2022, which saw NATO firmly lined up as a supplier of arms, training, and military intelligence, but not troops, to Ukraine.

The first cold war was bipolar, but this one is tripolar militarily (the United States versus the "aligned" Russia and China) and tripolar economically (China versus the aligned United States and the European Union). By the late 1960s, it was clear that US industrial might would overwhelm the USSR. Now China continues to grow at more than double the US rate with more than double the US population, and Russia (though weak economically) is investing heavily in its military capacity and in cyber warfare.[70]

The United States, China, and Russia stand out but are far from geopolitically equal. Russia is a great power only militarily; otherwise, it is more the weight of Mexico in economic terms. The United States vastly outspends China and Russia in military spending, but Russian and Chinese nuclear standing, much higher rates of increase in military spending, and revisionist strategies make them the clear rivals. Recently, Russian advances in "hyper-weapons" (the "Avangard," a very fast, maneuverable reentry vehicle) are likely to spark an arms race in these deadly weapons capable of evading existing defenses.[71]

While global military geopolitics is tripolar, Russia and China are now effectively aligned (even though mutual rivalry has characterized their past and could reemerge). Similarly, the United States and the European Union are aligned, though this alignment rapidly eroded when Trump's right-wing populist sympathies and his aggressive trade strategy put this traditional alignment under great strain. By 2022, spurred by the war in Ukraine, Biden was attempting to reestablish the transatlantic liberal democratic community. A fourth "power," the European Union, is an economic superpower, but it is overwhelmingly civilian in its orientation and less than united in its global foreign policies.[72]

Cold War II so far is much less global in its reach and the sides are less clear-cut. Nonetheless, this new cold war is spreading geographically and dividing states ideologically. China established in 2020 an arrangement with Iran and incorporated it in the Belt and Road network of investments (in return for heavily discounted oil). Accompanying the contentious summit in Alaska in 2021 between the Biden and Xi foreign policy teams, the United States has sought to mobilize a Quad of democratic powers in Asia—Japan, Australia, India, and the United States—to confront China.

Importantly, this burgeoning second cold war is not yet as extreme or as extensive as its predecessor. None are as implacably hostile to each other as they were during the Cold War. China particularly denies that it is in a cold war. During a 2020 visit to Paris, Chinese foreign minister Wang lamented that the United States has been "coercing other countries to take sides" and stoke conflict. "We never wanted to engage in a new Cold War with anyone."[73] President Biden said basically the same thing at his speech before the UN General Assembly in September 2021: "We are not seeking a new Cold War or a world divided into rigid blocs."[74] (He then went on to declare that championing the "universal rights of all people" is "our DNA as a nation" and highlighted Xinjiang and Chechnya as instances of abuse.)

Indeed, a very good case can be made that the looming cold war will not be like the post–World War II Cold War between the West and East, the United States and the USSR, NATO versus the Warsaw Pact.[75] The

Cold War was bipolar, dominated by the unusual predominance of the United States and the USSR after the defeats of Germany and Japan and the devastation of France, Britain, and China. Today, while the United States and China predominate (as the next chapter will discuss), Russia is a significant military power, and the European Union is a significant economic one.

Neither the United States nor China has as yet organized tight alliances against the other, and neither is defined to the same degree by ideology. The Cold War was a contest of superpowers but also a revolutionary confrontation between capitalism and Communism, democracy and dictatorship. Democracy versus autocracy does shape our current divide, and the economic systems of capitalism and corporatism do clash (both explored in the next chapter), but China surpassed the United States in 2022 in the number of billionaires its economy has produced. China is not seeking to spread autocracy for its own sake, and both China and the capitalist economies of Europe, Japan, and the United States understand that they are each other's best customers and suppliers.

Russia and China represent distinct challenges to US national security. Russia is said to be a "rogue"; China, a rival peer.[76] Russia is not a peer or near-peer competitor but rather a well-armed rogue state that seeks to subvert an international order it can never hope to dominate. It can militarily dominate its neighbors (as it is trying to do with Ukraine) and its clients (such as Syria). In contrast, China is a global peer competitor that wants to shape an international order that it can aspire to dominate. Both countries seek to alter the status quo, but only Russia has in recent years attacked neighboring states, annexed conquered territory, and supported insurgent forces seeking to detach yet more territory. Russia assassinates its opponents at home and abroad, interferes in foreign elections, subverts foreign democracies, and works to undermine European and Atlantic institutions. In contrast, China's growing influence is based largely on more-positive measures: trade, investment, and development assistance. These attributes make China a less immediate threat but a much greater long-term challenge. It would be pleased to dominate the IMF, World Bank, or other multilateral institutions, not destroy them.

In the military realm, Russia can be contained, but China cannot. Its military predominance in East Asia will grow over time, compelling the United States to accept greater costs and risks just to secure existing commitments. But it is geoeconomics, rather than geopolitics, in which the contest for world leadership will play out. It is in the domain of geoeconomics that the balance of global influence between the United States and China has begun shifting in China's favor. An influential RAND study has concluded that as China's per capita GDP approaches Russia's, as its population is eight times Russia's, and as its growth rate is three times Russia's, China is a greater geoeconomic challenge to the United States than Russia. As of 2017, moreover, China's economy was the second largest in the world, behind only that of the United States. Russia's was eleventh.

Russia's military expenditure is lower than China's, and that gap is likely to grow. Russia, the authors of the RAND study note, dominates militarily all its neighbors (except China) but is "vulnerable to a range of nonmilitary deterrents," such as multilateral sanctions on the Russian economy focused on exports of fossil fuels. In contrast, "militarily, China can be contained for a while longer; economically, it has already broken free of regional constraints."[77]

Yet the threat of cold war is real and increasing. China's new "wolf warrior" diplomacy is embroiling China in deep conflicts that are driving alignments along ideological fractures. When Chinese foreign minister Wang threatened Czech politicians with dire consequences if they visited Taiwan, it provoked the Czech foreign minister to declare "I am Taiwanese"—consciously echoing President Kennedy's famous Cold War words "Ich Bin Ein Berliner" at the Berlin Wall.

China, however, expresses no interest in exporting Xi-ism around the world and professes to want only prosperity for its citizens and security from foreign interference in its domestic affairs. There is no reason to question the sincerity of this claim. But complicating it is the fact that China regards the South China Sea, Taiwan, Hong Kong, Tibet, and the Uighurs as domestic matters in which no foreign interference will be tolerated. But to China's southern neighbors (and the United States and other seafaring nations), the South China Sea is international. Taiwan is functionally independent and blanketed in the Shanghai Communiqué foreclosing the use of force, and Hong Kong is cloaked in the "One Country, Two Systems" agreement that was thought to protect its domestic autonomy in court proceedings and other matters. And the Uighurs and Tibet are matters within the scope of the international community's concern with human rights. All this is ripe for tension.

Thus while China is a rival not a rogue, its international order would not just be the same order as is now dominated by the United States, Europe, and the democracies with just a new driver in the front seat. Instead, it would be committed to an authoritarian international order[78] in which human rights would no longer be the "common standard of achievement for all peoples," international financial institutions would no longer encourage market economies, and the United Nations would no longer formally support democratic governance.

Moreover, as discussed in Part Two, Trumpism, with its fandom for authoritarian rulers like Putin or Kim Jong-un, complicates ideological bifurcation. Nonetheless, Secretary Pompeo spent his 2020 trip to Western Europe attempting to garner support for a "coalition of democracies" that would confront China.

Adding further to the complexities of the second cold war, the rivalry is not a simple ideological divide like the contest between Communist Socialism and liberal capitalism. Communism, like some versions of liberalism, was a universalistic ideology. All persons should be liberated. Putin's or Xi's autocratic nationalism is a Russia-first or China-first philosophy, not a universal appeal to join a new wave of authoritarianism.[79] But, as Robert Legvold persuasively suggested in his account of the new cold war between Russia and the United States, nationalism and xenophobia can fuel a cold war conflict over legitimacy, as it has the long conflict between revolutionary Iran and the United States since the Iranian revolution.[80]

Many middle powers, moreover, resist cold war–style bifurcation. Thailand, Brazil, Mexico, South Africa, Indonesia, India, and many other developing countries were part of the sizeable minority that abstained on the UN General Assembly votes condemning Russia for the 2022 invasion of Ukraine and the expulsion of Russia from the Human Rights Council. Some recall destructive US-led interventions such as Iraq in 2003 and Libya in 2011 that left their regions in turmoil. Some have human rights vulnerabilities that make them worry about a world order that might emerge if the United States were dominant in the globe after defeat of Russia or China. India fears pressure over Kashmir; Mexico has a long-standing, brutal drug and cartel war. Others are semi-democratic and welcome an alternative, autocratic source of financing and trade. Even others, like Tanzania, find that Chinese Belt and Road financing means that they no longer need to accommodate US or Western European demands. And, still others doubt the staying power of Biden-style global engagement for democracy and imagine a United States where Trump's Republicans, close friends of Putin, return to power.[81] And many simply seek to gain whatever benefits are available from both sides without having to choose. Thus, fittingly, a "new third world," analogous to the Cold War Third World between the NATO First World and Warsaw Pact Second World, is emerging for the "new cold war."

There are, moreover, areas of common strategic interest between current actors. The United States and China both worry about the nuclearization of North Korea; the European Union and China are both troubled by climate change; the United States, European Union, and Russia are connected in efforts against Islamic State terrorism. As outlined in the next section, a new arms race will strain these affiliations and perhaps break them.

All these actors are much more economically interdependent than during the original Cold War, and tensions between them are thus much more costly. Hollywood, US agriculture, US consumer manufacturing, German auto companies, and European gas consumers will all push back against a new economic iron curtain with China and Russia. The US cyber and tech sectors battling for dominance of 5G on the other hand may welcome an isolation of Chinese competition.

Lastly, the second cold war, unlike the first, seems to be a partisan lightning rod in US domestic politics. Domestic politics no longer stops at the water's edge. President Trump seemed blind to Russian incursion (regarding criticism of Russia as criticism of himself and his narrow electoral victory in 2016). Democrats were said to be favored by China (according to the Trump administration in its electoral rhetoric in 2020).

The Impact of Cold War on the Rest of International Politics

The Cold War rapidly eroded cooperation with the Soviet Union and produced severe effects on world order; the new cold war has more to unravel but seems to be beginning to have similar effects.[82]

This is of special concern because many facets of globalization—ranging from public health crises to the emergence of violent, revolutionary non-state actors—are producing emerging threats in the current international disorder. Globalization also has and will encompass enormous opportunities, but, in various ways, international cooperation will be difficult as the following phenomena test its stability. Globalization increases interdependence and thus complicates cooperation in the face of ever-growing connections. No problem can be addressed on its own.[83]

- Public health crises and epidemics, most strikingly today COVID-19, have exposed the lack of global capacity to prevent the spread of infectious diseases.
- Financial crises and international and domestic inequalities threaten to undermine social cohesion and increase popular discontent as horizontal inequalities among ethnicities or regions correlate with increased violence and conflict.[84]
- Cybercrime and cyberterrorism feed on rapidly evolving technological innovations that have tied the world together in one informational space, creating vast new opportunities for development that also create new risks by allowing non-state actors easier access to lethal technology, such as armed drones and weapons of mass destruction.
- Migration and urbanization, including the predicted 405 million cross-border migrants by 2050,[85] will add productivity to the econ-

omies, but also put at risk the social cohesion of host countries. Humanitarian disasters—man-made and natural—add a layer of complexity to this dynamic. For example, the humanitarian catastrophe emanating out of Syria—with 4.086 million refugees—places immense pressures on Turkey, Jordan, Lebanon, Iraq, and Egypt[86] and on the European asylum system as Syrian refugees swamped reception capacities and took ever more dangerous routes through the Mediterranean and Balkans.

- Climate change ties the world ever more closely together in a common fate: an increasingly limited supply of necessary food, water, land, and clean air. Yet the demand for these resources is rising because of an increase in population.[87] According to the United Nations, by 2030 the world will need at least 30 percent more water, 50 percent more food, and 45 percent more energy than we use today.[88] All these have the potential both to stress the planet and to provoke a conflict over resources.

- Lastly, the rise of new non-state actors poses its own challenges and threats to the multilateral system by increasing the number and character of participants in the international arena and adding radical and violent preferences to the conflict mix. At the extreme, this includes attacks and casualties due to terrorism (understood as non-state attacks on noncombatants).

Exacerbating and radically complicating the preceding insecurities is the fact that they are parts of the more general crisis facing the international order, both today and in the foreseeable future. States must try to protect their citizens from terrorist attacks and cybercrimes. But, as John Mueller and others have argued, this should be seen primarily as a policing matter, not a geopolitical threat.[89] Regional crises, including the devastation of Syria after 2011 and the 2018–2019 crisis in Venezuela, have all been deeply traumatic for those who have experienced them, but their wider impact is shaped by the overarching rivalry between the United States and Russia and China. It is the rivalries among these states that provide an additional hostile global valence to each of those individual problems. Those global rivalries will drive an arms race and pose warlike (but not necessarily kinetic) threats to the fundamental rights of "political independence and territorial integrity" promised to all states in the UN Charter (Article 2.4). Indeed, at the worst, we may look back with longing to an era when we merely experienced disorder and ungovernability, rather than a world split into blocs in which what were merely problems became instruments of strategic destabilization.

A threatened new cold war questions underlying principles of legitimate, problem-solving cooperation. It encourages states to exacerbate rather than ameliorate crises in order to pressure rivals. It makes each of the six challenges noted above less likely to be addressed in a spirit of problem solving.

Josep Borrell (EU foreign policy chief) diagnosed the resulting problem in this way: "The demand for multilateral solutions is much greater than the supply," he said, pointing to "more divisions, more free-riding and more distrust than the world can afford." "We need global cooperation based on agreed rules because the alternative is the law of the jungle, where problems don't get solved," he said. "Every day we see the cost of the absence of multilateral action in reduced access to vaccines and insufficient climate action, and peace and security crises that fester."[90]

A pertinent example is the dispute over the new Russian-led global cybercrime treaty introduced in the UN General Assembly in November 2019. The treaty would replace the Budapest Convention (2001) on cybercrime policing. Few dispute the danger of cybercrime noted above, but a coalition of Western states describes the proposed new treaty as a license to police Internet freedom of access and transmission in the name of vague "emergencies" to protect governments from criticism. Described by one US official as a "digital Iron Curtain," it has mobilized a new authoritarian versus liberal divide with China, Russia, North Korea, Myanmar, Nicaragua, Syria, Cambodia, Venezuela, and Belarus leading the new effort to control the Internet and the United States, Japan, Morocco, Costa Rica, and all but two of the European Union countries defending the existing treaty.[91]

Another example is the sanctions regime for North Korean nuclearization. In May 2022, the UN Security Council voted on a draft resolution updating and strengthening the Security Council Resolution 1718 Democratic People's Republic of Korea (DPRK) sanctions regime. China and Russia both cast a veto, even though all the previous resolutions on North Korean nuclearization had passed with Permanent Five (P5; United States, Russia, China, France, United Kingdom) support. The remaining thirteen council members voted in favor of the resolution.[92]

Even the global catastrophe of the COVID-19 pandemic has become an instrument of Cold War–style rivalry, with Russian and Chinese spy agencies preying on US and European labs to steal vaccine research (we are not aware whether Western spy agencies are reciprocating or not).[93]

Cold War Divided Multilateralisms

Human rights (as established in the Universal Declaration of Human Rights [UDHR]), peacekeeping, and NATO were all born between 1948 and 1949. The first two preceded, and the last directly reflected, an escalating Cold War.

The UDHR was endorsed in 1948, just as the era of the World War II "United Nations" alliance was fading and Cold War tensions were rising. It reflected many ideologies: Western liberalism and social democracy, Global South developmentalism, and Soviet Communism. Eleanor Roosevelt's social democracy, John Peters Humphrey's liberalism, and Charles Malik and René Cassin's cultural humanism kept these ideologies together enough to produce the UDHR amalgam. The UDHR passed in 1948 with no negative votes, forty-eight positive, but with eight abstentions (the USSR, Byelorussia, Ukraine, Poland, Yugoslavia, Czechoslovakia, and—for obvious reasons—South Africa and Saudi Arabia). This soon produced divisions on human rights, with the West sponsoring civic and political rights and the East social and economic rights—all of which had been united in the UDHR.

A Cold War stalemate between East and West at the UN Security Council also limited the scope of peacekeeping. "First-generation" peacekeeping emerged in 1948, designed to launch interpositions between warring parties to monitor truces. However, its reach was limited to the few conflicts that both the United States and the USSR wanted to isolate, and its functions were limited to monitoring truces—with the notable exceptions of the peace operations in the Congo and Lebanon.

On the other hand, NATO, created in 1949, directly reflected and flourished in the Cold War. It was not merely a military alliance, as suggested by the preamble to the North Atlantic Treaty, which stipulated that:

> The Parties to this Treaty . . . reaffirm their faith in the purposes and principles of the Charter of the United Nations and are determined to safeguard the freedom, common heritage and civilisation of their peoples, founded on the principles of democracy, individual liberty and the rule of law.

The Cold War stimulated, reinforced, and gave shape to NATO's confrontation with the Warsaw Pact across Europe, which was replicated and mirrored in numerous regional conflicts and in the alphabet soup of alliances including CENTO (the Central Treaty Organization [for the Middle East]) and SEATO (the South East Asia Treaty Organization).

Post-Cold War Global Multilateralism

The Cold War ended with Gorbachev's loosening of the restraints on Eastern Europe: the famous "Sinatra doctrine" (each country could now do it "my way"); his announcement that open democracy was the crucial foundation of genuine socialism (1985 Party Congress Speech); and, most strikingly, his announcement that human rights were not Western, but were rather "human values," owned and acknowledged by all human beings.[94] The end of the Cold War was reinforced by the movement toward glasnost and perestroika in the USSR and ultimately secured with its collapse in 1991.

After the Cold War, human rights doctrines flourished, the high point being the Vienna Declaration's consensus that human rights are "universal, indivisible, interdependent, and interrelated"—rhetorically amalgamating civic and political rights with their economic and social counterparts. Similarly, with the Agenda for Peace (1992), peacekeeping flourished with a rapid escalation in the number and depth of missions. This included the move from first-generation ceasefire monitoring to second-generation multidimensional peace building and third-generation peace enforcement (including the protection of civilians). Before 1988, there were thirteen UN peacekeeping operations (an average of just over three per decade), and between 1988 and 2010 there were fifty-three (about twenty-six per decade).

While human rights and peacekeeping operations blossomed, NATO entered a period of identity crisis. It had been designed to deter the Soviet Union and the Warsaw Pact and to stop the spread of Communism. What should it do once these threats were gone? Indeed, many scholars of international relations predicted its rapid demise.

NATO, however, did not die. Rather, it expanded in numbers and evolved by undertaking new roles, including peacekeeping in the Balkans and then peace enforcement in Afghanistan. Institutions rarely do die. The United States still has two powerful regiments called cavalry, though now they ride helicopters. But NATO budgets did fall, and readiness slipped.

New Cold War Plurilateralism

Since 2012—the year of Putin's return to the Russian presidency and Xi's ascendancy in China, both of which sparked alarm in the United States and Europe—we have seen the signs of the emergence of another cold war.

At its most general, we see the emergence of two different "plurilateral" approaches to global multilateralism.[95] In the words of a valuable 2019 report from the Center for a New American Security, China's approach:

1. Promotes a particularist view of human rights, in which each country's unique conditions can provide justifications for the government to disregard individual or minority claims.
2. Redefines democracy in terms of so-called "economic and social rights," rather than inalienable political rights.

3. Makes state sovereignty inviolable and reestablishes states as the only legitimate stakeholders in global governance.
4. Resolves political issues through bilateral negotiations, where China can use its full panoply of leverage to get its way over smaller, weaker states.

The liberal democratic approach, traditionally (before and after Trump) that of the United States and its allies:

1. Supports a universal view of human rights in which civil liberties are inalienable rights regardless of a country's internal political circumstances or considerations.
2. Affirms that representative systems of government support peoples' aspirations to peace and prosperity and that countries need not choose between democracy and development.
3. Supports the independent role of civil society in shaping international organizations' responses to political problems.
4. Strengthens rules-based multilateral approaches that provide big and small states alike with avenues to advance their interests, subject to clear consensus principles.

But with the advent of the Trump administration, human rights came under attack by all sides. Indeed, the combination of rising Cold War–style tensions and Trump's illiberalism greatly harmed the human rights project. The United States withdrew from the UN Human Rights Council (to then rejoin under Biden). China's action against Uighurs and Putin's attack against freedom of speech (criticism of state and government is now illegal) were both condemned by the European Parliament.

A vote in 2020 in the UN Human Rights Council became emblematic of both the emerging divide and China's rising clout. China was able to secure a lopsided victory in support of its crackdown on civil rights in Hong Kong under the new National Security Law. Fifty-three states voted with China; twenty-seven opposed.

Supporting: China, Antigua and Barbuda, Bahrain, Belarus, Burundi, Cambodia, Cameroon, Central African Republic, Comoros, Congo-Brazzaville, Cuba, Djibouti, Dominica, Egypt, Equatorial Guinea, Eritrea, Gabon, Gambia, Guinea, Guinea-Bissau, Iran, Iraq, Kuwait, Laos, Lebanon, Lesotho, Mauritania, Morocco, Mozambique, Myanmar, Nepal, Nicaragua, Niger, North Korea, Oman, Pakistan, Palestine, Papua New Guinea, Saudi Arabia, Sierra Leone, Somalia, South Sudan, Sri Lanka, Sudan, Suriname, Syria, Tajikistan, Togo, United Arab Emirates, Venezuela, Yemen, Zambia, and Zimbabwe.

Opposing: Australia, Austria, Belgium, Belize, Canada, Denmark, Estonia, Finland, France, Iceland, Ireland, Germany, Japan, Latvia, Liechtenstein, Lithuania, Luxembourg, Marshall Islands, Netherlands, New Zealand, Norway, Palau, Slovakia, Slovenia, Sweden, Switzerland, and the United Kingdom.

Only three of China's supporters were rated "free" by Freedom House: Antigua and Barbuda, Dominica, and Suriname (combined population, about 700,000). All three, and at least forty of the other signatories, have signed onto China's Belt and Road infrastructure project. Many of the African signatories are trying to renegotiate debt payments to China amid sharp COVID-related downturns.[96] Not all the supporters regularly align with China and other authoritarians; some indeed, such as Saudi Arabia, are close US allies. But the autocratic liberal divide is there to be exploited in the new cold war contest.

Another significant vote occurred in May 2021, when the UN General Assembly voted to re-endorse the principles of "Responsibility to Protect," the UN doctrine first adopted in 2005 that holds states responsible for protecting their populations from atrocity crimes and authorizes the UN Security Council to act when states fail to do so. The vote was 115 in favor, 15 against, 28 abstentions (and 35 nonvoting).[97] Those against included a significant grouping again reflecting the emerging counter-alignments. They included Russia, China, Belarus, Nicaragua, Cuba, Venezuela, Bolivia, Burundi, North Korea, Egypt, Eritrea, Kyrgyzstan,

Zimbabwe, and Indonesia. The key complaint from China and Russia was that "Responsibility to Protect" has been and would be manipulated. But clearly, this was ideological line drawing. No action by the UN Security Council can be taken unless both Russia and China approve.

A rivalry for control of the United Nations has emerged between the United States and its liberal allies, on one side, and Russia and China and its allies on the other. China is taking charge of the committees that appoint human rights rapporteurs in order to ensure that its view has influence. It has also taken over the COVID-19 investigation in the World Health Organization.[98]

A commitment to peacekeeping has also been collateral damage of escalating tensions. There have been only five UN peacekeeping operations launched since 2012, and because of Russian and Chinese vetoes, the UN Security Council has been AWOL on Syria.

A report from the International Crisis Group (ICG) highlighted important trends. In 2019, the UN Security Council's

> members sparred bitterly over Venezuela, struggled to sustain the Yemeni peace process, and failed to come to common positions on events in Sudan and Libya.... The Council has not discussed Venezuela at all since May (even members that want it to do more think the crisis is too polarising) and found it hard to respond to fresh outbreaks of violence in Yemen. It has done little to stop the ongoing fighting in Libya and—other than agreeing to keep UN peacekeepers in Darfur—made a scant contribution to Sudan's political transition. It has responded indecisively to other challenges, including the Kashmir crisis and Turkey's incursion into Syria.

The ICG continued, identifying three trends. "The first is a gradual but significant souring of relations between China and the Council's Western members. The second is the deepening of divisions between the U.S. and its European allies about the forum's role in responding to trouble spots such as Syria and the Democratic People's Republic of Korea (DPRK).

The third is the growth of disputes over how the Council deals with crises in Africa—which have created divisions both between African and
non-African diplomats and also among African officials themselves."[99]

As an example of the costs of the new cold war divide, consider arms
control diplomacy with North Korea. In December 2017, the UN Security
Council agreed that another test of a North Korean ballistic missile capable of reaching the United States would result in new fuel sanctions to
coerce Kim Jong-un. But in March 2022, when Kim tested just that kind
of missile, the Security Council flinched. China and Russia refused to
sanction a North Korea that had become an ally in their coalition against
NATO's response to the Russian invasion of Ukraine.[100]

Even when it comes to basic global public goods such as disease containment, the new cold war is eroding cooperation. According to UN
secretary-general Guterres, a "dysfunctional relationship" between
members of the UN Security Council has hindered an effective global
response to the new coronavirus. He added: "Each country went its own
way, with the epicenter moving from country to country. . . . We see that
the very dysfunctional relationship that exists today between the United
States-China, United States-Russia, makes it practically impossible for
the Security Council to take any meaningful decision that would be
fundamental."[101]

One might thus expect that NATO, as during the Cold War, should now
be reviving. However, although European and Canadian defense expenditure, after falling during the Great Recession, sharply rose in 2014, NATO
too may be in crisis. Until the invasion of Ukraine revived the institution,
NATO was subject to deep divisions between its Western European members and the United States. To quote two prominent diplomats, Nicholas
Burns and Douglas Lute:

> The single greatest challenge NATO faces today is the critical need
> for reviving strong, reliable American leadership. . . . At the most
> basic level, the next American president must reaffirm U.S. com-
> mitment to the Alliance, especially the Article 5 collective defense
> pledge, in both words and deeds. Given the opportunity to do so

within months of his inauguration in May 2017, President Trump refused to honor the U.S. commitment to Article 5, even while unveiling a memorial at the new NATO headquarters commemorating its historic invocation after 9/11.[102]

Ironically, then, the new cold war seems to be producing problematic prospects for all three pillars of the post–World War II international order. Peacekeeping operations and human rights are harmed by the new cold war rivalry, while NATO was damaged by Trump's presidency, and a return of similar policies would have similar effects.

Part Two

THE
SOURCES
OF CONFLICT

■ THE COLD WAR WAS "FOUGHT"
predominantly through arms races between NATO and the Warsaw
Pact, through covert action and through proxy wars, such as in Vietnam,
Angola, and Afghanistan.[1] As the previous chapter argued, the looming
new cold war is mostly fought directly and limitedly, again with the large
exceptions of Syria and Ukraine, and transnationally, through political
subversion, industrial competition, and cyber warfare. The Cold War was
bipolar; the new cold war is tripolar militarily (United States, Russia, and
China) and tripolar economically (European Union, United States, and
China). But, net, the United States and China emerge as a bipolar rivalry
that is both military and economic. At the same time, global politics is
bifurcated into two alliances: one liberal, led by the United States, and
one autocratic, the alignment of Russia and China.

By the late 1960s, it was clear that US industrial might would overwhelm the USSR. Now China continues to grow at more than double the US rate with more than double the US population, and Russia
(though weak economically) dominated the contest over Syria and in
2022 invaded Ukraine while investing heavily in military capacity and
cyber warfare.[2]

Three powers stand out but are not (yet) geopolitically equal. The
United States vastly exceeds China and Russia in military spending, but
Russian and Chinese nuclear standing, much higher rates of increase in
military spending, and aggressive strategies make them the clear rivals.
The fourth "power," the European Union, is an economic superpower,
but it is overwhelmingly civilian in its orientation. Its member states have
aligned in NATO with the United States but, until Putin's invasion of
Ukraine mobilized a spirit of unity in NATO, its members were far from
united in their global foreign policies.[3]

Amy Zegart, an intelligence specialist, nicely summarized the varying aspects of threats the United States (and the liberal West) faces:

> In the old days, power and geography protected America. Not anymore. Cyberspace is enabling adversaries to attack us across long distances without firing a shot, hacking machines as well as minds. China has prosecuted a sustained and successful campaign to steal huge amounts of American intellectual property for economic and military advantage. Russia is using cyber-enabled information operations to interfere in elections and undermine democracies from within. Criminal groups are waging ransomware attacks against American cities, energy suppliers, and other crucial infrastructure. The array of threats facing the country has never been greater because cyberspace is strengthening the weak and weakening the strong. Advanced industrial democracies are exceptionally vulnerable to cyber breaches of all kinds because they are the most digitally connected and because their freedom of speech enables nefarious actors to deceive at scale.[4]

China's rival power, Russia's rogue behavior, and various sources of disruption pose significant but diverse threats. Together they pose a significant threat of an emerging new cold war between liberal and authoritarian blocs. What are its sources? To what extent are these sources international (interstate among the separate powers and blocs) and transnational (spilling over into and from domestic politics and economics)?

I start with the general challenges of cooperation in international relations. In Chapter Three, I explore the special circumstances of interstate competition as power shifts from a hegemon to a rival. In Chapters Four and Five, I address the transnational systemic rivalries of authoritarian and democratic political systems.

The Challenge of International Cooperation

Cooperation is always difficult in world politics. The absence of world government makes aligning interests a challenge because "harmony"—

when interests and strategies all align—is very rare. Coordination too is a problem even when interests and values overlap, because states rationally have an interest in shifting the costs of cooperation onto other states even when they agree on the goal. Misinterpretation and the inability to rely on promises of future action also create incentives to choose immediate advantage over cooperative action even when the benefits of cooperation are larger than the payoff to individual action, again because of the uncertainty over whether other states have compatible interests and, if they do, whether they too will cooperate.

When one adds to anarchy the assumptions of Hobbesian human motivations—fear, glory, and material advantage—the condition of the "state of nature" becomes a "state of war" (where the possibility of battle is known) and in Hobbes's famous phrase, "the life of man, solitary, poor, nasty, brutish, and short."[5]

That is the heart of the structural realist story of world politics where states in an international system are analogized to Hobbesian individuals in a state of nature lacking government. Cooperation can be achieved but only when either anarchy is controlled or motivations are changed. One thus needs to change—in the words of the traditional international relations metaphors—either the "forest" (the system of states) or the "beasts" (the states themselves) or both.

Cooperation under anarchy can be advanced by international coercion (empire or hegemony) or rational strategies that change the system. Empires impose order (favoring the dominant state) as do hegemonies.

Under more equal circumstances, while states often have competitive interests and some seek glory, the deeper difficulty of cooperation in an interdependent world is that even when states have common interests, those interests are not sufficient to produce cooperative outcomes. All parties can benefit from a cooperative solution, but no cooperation will be forthcoming unless they (or a sufficient number of them) can be individually motivated to act. This is the famous "tragedy of the commons" problem of collective action. Each party will rationally shift the responsibility and free ride rather than volunteer to bear proportionate costs because it will assume that someone else will bear the costs. Alternatively, if a party does cooperate, it will assume that the cooperation of others cannot be guaranteed, and thus its investment in cooperation will be wasted.

Cooperation becomes likely, therefore, only when one predominant actor can bear the entire cost with the expectation that the benefits it receives are greater than the entire cost (letting others free ride). Alternatively, a very few, rational and interdependent actors sufficiently bound together can act in concert ("one for all and all for one").[6] During the Cold War, US predominance in the West is said to have provided that first kind of leadership.[7]

Repeated interaction and iteration among equals can also produce cooperation when states adopt tit-for-tat strategies (punishing defection, rewarding cooperation) and information is perfect, numbers of states are small, interdependence is clear, and the "game" has no expected end point. All these demanding assumptions are necessary so that the calculations of consequences are clear.[8] Clearly, the challenge of effective cooperation is real.

Changing the "beasts" is an alternative famously explored in liberal theory (and some Marxist Socialist theories) that envisions changes in values and interests produced by domestic structures (democracy, constitutionalism, Socialism) that create reliable ("self-enforcing") incentives to cooperate. Thus in the "democratic peace thesis" inspired by the great eighteenth-century German philosopher Immanuel Kant, liberal democracies respect fellow liberal democracies because they are also committed to respecting individual liberties, and they are internally constrained by constitutional provisons encouraging deliberation and by the representation of voters who bear the costs of war as soldiers and taxpayers.

Actor and process theories have explored how these changes work in various combined settings, as was done by Elinor Ostrom in her Nobel Prize–winning work.[9] In it, she outlined the large number of attitudes and processes that might contribute to successful cooperation. Similarly, Robert Ellickson developed an illuminating account of remarkable cooperation among otherwise competitive Shasta Valley ranchers and farmers. One implication of Ellickson's argument is thus that cooperation is possible and effective without external (i.e., global) regulation and courts. The question then is what it takes for nations to become reliable "neighbors" like the Shasta ranchers and farmers.

The keys to successful cooperation for Ellickson appear to have been three: minimal "social distance" (shared circumstances and compatible values); lower or disaggregated rather than higher and existential stakes; and mutual interdependence (the absence of third parties on whom the consequences and costs can be off-loaded).[10]

Today the international system lacks the standard Ellicksonian prerequisites of cooperation. It has shared circumstances (including climate change) but not noticeable shared values (autocracy versus democracy); the stakes are potentially very high if cooperation fails; and, while mutually interdependent, there are multiple actors (to blame for failed cooperation). US hegemony has fallen since the Cold War, reducing systemic sources of imposed cooperation, and the emerging discord between autocracy and democracy reduces the potential for cooperative values and credible commitments.[11]

Generalizable theories thus suggest rocky roads lie ahead. And when we look into the specifics of systemic rivalry and transnational competition, the prospects look even more challenging. We are in the middle of a dynamic evolution that sees the rise of China in influence, challenging the rules established by the United States and its allies after World War II. China is insisting, sometimes reasonably, on new standards and additional hands on the wheels of global trade, finance, and the management of the multilateral institutions like the United Nations, the global seas, and global infrastructure investment. And, as President Biden recently warned, we are experiencing a contest of political institutions and ideologies, democracies versus autocracies. All make global cooperation vastly more difficult, as I elaborate in this part of the book, which traces the sources of the emerging international dis/order.

CHAPTER THREE

Superpower Systems, Hegemonic Transitions, and Multidimensional Polarity

What sort of international system are we likely to experience? Unipolar, bipolar, or multipolar... or multidimensional? And with what effects?

As noted earlier, superpower hegemony can enhance multilateral cooperation among self-interested states when the private benefit of cooperation to the predominant state exceeds the collective costs of providing cooperation. Hegemonic cooperation presupposes that hegemonic states share with other states a common cooperative goal from which all benefit. This form of cooperation is especially prevalent in bipolar systems that enhance solidarity within blocs while exacerbating rivalry between them.[1] Thus, the relative decline of old superpowers (most strikingly the collapse of the USSR and the Warsaw Pact) opened a brief period in the 1990s and early 2000s in which the United States was the sole superpower in a unipolar system in which US hard and soft power predominated. Liberal optimists, such as Francis Fukuyama, then announced an "end to history."[2] Today, the relative decline of US hegemony (accompanied by the rise of new powers such as China) presents linked problems of both a decline of hegemonic cooperation and an increase in the diversity of ideologies and preferences that make all forms of cooperation more difficult.

The power structure of the international system affects how hostile or cooperative relations are among its component states. Systems are seen as unipolar, bipolar, or multipolar, depending on the number and relative power of the leading states.[3]

Unipolar superpower hegemony can enhance multilateral cooperation among self-interested states, particularly when the benefits of free trade, monetary cooperation, or multilateral security overwhelmingly accrue to a large state (measured in GDP). That hegemonic state can then subsidize the others' share in the costs of maintaining cooperation and still come out ahead. Other states will free ride or the hegemon may choose to impose costs for noncooperation that ensure the cooperative arrangement. Many saw both the Cold War in the West and the post–Cold War 1990s more globally reflecting these dynamics.

Unipolar systems thus can be stable,[4] but only if the security incentives to balance against the hegemon are curtailed. Hegemonic cooperation presupposes that hegemonic states share with other states a common goal from which all would benefit if they cooperated.[5] However, concerns about national security can easily overwhelm the profits derived from trade or investment or other forms of cooperation, so it is vitally important that states possess a credibly assuring, nonthreatening foreign policy. This form of cooperation tends, for obvious reasons, to be especially prevalent either in bipolar systems that enhance solidarity within already aligned blocs, while exacerbating rivalry between them, or among similarly identified domestic orders (such as fellow liberal democracies). Thus, the post–World War II international order became bifurcated, with international liberal cooperation flourishing in the West, led by the United States, and a (much more imposed) international Communist order flourishing in the East.

What sort of an international order are we entering today?

Unipolarity seems over (unless China collapses in internal strife). Tripolarity is unlikely (unless the European Union suddenly unites into a single federal power). The BRICS (Brazil, Russia, India, China, and South Africa) nations not surprisingly talk about a new multipolar order composed of themselves with the United States. But the material trends, as measured by comparative GDP, appear to favor bipolarity.

According to the US Department of Agriculture's most recent macroeconomic projections, China will continue to boast the world's second-largest economy in 2030, a close second to the United States (Table 2). India is projected to have the third-largest economy by that same year, but the projections for the United States and China are three to four times as large. To the extent that basic material forces shape the international order, this indicates a bipolar world order is more likely than a multipolar or unipolar world order in the next fifteen years.[6]

Table 2. Real Gross Domestic Product (GDP) in 2010 US Dollars (in Trillions) for Richest Countries: 1969, 2014, and 2030[7]

Ranking	1969	2014	2030 (Projected)
1	USA, 4.8	USA, 16.3	USA, 24.8
2	Japan, 1.9	China, 8.1	China, 22.2
3	Germany, 1.4	Japan, 5.6	India, 6.6
4	USSR, 1.10[8]	Germany, 3.5	Japan, 6.4
5	France, 1.0	France, 2.6	Germany, 4.5
6	UK, 0.89	UK, 2.4	Brazil, 4.0
7*	Italy, 0.87	Russia, 1.67[9]	Russia, 2.43[10]

*See notes for Russia.

Still other estimates project China's GDP at double that of the United States (when measured in current dollars) in 2030.[11] Another estimate using purchasing power–based conversion in 2010 dollars (that is, when account is taken of the same value in actual goods) puts the differences as shown in Table 3.

Table 3. GDP in Trillions of US Dollars, Purchasing Power Parity (2010 Conversion)[12]

Country	2020	2040
China	17.7	36.5
Russia	3.0	4.7
USA	17.7	27.5
Japan	4.3	5.5
"EU 15 plus UK"[13]	13.8	20.2

Of course, GDP is not a direct source of geopolitical power. Moreover, estimating long-run trends in GDP is far from an exact science.[14] Purchasing power parity (what an equivalent basket of goods costs) is relevant for the costs of troops, not for the costs of satellites, which is better measured by market exchanges that reflect global prices for high tech. GDP estimates thus reflect irreducible uncertainties, together with differences of methodology.

Complicating that is whether we can simply project current trends. China has been growing impressively in both GDP and GDP per capita. But some prognosticators worry that the age imbalance in China, which in the past has advantaged China with a disproportionately large young and productive population, will shift, producing a disproportionately large elderly population, reducing productivity, and increasing the health-care and other costs associated with age. This has led knowledgeable commentators, including Minxin Pei, to warn that extrapolating Chinese growth in ways that see its economy surpass that of the United States misses significant limitations to Chinese economic development. Pei stresses the impact of an aging population, which could include a population decline from 1.4 billion to 587 million by 2100. He also identified the drag on innovation and efficiency imposed by centralized party control, commenting: "The party's existential fear of losing control will impel it to maintain a tight grip on the economy, making it less efficient. Giant but ossified state-owned enterprises will continue to waste resources."[15] He then added that the United States has the advantage of allies across the globe, and China is faced with nearby rivals in Japan and India.

Another source of uncertainty is that GDP is a weak predictor of power. If power is demonstrated influence, then aspects of what Joseph Nye has called "soft power"—including norms, ideas, and culture—make a difference.[16] Moreover, even hard power depends on context and strategy: Influence depends on what you are hoping to do (to whom, when, and how).[17]

Well short of the vague (but important) effects of soft power, military "hard power" still counts. Weapons acquisition and an arms race also shaped the bipolar confrontation of the 1960s. (In 1969, the United States had 26,910 nuclear weapons, while the Soviet Union had only 10,538.)[18] The military dimension of power retains its significance and has, in fact, become less determined by purely economic resources. Commitment makes a difference. Russia currently magnifies its global standing in the military area with almost 6,000 nuclear warheads, more than the ~5,500 currently in the US arsenal. Indeed, the imbalance between its reduced economy and continued nuclear eminence is dangerous.

The United States clearly dominates China today in global military capabilities. The United States has 20 times the nuclear warheads; 11 nuclear powered aircraft carriers to China's 2 (soon to be 3) conventionally powered carriers; and 2,000 modern fighter jets to China's 600.[19]

Relative commitment also makes and will make a difference. Reflecting just important differences in military resources and commitment, military expert Michael O'Hanlon of Brookings estimates US military spending at 3.3 percent of GDP in 2018 ($604.5 billion), Chinese at 1.5 percent ($220 billion), and Russian at 3.7 percent ($46.6 billion). With similar levels of commitment, military spending in 2040 is thus likely to be as shown in Table 4.

Table 4. Projected Military Spending in 2040[20]

Country	2010 US Dollars (Billions)
China	550
Russia	170
USA	700
Japan	50
"EU plus UK"	300

Extrapolating further from Table 4, it is easy to imagine that—if relations became even more contentious and cold war-ish—a much richer China could begin to spend at the US rate, pushing its spending to around $1,210 billion. This raises the prospect of a near equality of spending between China and Russia, on the one hand (totaling $1,380 billion), and the United States, Japan and the European Union on the other (totaling $1,050 billion).

What all the estimates seem to agree upon is that over the next twenty years, a multipolar, relatively equal "classical" balance of five or more powers is the least likely scenario. It is also feasible that (should the United States experience an economic crisis) China will be the unipolar power or (should the European Union unite to become a single sovereign power) a tripolar order will emerge. But neither of those two scenarios are as likely as is some form of bipolarity between the United States and China, reinforced by allies such as Russia for China and Japan and the EU states for the United States.

At the same time, given the complexities of what constitutes power—hard and soft—and Russia's military hard power and the European Union's capacities as an economic and soft power, the best descriptor seems to be global bipolarity with parallel, multidimensional, multipolar "chessboards" playing differing geopolitical games at different times and places.[21]

For a variety of reasons described in the next section, none of these scenarios is promising for international cooperation. The relative decline of old superpowers (most strikingly the collapse of the USSR and the Warsaw Pact) and the rise of new ones present linked problems of both a decline of hegemonic cooperation (by the United States in the West) and an increase in the diversity of ideologies and preferences that make all forms of cooperation more difficult.

Multipolarity and Bipolarity

Multipolar balance-of-power systems have often been seen as moderating tensions and stabilizing international security because of their flexibility.[22] They moderate because shifting alliances (as states seek to counter threats from other states) can substitute for preventive wars or the costly efforts required to build military capacity. And they curb ideological confrontation because states of opposing ideologies but nearly equal power can find that they need to cooperate in new alliances across ideological divides for the sake of opposing other coalitions of states. These systemic features (together with eighteenth-century Europe's shared culture and aristocratic governments) made for the vaunted moderation of the classical balance of power.[23]

Countering this moderation are the dangers of "chain-ganging" and "buck-passing" as described in a classic article by Thomas Christensen and Jack Snyder.[24] When offensive weapons are perceived to be dominant and consequently there are advantages to striking first, multipolarity encourages chain-ganging as alliances preemptively strike to avoid the defection of members (as seemingly occurred at the start of World War I with Germany's decision to back Austria, and France and the United Kingdom's decisions to back Russia). When the defense dominates, alliances buck-pass and appease as each member seeks to hide behind the defenses of others, and potential aggressors can grow in power by picking off alliance members selectively (as occurred in pre–World War II appeasement of Nazi Germany).

Bipolarity also lays claim to stability, as described in a famous article by Kenneth Waltz.[25] In effect, bipolarity allegedly resolves the problems of multipolar chain-ganging and buck-passing. Chain-ganging is addressed because no member of an alliance with a polar state is of a power weight so important as to warrant protection at the cost of an otherwise unnecessary war. Buck-passing is precluded because there is no other power but the polar power that can meet a threat from the other pole; the polar powers are thus always attentive and prepared, partly because they can focus on just each other. In another famous analogy, while one "scorpion in a bottle" is secure, two are more likely to survive through vigilant deterrence than any other larger number because of the threat of accidental contagious contact leading to mutually destructive war.

Countering bipolar stability, or at least bipolar moderation, are two other more powerful tendencies. One is the very concentrated quality of the bipolar standoff. A bilateral context tends toward the extremes: Survival is victory, and defeat is destruction. Carl von Clausewitz, the Prussian strategist, brilliantly conveyed in his classic tome, *On War*, the tendency of such two-sided wars to continue until total destruction. Each defeat tempts the losing power to renewed effort in order to avoid ultimate destruction, and each victory tempts the victor to escalate in order to avoid the defeated recovering its military capacity and fighting again.[26]

The second is the tendency of bipolar systems to exacerbate (even, according to some, to originate) ideological conflict. The classic source is the wonderful satire *Gulliver's Travels* (1726) by Jonathan Swift.[27] The relevant passage from it (Part I, Chapter 14) runs as follows:

> It is allowed on all hands, that the primitive way of breaking eggs before we eat them, was upon the larger end: but his present Majesty's grandfather, while he was a boy, going to eat an egg, and breaking it according to the ancient practice, happened to cut one of his fingers. Whereupon the Emperor his father published an edict, commanding all his subjects, upon great penalties, to break the smaller end of their eggs. The people so highly resented this law, that our Histories tell us there have been six rebellions raised on that account, wherein one Emperor lost his life, and another his crown. These civil commotions were constantly fomented by the monarchs of Blefuscu, and when they were quelled, the exiles always fled for refuge to that Empire. It is computed, that eleven thousand persons have, at several times, suffered death, rather than submit to break their eggs at the smaller end. Many hundred large volumes have been published upon this controversy: but the books of the Big-Endians have been long forbidden, and the whole party rendered incapable by law of holding employments. During the course of these troubles, the emperors of Blefuscu did frequently expostulate by their ambassadors, accusing us of making a schism in religion, by offending against a fundamental doc-

trine of our great prophet Lustrog, in the fifty-fourth chapter of the Brundecral (which is their Alcoran). This, however, is thought to be a mere strain upon the text: for their words are these; That all true believers shall break their eggs at the convenient end: and which is the convenient end, seems, in my humble opinion, to be left to every man's conscience, or at least in the power of the chief magistrate to determine.

The passage is a satire on the insubstantiality of conflict between Protestants and Catholics (or Whigs and Tories) in early eighteenth-century Britain and of the fierce rivalry between England and France. The systemic point is the way in which Blefuscu (France) protects the Big-Endians (Tories) and foments Big-Endian rebellion in Lilliput (England). (And we can presume vice versa.) The domestic binary ideological conflict is sustained by the parallel bipolar distribution of international political strife. Each ideology becomes a partisan of the other external power, making every civil war international and every international war a domestic civil war ... while exacerbating strife and violence all around. Many, of course, see similarities to the post–World War II Cold War between the democratic capitalist US/NATO and the autocratic Communist USSR/ Warsaw Pact.

Bipolarity also significantly facilitates informal empire. In a bipolar system, each pole controls subordinate countries by ensuring the rule of a favorable faction. This international control is made more secure because defection is equivalent to revolution, placing in power the other, hostile ideology.[28] This permits informal rule through effective control while maintaining the nominal independence of the subordinate state and has similarities to US-controlled anti-Communism in capitalist Central America and to Soviet-imposed anti-capitalism in Communist Eastern Europe.

When informal empire is facilitated in this way, the system encourages the extension of bipolar conflict into the peripheries, globalizing the original conflict between the two poles. Bipolarity also ensures that the conflict escalates and spreads beyond power politics to other egg-endianisms such as economics, ideology, culture, sport, and any other human activity that can conceivably produce winners and losers.

Hegemonic Transition

The last major international systemic effect is transition from one hegemon to another. It has long been seen as deeply destabilizing. Attention to this dynamic has been traced to Thucydides's warning in his *History of the Peloponnesian War* that the rise of Athens and the challenge it posed to Spartan hegemony precipitated war. When the old hegemon seeks to hold on to the privileges of preeminence and the rising challenger insists on imposing its own international order, war becomes the decider.[29]

Today, geopolitical strategists thus worry about the threats to the West emanating from the destabilizing power dynamics caused by the rise of China, the decline of Russia, and the threat to the United States. This is labeled the "Thucydides Trap" and is currently the subject of a popular book by the American political scientist Graham Allison.[30] In it he documents how only four out of sixteen historical "Thucydides Traps" were resolved peacefully. In the other twelve, ruling powers, such as the United States, struck to preserve preeminence or rising powers, such as China, struck to claim the privileges of leadership denied to them.

Not surprisingly, Xi Jinping's pronouncement that "The East is rising, while the West is declining," has set off alarm bells.[31] National glory and economic prosperity continue to sustain an ambitious agenda in which Xi appears determined to maintain China's rise and claim full equality with the United States, at the minimum, and, according to a RAND study, regional hegemony over East Asia and global leadership, at the maximum.[32]

The rise of China will be particularly problematic, the pundits note, if China decides not to cooperate with the West and insists upon radical change in the multilateral order. China is the second biggest military spender in the world. China and the United States are the only countries to have triple-digit defense budgets (in billions of US dollars).[33] Moreover, China is also not transparent about the allocation of its defense budget[34] and often appears disinclined to follow the rules of the multilateral legal order, as evidenced by its actions regarding the South China Sea.[35]

Hegemonic transitions also generate important informational asymmetries that foster strife. The old hegemon has a structural incentive to sound the alarms in order to mobilize domestic and international support to resist the rise of the challenger. The challenger has an equivalent structural incentive to convey an image of accommodation—until it is ready to overturn the old order. Both thus produce the appearance of misinformation that exacerbates strife. Given those incentives, neither is believed. As noted in the previous chapter, we saw this in Biden's drawing of sharp lines between autocracy and democracy and in Xi's vehement denials of any interest in a cold war.

Contrarian Complexities

Other structural factors push back against bipolar confrontation. The Russian-Chinese alignment is not free from tension (as over Siberia). And US allies, especially in Europe, are reluctant to see confrontation increase. And, as noted earlier, debate continues on just how "rising" China is. Hal Brands, a well-known US national security historian, has questioned how reliable China's putative rise is. The economy seems to be faltering even though military capacities are climbing. This could produce a moderation in the perceived China threat by the US or it might produce a "worst of both worlds" scenario in which the United States sees China as a rising challenger and China sees itself as a declining power with an incentive to strike soon before its power wanes.[36]

NATO allies have long been able to shelter under and free ride on the security that US global balancing against the USSR/Russia and China has offered. Knowing the United States will confront Russia, Europeans have felt little need to pay their proportionate share on NATO defense expenditures.[37] Concerned that subservience to the United States would write a blank check for a more adventurous foreign policy, they recall Iraq 2003 when the United States went to war over French and German opposition and without a UN Security Council authorization. Adding to that, in 2021 France experienced the sting of the Australia, UK, US Alliance (AUKUS) spurning of the French submarine "deal of the century" (Australia instead chose to replace French diesel subs with US nuclear ones). Pulled by profitable trade arrangements with Russia and China, Germany was reluctant to risk very profitable ties that bring cheaper Russian natural gas through Nord Stream 2[38] to Germany at the same time as China accounted for more than half of the sales of Volkswagen and other German firms.[39] Moreover, dangerous as reliance on Chinese Huawei technology might be, Europeans are reluctant to further a US monopoly of cyber technology.

Much of that changed in 2022 when Putin invaded Ukraine and—to the wonderment of many—the NATO alliance cohered and strengthened as the allies agreed on severe sanctions against Russia, the Biden administration worked to consult with all NATO, Germany raised its defense spending above the 2 percent GDP target, Finland and Sweden applied to join, and France's President Macron coordinated his diplomacy with his allies. Global condemnation of the Russian invasion was overwhelming. Nonetheless, some African countries appeared reluctant to join the opposition to Russia's invasion. Sixteen out of 35 abstained in the UN vote; some out of memory for the key role Soviet support offered during the long struggle against colonialism and apartheid.[40]

Structural factors between blocs thus have pulled toward confrontation, and tensions inside the blocs have favored conciliation. So far, the interbloc tensions seem to be predominating.

CHAPTER FOUR

Corporatist, Nationalist Autocracies

F urther complicating the emerging international order, and threatening a new cold war, are differences in domestic regimes and ideologies that produce transnational political strife. While bipolar systems may both moderate or exacerbate tensions, bipolar systems with divergent ideologies strongly tend toward cold war–style confrontations rather than global cooperation.

Political authority in the United States is legitimated by civil and political freedoms (such as freedom of expression and assembly), democratic elections, private property, and private ownership of the means of production; in China by material progress, bureaucratic authority, state control of the economy, and evocations of Confucian and Communist values (in a perplexing mix); and in Russia by nostalgic sentiments of past imperial power, nationalist resentment against the West, and the popularity of Putin's revival of the economy. These different conceptions of legitimacy are the sources of potential suspicion between these states and thus misunderstandings and conflict. Thus the overriding rivalry so far is one between corporatist, nationalist autocracies (CNAs: Russia and China) and liberal, capitalist democracies (LCDs: the United States and its key European Atlantic and Pacific allies).

At the end of the Cold War, "triumphalists" assumed that Russia and China would rapidly evolve into liberal democracies. Some argued that liberal, capitalist, consumerist democracy was the "end of history," a form of social organization that offered ultimate satisfaction for material wants, political legitimacy, and spiritual satisfaction.[1] In the past few years, a new and different reality has begun to emerge. We in the West have come to acknowledge that Russia and China are not liberal democracies in the wings, at least not anytime soon. They have their own political systems, interests, and ideologies that are deeply ingrained. And Russia and China are not like the rich democracies of the United States, Germany, Japan, the United Kingdom, France, or even the poorer ones of India, Brazil, or South Africa. Nor are their foreign policies similar: The democracies did not balance against the unipolar United States following the end of the Cold War. Nor have they yet, despite the provocations of George W. Bush adventurism or Trumpian trade and foreign policy.

The great irony is that Chinese autocracy appears to have had transformative influence on the United States, rather than US liberal democracy having transformed China. The hollowing out of the American middle class (in part driven by trade competition) has eroded the bases of stable democracy, giving rise to the autocratic-friendly presidency of Trump and political polarization. Moreover, competing with China has encouraged the United States to engage in more rather than less state direction of the economy, including trade quotas and international investment restrictions, all in the name of national and cyber security.

Beyond the rise of China, other powers continue to shock the multilateral order. As evidenced by the US invasion of Iraq in 2003 under President George W. Bush, superpowers have unique capabilities to destabilize regions and disregard multilateral principles. More recently, the global multilateral order was again reminded of this special role of militaristic conflict by Russian actions (the annexation of Crimea, invasion of Ukraine, shielding of Assad in Syria) under President Vladimir Putin.

When we look to the domestic sources of tension and the way in which those interact transnationally across borders with other domestic sources, three developments stand out. The first is the return of corporatist, nationalist autocracies (CNAs) highlighted in the transformations in China and Russia since 2012. The second is the ongoing effects of liberal expansionism, embodied in foreign policies inspired by liberal principles, capitalist interests, and democratic institutions of the United States. The third is the anomalous election in 2016 (and the possible return in 2024) of Donald Trump, who resembled (and seemed to admire) the style and values of Putin and Xi more than he did any previous modern US president.

While leadership personalities do make a difference, the roots of hostile conflict coming from Russia and China are structural. Both systems, once Communist and totalitarian, have become corporatist, with the state shaping the private sector and responding to an influential oligarchy of corporate wealth. Both reflect strong nationalism, responding to resentment of the loss of their own empires and memory of imperial aggression inflicted by the West. And both have become dominated by autocratic government, increasingly determined by the will of one supreme leader. Together the three traits increasingly resemble classic twentieth-century Fascism, but differences are equally important, including the absence of the Socialist-Communist alternative that determined so much of Fascism's support and evolution and the absence in both cases of mass-based radical political parties. It is equally important to highlight the differences between Russian and Chinese CNAs, with the latter having a much stronger state and party form of rule, and the former a much more independent (though repressed) civil society.[2]

Although different, Russia and China share substantial features of corporatism, autocracy, and nationalism. Each separately can cause tension in relations with liberal capitalist democracies. But what is most important and corrosive is the combination of the three, which I explore in the paragraphs that follow.

Corporatism

In the modern classic discussion of corporatism, Philippe Schmitter defines and outlines the varieties of corporatism:

> Corporatism can be defined as a system of interest representation in which the constituent units are organized into a limited number of singular, compulsory, noncompetitive, hierarchically ordered and functionally differentiated categories, recognized or licensed (if not created) by the state and granted a deliberate representational monopoly within their respective categories in exchange for observing certain controls on their selection of leaders and articulation of demands and supports.[3]

At its most straightforward, we can think of the differences between, on the one hand, conventional market-based industrial relations in which corporate management (representing shareholders) bargains with labor acting either individually or represented by unions and, on the other hand, companies managed by joint manager-worker committees. At a more aggregated level, we can think of the differences between companies competing in a market and companies organized into cartels to divide the market and, at the highest level, private ownership versus state-owned or directed ownership.

Within this overall concept, one then can then distinguish, as does Schmitter, between "monist" forms of organization (monopolized control by the state or party—think Soviet Communism) and "syndicalist" forms (where there is no monopoly, much voluntarism, and no control by the state—think various forms of corporate co-determination and stakeholder democracy as can be found in Sweden or Germany). This distinction also relates to distinctions between "societal corporatism" (where control comes from below) and "state corporatism" (from the state, above) and, finally, between "revolutionary" (part of a rapidly imposed new order) and "evolutionary" (derived over time by bargains among social forces).[4]

Schmitter's key point is that corporatism is a form of organization compatible with a variety of political regimes and characterized by various effects. All tend to reflect a response to various crises of the market and the societal response to market instability and the adverse effects the market can have on everyone from the elite to the mass. Its major alternative is pluralism, which relies on the market and independent social response organized along class, civil societal, or employment lines (unions, organizations of businesses or professions, not joined in functional units within a single corporation or industry).

One source of corporatism was articulated in one of the great books of the twentieth century, Karl Polanyi's *The Great Transformation*.[5] His book is a profound study of the effects of the market economy both domestically and internationally. Polanyi's argument, in summary, holds that marketization makes market society unsustainable by undermining social stability.

He acknowledged that, indeed, the combination of the domestic market economy, political representation, the gold standard, and the international balance of power did create a sustaining circle of mutually reinforcing economic contacts that helped produce societal stability and even the peace of the nineteenth century—the "Long Peace of 1815–1914." But trade is not just an exchange of commodities at arm's length or at the border. It is a revolutionary form of exchange. Exchanging commodities changes prices and produces revenue that alters the demand for various "factors"—inputs of labor, capital, and land—that go into producing the commodities that are exchanged. As was later elaborated in a set of theorems concerning "factor price equalization," trade in commodities has potentially revolutionary effects in changing the returns to land, labor, and capital that go into the production of these commodities. Countries tend to export commodities that intensively use the factor inputs with which they are most endowed and import commodities that embody scarce domestic factors. Foreign trade thus increases demand, price, and, eventually, return for relatively abundant factors as it shrinks demand, price, and return for scarce domestic factors that now have to compete with cheaper imports. Together this tends toward global factor price equalization (in theory, with many assumptions, and thus real-world qualifications).[6]

Market ideology sometimes assumes that trade is arm's-length commodity exchange, neglecting the potential effects of commodity trade on the inputs that go into the production of the commodities exchanged (land, labor, and capital). Why is this important? Trade, whether national or international, by changing the returns to land, labor, and capital disrupts relations that had become embedded in social hierarchies and in political power. Treating land, labor, and capital merely as commodities misses the dislocation experienced by established communities, village life, regional life, and the relations among classes, industries, and sectors and eventually changes the international balance of power. Trade therefore produces a reaction. Farmers do not like to have the prices of their farm products drop to the prices set by more competitive rivals. Consumers might prefer the lower prices, but the usually better organized producers resist. Laborers and manufacturers do not want to compete with labor that makes one-tenth of their income or with firms that have costs a fraction of their own, whether in a newly integrated national or international market.

When peoples' livelihoods are marginalized, they tend to react. Polanyi recounted that, at the end of the nineteenth century, the reaction to the market took the form of political corporatisms of either social democracy on the left or Fascism on the right. National economies attempted to protect themselves from the swings of the global economy by raising tariffs in order to protect national consumption or by launching imperial conquests to expand national resources. The resulting rivalry produced, Polanyi continued, Socialism, Communism, and Fascism domestically, and World War I, the Great Depression and its competitive devaluations, and eventually World War II. Peace, prosperity, and democracy collapsed under the weight of heavy interdependence.

Russian Corporatism

Russian Communism in 1918 was an extreme example of the collapse of market society under the onslaught of World War I. Russia today has many of the features of corporatism, though not Communism. Emerging from the state-controlled version of top-down corporatism that was

Communism, Russia's privatization and marketization were far from complete in the 1990s. Today, at the factory level, the economy still lacks a fully pluralist operation of labor-market industrial relations.[7] In the words of one of the leading commentators on Russian industrial relations: "Russian trade unions have failed to establish a new identity as bodies representative of their members' interests because of their twin dependence on management and on the state."[8] At the level of intercorporation competition and relations between corporations and the state, the picture is complicated. Today even private firms rely heavily on state patronage and are subject to many controls. As Tim Frye has suggested, a delicate equilibrium of "legal dualism" has emerged in which the state allows substantial operation of market relations and access to the rule of law in order to encourage growth while at the same time retaining sufficient influence on markets, ownership, and the courts to make sure that firms serve the interests of the factions (since 2001, Putin's United Russia Party) currently in power.[9]

Under the Russian version of oligarchic corporatism, the state and the oligarchy co-direct and co-own the economy with the United Russia Party protecting oligarchic control and the oligarchs funding the ruling party. Externally, the oil and gas sector has become the vital source of both revenue and international influence and is actively controlled by the Putin government. More broadly, between 63 and 70 percent of the capitalization of the Russian economy is now in state-owned enterprises (SOEs), and the number of government-owned "unitary enterprises" has tripled in the past three years. Together, between 40 and 50 percent of Russian GDP is said to be state controlled.[10] State control helps ensure that the Russian government retains the support of the populace, many of whom would lose their jobs if they dissented.

Perhaps more significantly, the Russian economy illustrates the "clientelist" version of corporatism. *The Economist* identifies a full 16 percent of the Russian GDP is absorbed in the (non-SOE) "crony" sector.[11] (SOE is State Owned Enterprises.) The US State Department recently stated: "SOE procurement rules are non-transparent and use informal pressure by government officials to discriminate against foreign goods and services. The current Russian government policy of import substitution mandates numerous requirements for localization of production of certain types of machinery, equipment, and goods."[12]

A recent example of how Russian corporatism works is the 2022 downfall of Oleg Y. Tinkov. Tinkov was worth more than $9 billion in November 2021 and was famous as one of the very few self-made business tycoons in Russia. Rather than energy and minerals (the operating grounds of Russian kleptocracy), Tinkov began as a beer brewer and became the founder of one of the world's most sophisticated online banks. But in 2022, he criticized the war in Ukraine in a post on Instagram. Tinkov called the invasion "crazy" and derided Russia's military: "Why would we have a good army," he asked, if everything else in the country is dysfunctional "and mired in nepotism, servility and subservience?" As the *New York Times* reported: "The next day, President Vladimir V. Putin's administration contacted his executives and threatened to nationalize his bank if it did not cut ties with him." He sold his 35 percent stake to Vladimir Potanin, a mining magnate close to Mr. Putin, in what Tinkov described as a "desperate sale, a fire sale" forced on him by the Kremlin."[13]

Chinese Corporatism

The Chinese economy is remarkable in many ways. It is *the* success story of contemporary globalization. Growing from the 1980s reforms at double-digit rates, China moved from a poor developing country to become the globe's second-largest economy, largest exporter, and the center of global construction. In ten years, from 2001 to 2011, China added 203 million people to its middle class.[14] China is also very far from Communism. In 2021, it surpassed the United States in the number of billionaires, with 1,058 of them.[15]

Much of this success has come from extensive market-oriented reforms initiated by Deng Xiaoping. Under the leadership of Xi Jinping, the 2013 Third Plenum of the 18th Party Congress of the Chinese Communist Party reaffirmed the role of the market as having the "decisive role" in revitalizing a lagging Chinese economy. But, as China expert Elizabeth

Economy has suggested, Chinese economic reality displays pervasive inertia. In 1978, SOEs generated 80 percent of China's industrial output. Privatization would reduce that considerably. Today the 150,000 SOEs employ only 40 million workers and produce 40 percent of the Chinese economy (but they control over $21 trillion in assets). Yet, more important, these SOEs are key components of state control of the leading sectors and the sectors most essential in maintaining political stability. They obtain favored financing, regulation, and investment support, irrespective of their efficiency or solvency. The key purposes of this form of corporate governance are multiple, offering the Chinese Communist Party "control for purposes other than the maximization of its wealth as a shareholder—purposes such as the maintenance of urban employment levels, direct control over sensitive industries, or politically motivated job placement."[16] Through regulation of property, approval of mergers and new construction, and access to domestic and foreign financing, the state exercises indirect control of most other companies, greatly to the benefit of well-connected members of the new corporate elite.[17]

Given this level of integration, these firms often serve as agents of the state. In a story Economy elaborates, Chinese iron ore companies appeared to follow state direction in coordinating to purchase shares in order to ensure that two Australian companies could not merge in a way that would make them a serious rival to the Chinese companies.[18] Even the more independent firms, such as the very successful Huawei, are alleged to play roles in intelligence collection and sustaining political beachheads (as Huawei allegedly did in creating an Internet network for North Korea).[19] And the state seems to reciprocate. In 2019, when a group of former Huawei employees alleged that Huawei was doing business in US-sanctioned Iran (contrary to the firm's assertions), the Chinese state stepped in and arrested the individuals.[20]

Further illustrating the deep integration of economy and political control, the construction sector is closely integrated with the Chinese state's overseas investment initiatives. And the Communist Party bureaucracy is deeply entwined in a mutually profitable embrace with finance and industrial production.[21]

In 2020, Xi announced an important effort to enhance party control over the entire economy. The General Office of the Central Committee of the Chinese Communist Party on September 15, 2020, issued the *Opinion on Strengthening the United Front Work of the Private Economy in the New Era*. It directed the party's United Front Work Departments (UFWDs) to increase their role in the private sector. This built on Xi Jinping's 2016 call to increase the party role in state-owned enterprises "integrating the Party's leadership into all aspects of corporate governance." Now the party intends for similar direction within private enterprises. Ye Qing, vice chairman of the All-China Federation of Industry and Commerce, called for building a "modern private enterprise system with Chinese characteristics." This would include giving a company's internal party group control over the human resources decisions of the enterprise and allowing it to carry out company audits, including monitoring internal behavior.[22]

In 2020, when famous Alibaba entrepreneur Jack Ma criticized constraints imposed on his new Ant Group's plan to fund the small-business, nonestablished sectors of the Chinese economy, Xi struck back, scuttling Ma's IPO (initial public offering). The newly established Financial Stability and Development Committee was tasked with ensuring (in the words of a "senior Chinese official") "whether you're aligning your interests with the state's interests"—as defined by Mr. Xi.[23] Ant soon fell in line, accepting designation as a regulated banking entity and promising to "spare no effort in implementing the rectification plan" that includes abandoning its "information monopoly" on the detailed consumer data it has collected, which it will surrender to the central bank.[24]

Some have begun to speculate that Xi is actually seeking a full-blown revival of Maoist Communism.[25] In this reading, Xi is restoring Communist Party control of the private sector in order to prepare for the Marxist stage of "state capitalism," which itself is the precursor in Marx's theory to the Communist (democratic, peaceful) revolution to full social ownership of the means of production. A more straightforward interpretation is that Xi seeks a strengthening of Communist Party control to avert resistance by an increasingly restive capitalist class and to restore the party's legitimacy in the eyes of the increasingly disaffected rural and urban poor. With the curbing of Alibaba, hundreds of new corporate regulations, and appeals to "common prosperity," the one sure effect is increased state control.

Two noted political economists describe recent trends as follows:

> Although industrial policy never completely went away, the commitment of resources to industrial policy accelerated steadily since the shift noted above that occurred around 2006. In addition to the ongoing focus on exports, new attention was paid to achieving competitiveness in a range of cutting-edge industries. The roll-out of a series of policy tools mobilized to support these programs was emblematic of the new state-led push to foster indigenous innovation and upgrade manufacturing. Moreover, these developments were taking place in sectors that not only had relevance for China's economic position but for its military modernization as well.[26]

In the World Trade Organization (WTO), which serves to regulate trade disputes among its members, liberal, capitalist economies are in significant tension with China. There are rules for private transaction and for government procurement. But as Vikram Khanna has noted: "problems arise in cases where the boundaries between state and private enterprises are blurred, as is often the case in China. It is then not easy to judge whether a preferential transaction is of a private commercial nature—which falls outside the WTO rules—or amounts to a state subsidy. At the heart of the problem is what constitutes a 'public body,' which in China is not as clear as in other countries."[27]

Indeed, under the guise of antitrust enforcement, the big Chinese tech and cyber firms, like Ant, Tencent, and Alibaba, have become "a mere appendage of the state." Chinese firms seeking a stock market listing in New York or Europe have to first submit to a "cybersecurity checkup" to guarantee compliance with Chinese state interests in view of potential conflict with the United States as well as make large well-publicized investments at home to reduce inequality in order to establish their bona fides as servants of the party.[28]

Thus we see clashes between market economies and corporatist economies—such as America's current trade war with China.[29] Key issues include intellectual property protection (technology theft and coercive technology transfer); currency manipulation; and, perhaps most challenging, trade subsidies, as Beijing provides direct subsidies to industries and the much more prevalent regulatory favors (for government contracts and local government supports) and subsidized loans for economic development purposes. All these are problematic under WTO rules. The United States wants China to stop them, but these measures are not just economic tools or market advantages; they are the essence of the corporative economic model of governance.

The recent campaign to eliminate Hong Kong's legal autonomy with the National Security Law (2020) illustrates how businesses have been mobilized both to cushion the impact of the flight of foreign investment from Hong Kong and to use corporations to police and punish their workers' political activities. Beijing has encouraged mainland big firms to expand their operations in Hong Kong, threatened international banks such as HSBC, and demanded that companies, including Cathay Pacific, discipline their workers who participate in street demonstrations.[30]

Even more concerning is the use of Chinese companies as intelligence sources for the Chinese government. The National Intelligence Law of June 2017 requires all Chinese entities to provide information on request to Chinese intelligence units. In 2020, this has implicated TikTok in a dispute with the US government over TikTok's acquisition of immense quantities of information on US citizens, all provided by its users.[31]

The Biden administration identified a new level of aggressive coordination that shapes China's digital threat to the United States. Identifying networks of private and state hackers working together to penetrate both governmental agencies and private firms in the West, Biden officials portrayed a new front of wide competition in which the Ministry of State Security played the central role. The network of government-affiliated hackers served state and private purposes stealing state secrets and technology and business information in what was described by Secretary of State Blinken as "an ecosystem of criminal contract hackers who carry out state-sponsored activities and cybercrime for their own financial gain."[32]

Competition even extends to information as democracies make economic data more available than do similarly developed autocracies. The underlying logic, according to a new study, is that "[t]ransparency attracts investment and makes democracies more resilient to breakdown. But transparency has a dubious consequence under autocracy": it leads to political instability, exposing the government to domestic and international dissent and thus making the autocratic elite reluctant to open up information.[33]

These corporatist tendencies have had three main effects.

First, it is nearly impossible to have primarily commercial, or market-based, relations with firms in a corporatist economy. Every conflict is inherently politicized, every competition extends beyond an economic transaction to involve state actors whose interests are directly affected. These actors moreover are unlikely to allow courts to resolve disputes, unless they control the court.

Second, corporations will as a matter of course call upon the state for support and direction in their competition with foreign firms at home or abroad; again, politicizing all economic transactions.

Third, security conflicts among states will lead them to impose corporatist kinds of controls. The 2022 obsession with "supply chain security" in the wake of the Russian invasion of Ukraine is illustrated in the dependence (and then cancellation) by Germany of Nord Stream 2 natural gas and oil flowing from Russia. The US dependence on China for everything from masks to ordinary consumer products during the COVID-19 pandemic is another instance of the political sensitivity of economic relations. But the phenomenon has much deeper roots in "trading with the enemy acts" and CoCOM controls on trade during the Cold War.[34]

Inequality and political power also combine in the United States. In 2013, the total net worth of the top 400 billionaires was an estimated $2.2 trillion; in 2022, the number has more than doubled to $4.5 trillion.

This kind of money buys influence. According to US political scientists Benjamin Page and Jeffrey Winters, who study income inequality in the United States, it can shape favorable tax policies and Internet regulation, among others. But,

> what makes American oligarchy different from its Russian counterpart is that it operates at significantly greater arm's length, driven by lobbying and campaign contributions rather than outright corruption. "Russian oligarchs who are close to Putin—that's a very special kind of thing," Page says. "They make a ton of money in pretty direct relation to the government. A lot of them make it from government-owned or -controlled or -regulated companies. That's substantially less true of the United States." Page acknowledges that American oligarchy is different—it is embedded in the political system. [35]

Nor are liberal market economics altogether removed from politicization, nor from reliance on SOEs.[36] The defense sector most strikingly reflects these dynamics. Boeing and Airbus are far from ordinary commercial firms. The difference is one of degree and scope. And clearly, competition between Boeing and Airbus has not prevented close and highly cooperative relations between the United States and Europe. We also can see crony capitalism at work, especially in dealings between the global oil sector and leading US, formerly public officials. At a 2021 investment conference in Saudi Arabia, the big draw was Saudi Arabia's $450 billion sovereign wealth fund, the Public Investment Fund. According to an article in the *New York Times*, Steven Mnuchin, former secretary of the treasury in the Trump administration, raised money from the Saudi sovereign wealth fund, and Jared Kushner, Trump's son-in-law and former senior advisor, attended in connection with his launching of an investment firm called Affinity Partners, also seeking a potential $2 billion investment from the Public Investment Fund.[37] The key distinguishing issue for corporatism is less crony capitalism than the way in which corporatism combines with nationalism and authoritarianism.

Nationalism

The concept of "nationalism" also ranges widely. At the most minimal, it covers someone who believes that fellow nationals rather than foreigners should govern the nation (national self-determination) and that the government should promote the interest of the majority of the nation rather than that of a minority (thus restraining political corruption).[38] At the most maximal, a nationalist is someone who believes that the nation is inherently superior to all other nations and that it should avoid corrupting contact with other nations. For some this also includes winning every dispute ("America First") even if that means (but rarely acknowledging) losing out in the longer run, or losing out on other more important deals, or losing absolute gains because another nation might be gaining more.

There are also different kinds of nationalism. Civic nationalism (often associated with patriotism) is pride in and allegiance to the principles and institutions of a country. The American "Pledge of Allegiance" is a notable example of this civic ideal: "I pledge allegiance to the Flag of the United States of America, and to the Republic for which it stands, one Nation under God, indivisible, with liberty and justice for all." (Though, the addition of "under God" in 1954 steps away from its previously purely civic character toward religious establishment.) Ethno-nationalism promotes only the interest of a particular ethnic group, or race, and at the extreme is one of the key tropes of Fascism and resonates in recent discussions of "white nationalism" in the United States.[39]

"Populism" is closely related and often the label of choice for many of the recent challenges to liberalism. At minimum, it claims to reflect the alleged interests of the majority of the people as opposed to the interests of an elite. It is also full of familiar ironies as in the United States in 2016 where Hillary Clinton won the majority of the US vote against "populist" billionaire Donald Trump, while in the United Kingdom, "Remain" is (in 2022) more popular in opinion polls than "populist" Brexit was in 2016.[40] In a leading social science study of populism, Federico Finchelstein identifies post–World War II Argentine Peronism as the ideal type of modern populism and notes its key features: electoral, authoritarian democracy (rejecting dictatorship); an apocalyptic vision of politics; a charismatic messianic leader; antagonism toward "enemies of the people"; opposition to pluralism and tolerance; radical nationalism; an affinity toward politics as entertainment . . . and the list continues.[41] Nadia Urbinati in a complementary recent study emphasizes the proclaimed direct, unmediated, political relationship between the elected leader and the part of the population that he or she identifies as the "true people."[42]

Populism and nationalism combine in special fashion in Putin's Russia. Partly this is a product of the sense of loss of the Soviet empire and the Soviet Union, a sentiment stoked by Putin and others. Partly it is a product of the sense of vulnerability without natural security borders (other than the Pacific and the Arctic) and with 25 million fellow Russians beached in the post-Soviet diaspora in the Baltics, Central Asia, Crimea, and Belarus.[43] And, partly, it results from the anger at the collapse of the Soviet/Russian economy under Boris Yeltsin.

Putin famously described the collapse of the Soviet Union in these words: "Above all, we should acknowledge that the collapse of the Soviet Union was a major geopolitical disaster of the century. As for the Russian nation, it became a genuine drama. Tens of millions of our co-citizens and co-patriots found themselves outside Russian territory. Moreover, the epidemic of disintegration infected Russia itself."[44]

The single best explanation of the invasion of Ukraine is that he is attempting to re-create the imperial space Russia lost when the Warsaw Pact and the Soviet Union collapsed. In Ukraine, it goes under the patently absurd label of "denazification" of the democracy led by a Jewish freely elected president. But its convincing roots are deeply wounded prestige at the loss of empire. Putin exploits this feeling to stay in power as the voice and restorer of imperial greatness.

Notoriously, the collapse of the Soviet Union and its economy became expressed in deaths of despair, linked to heart disease and alcoholism, almost as if large numbers of the adult male population were committing slow-motion suicide. Declining longevity had characterized the USSR after its 1960s peak (when it matched US longevity rates), but

Mikhail Gorbachev had achieved a remarkable revival through a public health campaign in the late 1980s, only to see male longevity tumble under Yeltsin.[45]

Russian anger also reflects a modern deterioration in reliable information jointly produced by state domination in the new autocracies and the global spread of chaotic mass media stimulated by the decline of the establishment press and the rise of unfiltered Internet access. Hannah Arendt captured many years ago the new spirit of the times eloquently in her remark: "In an ever-changing, incomprehensible world the masses had reached the point where they would, at the same time, believe everything and nothing, think that everything was possible and that nothing was true."[46] Timothy Snyder, historian of Russia, illustrates this phenomenon in Putin's invasion of Ukraine in 2014. Putin officially denied the presence of Russian soldiers in Ukraine on the very day the Russian soldiers there announced: "We are special forces from the GRU" (the Russian military intelligence directorate). Russian foreign minister Sergei Lavrov denounced claims from Western media identifying Russian troops as "information warfare." Seventy-nine percent of the Russian public in a 2014 poll agreed that "the West will be unhappy no matter what Russia does, so you should not pay attention to their claims."[47]

In recent polling, Putin garners up to 60 percent approval ratings. Partly, of course, Russians dependent on the state sector have little choice but to support the government, but many also seem to appreciate the prestige Putin's foreign adventures, whether in Ukraine or Syria, earn Russia. Others think that no one else could hold Russia together.[48]

In 1972, the philosopher Isaiah Berlin explained that this kind of nationalism "expresses the inflamed desire of the insufficiently regarded to count for something among the cultures of the world." He identified modern nationalism with Germany's nineteenth- and twentieth-century vulnerabilities and resentments, but the sentiment is not unique to any one nation.[49] Putin and his circle have fostered a striking version of populist nationalism.

Tim Snyder has identified a new label for Russian nationalism widely used in Ukraine, "ruscism." It mixes "Russian" and "Fascism," focusing on the Russian tilt toward fascist practices, including "cults of the leader and of the dead, the corporatist state, the mythical past, the censorship, the conspiracy theories, the centralized propaganda and now the war of destruction."[50]

Russian hyper-nationalists have come to rely on three tropes. One is "Eurasianism" as an authoritarian alternative to the European Union for the former Soviet or Eastern bloc states that could not or would not join the European Union but would join with a Russian-style economy and polity.[51] The second trope is a hyper-nationalist, anti-rationalist ideology with roots in Russian variants of European Fascism. Its prophet was Ivan Ilyin, who was given to obscure and nihilistic sentiments and wild exhortations such as "Politics is the art of identifying the enemy" and "The fact of the matter is that fascism is a redemptive excess of patriotic arbitrariness."[52] In order to enforce the new populist nationalism, Putin in 2019 signed into law new rules that criminalize any "disrespect" for Russian society, the government, official symbols, the constitution, or any state body, as well as what the authorities deem to be "fake news."[53] In the course of the invasion of Ukraine in 2022, Putin passed a "fake news" law criminalizing anti-regime messaging, including calling the invasion of Ukraine a "war" instead of "special military operation." The third trope is great power prestige. The failure to jump start a more productive industrial sector (to balance oil and gas) has left Russia's military success and great power standing as the lead currency of its regime's prestige. Putin clearly enjoys his/Russia's "return to the top table" through coups in Crimea, destabilization in Ukraine, and success in dominating the diplomatic and military field in Syria, and most recently the invasion of Ukraine.[54]

Chinese nationalism shares with Russian chauvinism resentment over lost imperial power, and it focuses on subsequent national humiliation under Western and Japanese imperialism in the nineteenth and twentieth centuries. The Chinese historical narrative is one of great prestige: 1,000 years, from 800 to 1800, of being the center of the universe followed by 100 years of national humiliation from 1840 to 1940. It differs, however, in focusing its current prestige on material progress, the rapid growth of the Chinese economy since the market reforms of the 1980s.

There have been discussions of new imperial Chinese visions derived from traditional sources such as "tianxia"[55]—"All Under Heaven"—which encompasses an assertion of a hierarchical international order all subject to China at the center. There are also allegations of ethnic Han-centric exclusivism in Tibet and Xinjiang (but these acts are better understood as politically motivated authoritarian control, as outlined shortly). A more constant theme is Chinese defensiveness. The Chinese model is not offered for export and is instead more a defense against liberal norms, which Xi and the rest of the Chinese leadership sees as deeply subversive of its continued rule and Chinese stability and growth.[56]

"Document Nine" of 2013, supposedly issued as a strategy document by the newly appointed Xi Jinping, summarized China's new approach to ideological struggle. The document criticized "Western values," focusing on "extremely malicious" ideals and the threat they posed to Chinese society and the continued rule of the CCP (Chinese Communist Party).[57] The document focused on the "threats" stemming from promoting "Western Constitutional Democracy," "universal values" (an attempt to weaken the theoretical foundations of the party's leadership), "civil society" (defined as the view that "individual rights are paramount and ought to be immune to obstruction by the state"); "Neoliberalism" (privatization); the "West's idea of journalism" (challenging Xi's view that media and publishing should be subject to party control and discipline); and others.

Many Chinese intellectuals, some inspired by Nazi theorist Carl Schmitt, are aligning behind this statist vision of unlimited sovereign, executive authority as a comprehensive alternative to Western "universal values and constitutional governance."[58] Others, such as Jiang Shigong, claim that empire, rather than national sovereignty, is the inevitable foundation of a world order that is "structured around markets, currencies, and superpower domestic policy masquerading as universal legal practice—The US had its turn and now it's China's." In his words:

[The current state of world empire] faces three great unsolvable problems: the ever-increasing inequality created by the liberal economy; state failure, political decline, and ineffective governance caused by political liberalism; and decadence and nihilism created by cultural liberalism. In the face of these difficulties, even the United States has pulled back in terms of worldwide military strategy, which means that world empire 1.0 is currently facing a great crisis, and that revolts, resistance, and revolution from within the empire are unravelling the system.[59]

The angry denunciations of democracy activists in Hong Kong in 2019 exemplify this distrust, with repeated accusations that the dissent could only be motivated by US subversion, rather than the actual dismay at economic burdens, the loss of Hong Kong autonomy, and reneged promises of Hong Kong democracy. The end result was the elimination of the "one country; two systems" model with the imposition of the Beijing-directed National Security Law in 2020.

Yet when one compares the modern nationalisms of Russia and China to the past, neither is as messianic or expansionist as Communism had been during the Cold War.[60] Communism was asserted to be both universal and in a life-and-death struggle with capitalism. The duty of the Communist Party and all Communists everywhere was to promote its revolutionary advance. No such claims are made today by Russian or Chinese nationalism, but each nationalism makes cooperation between them and the liberal West more difficult.

Summing the current effects of the nationalisms, we see that the residue of historic grievance and current suspicion can reduce the value of cooperation (none of the "shared values" that brought the Shasta farmers and ranchers together) and make the act of negotiated compromise more challenging (as meanings and metrics diverge, while rival valuations of success make conflicts more zero-sum).

Authoritarianisms

The nineteenth and twentieth centuries saw the evolution of three dominant political systems—liberalism, Fascism, and Communism. The political sociologist Barrington Moore, Jr., in his magisterial *Social Ori-*

gins of Dictatorship and Democracy: Lord and Peasant in the Making of the Modern World outlined how modern politics evolved.[61] Moore identifies three trajectories from traditional agrarian society to the modern industrial world. In the liberal capitalist democratic path, exemplified by England, France, and the United States, the peasantry was politically weak (or converted into an entrepreneurial class of independent farmer-owners, as in the United States), and a strong middle-class bourgeoisie emerged. The aristocracy (where it still ruled) then allied itself with the bourgeoisie or failed to oppose its democratizing efforts. Democracy flourished. In the capitalist reactionary route, exemplified by Germany and Japan, the peasantry remained in place and posed a threat to the interests of both the bourgeoisie and the aristocracy, which consequently formed a conservative alliance against the peasantry. This alliance formed the basis for an autonomous, authoritarian state capable of being co-opted by a Fascist leader in a revolution from above. Lastly, in the Communist trajectory, exemplified by China and Russia, the bourgeoisie failed to emerge, but the peasantry was pervasive and independent enough from the aristocracy to form the roots of a radical revolution from below against the centralized agrarian bureaucracy.

Illuminating the broad development of alternative systems of government as the insights do, world history is of course more complicated. Modern democratic India fits poorly in this template; and, as important, the trajectories miss the widespread contemporary emergence of mixed regimes, such as modern authoritarianism, which are neither liberal nor (unlike Communism and Nazism) totalitarian.

Juan Linz fills in these gaps and memorably characterized these latter authoritarian regimes as:

> Political systems with limited, not responsible, political pluralism, without elaborate and guiding ideology, but with distinctive mentalities, without extensive nor intensive political mobilization, except at some points in their development, and in which a leader or occasionally a small group exercises power within formally ill-defined limits but actually quite predictable ones.[62]

Strong central government prevails and yet, unlike totalitarian regimes, the state does not completely control society. The government lacks genuine accountability other than to a narrow "selectorate" whether of party bureaucrats, military officers, or economic elites who control the state. But while the selectorate influences the government, it usually lacks the ability to reform or direct society. They range from autocratic (one-person rule) to bureaucratic (by a committee or party or military) variations. Most tend to rely on emotive appeals and engage in combat against external or internal enemies (to rally nationalist support) as a substitute for democratic or traditional legitimacy. The most successful, such as China, maintain stability by economic success—they deliver prosperity—and they employ targeted coercion against dissenters, potential and actual.

Populist authoritarianisms often result from mobilization against colonial rule, by both incorporating formerly excluded groups and ridding society of "agents" of colonialism. Bureaucratic authoritarianisms reflect a conservative military-bureaucratic alliance against political and economic instability in order to protect military privileges or property and (often) to attract foreign investment.

In both Russia and China, which mix elements of those regimes, democratic elections are limited to a single party or a party controls the media and intimidates any rivals. They lack open markets, the effective protection of property rights, and democratic precepts such as equal protection of the law.

The legitimacy of these political systems thus must be bolstered by political repression of dissidents, by strong economic performance (poverty or economic crisis is but a generation in the past), or by extreme nationalism—or all three. Both Russia and China have popular bases that should not be underestimated, but measuring true support is difficult given the repressive mechanisms that both states employ. Both regimes feel they have been slighted globally through the loss of empire: the Chinese by Western and Japanese imperialism in the late nineteenth and early twentieth centuries; the Russians by the collapse of the USSR.

Both now enjoy ever increasing access to the "Autocrat's Toolkit."[63] Exceptional increases in the ability to monitor the acts and preferences of their subjects (including mass facial-recognition technology) and large increases in the capacity of artificial intelligence to engage in "automated microtargeting" offer significant advantages to autocrats seeking to stay in power. The hoary "dictator's dilemma"—the bureaucratic controls that keep a dictator in power undermine the capacity of markets to produce the prosperity that keeps subjects quiescent—may soon be overcome. As Zeynep Tufekci poignantly declared: "people in power [use] these algorithms to quietly watch us, to judge us, to nudge us to predict and identify the troublemakers and the rebels."[64]

Clearly, democracies also have access to a similar digital toolkit. The difference is that the tools are not monopolized by the government. Available to a variety of political parties and private actors, they contribute to polarization, not to a political monopoly.

But corporatist and nationalist authoritarian systems are not all the same.

In Russia, before Putin, oligarchs dominated the state. Since his consolidation of power in 2012, Putin is successfully asserting the dominance of the Russian state by intimidating opponents (and assassinating others). Whether he will succeed or just emerge as another—albeit, the wealthiest and most powerful[65]—oligarch is an open question, one insightfully explored in important books by Karen Dawisha and Michael McFaul.[66]

As Matthew Schmidt summarized, Putin dominates but he also "rules in a coalition with powerful oligarchs and at the acquiescence of a public that's been effectively both bought off with higher standards of living from oil profits and kept in a kind of deliberate ignorance of the government's corruption because the formerly free press was systematically and brutally suppressed."

The 2022 invasion of Ukraine may put strains on the stability of the Putin regime. The Levada Center—one of the few independent polling centers in Russia—reported in April 2021 that "among the military-age cohort (18–24), a full 41% thought a war with Ukraine would hurt Putin's standing. 35% of the young-parent-age cohort (25–39) agreed, and it was nearly the same for the middle-age cohort."[67]

Surveying the longer development of the Putin regime and his oligarchs, Karen Dawisha identified a "kleptocratic tribute system."[68] In 2000, when Putin took power and established a semblance of order, the *autoriety* (the amalgam of organized crime and legal business) was absorbed into the state. "In many ways, the Kremlin's unspoken truce with the criminal class paralleled Putin's taming of the oligarchs, the mega-rich businessmen who had become such a politically powerful force under Yeltsin."[69] The ruling system is organized from the locality up in a chain of clientelist networks, mixing public officials and quasi-private corporations, at whose peak is Putin. And where intimidation does not guarantee order, assassinations have been employed as against Boris Nemtsov, a leading opposition figure and critic of the 2014 invasion of Ukraine. Reflecting on the fear of foreign subversion tendency in Russian politics, former US ambassador to Russia Alexander Vershbow described the assassination as follows:

> The terrain is not just the field of geopolitics, but Russian domestic politics as well. President Putin's aim seems to be to turn Ukraine into a failed state and to suppress and discredit alternative voices in Russia, so as to prevent a Russian "Maidan" [the popular Ukrainian 2013 uprising that toppled the corrupt and pro-Russian Yanukovych regime]. We've seen that the victims are not just in Eastern Ukraine, with the brutal murder of Boris Nemtsov last Friday. While we don't know who pulled the trigger, we do know that Boris Nemtsov was a powerful voice for democracy and against Russia's involvement in Ukraine who was among those vilified as "traitors" and "fifth columnists" in Russia's official propaganda.[70]

In 2019, the Federal Security Service launched a "wave of arrests against journalists, opposition activists, doctors and religious believers" as Russia's competing law-enforcement bodies scrambled to prove their status against rival public enforcers in order to "secure their future in a country they all view as a fortress besieged by enemies at home and abroad." This led to "nationwide raids on news outlets critical of the Kremlin and on the homes and offices of people affiliated with the opposition leader, Aleksei A. Navalny."[71] Navalny was then the target of an assassination attempt in the summer of 2020 bearing the hallmarks of previous Russian state assassinations.

Another tactic treats dissent as foreign subversion. Putin's officials have designated a popular independent media outlet and two rights groups as "foreign agents." The Justice Ministry slapped the "foreign agent" label on Mediazona, a news site known for its extensive coverage of high-profile court cases, on OVD-Info, a prominent legal-aid group that focuses on political arrests, and on Zona Prava, another human rights group.

Along with the three entities, twenty-two individuals—including members of the protest group Pussy Riot—have also been added to the ministry's registry of "foreign agents."[72]

The media itself serves as a successful channel for Putin's propaganda. In a media landscape in which the state media dominate and crowd out dissent, even messages that citizens understand to be propaganda nonetheless shape positive perceptions of state effectiveness. Citizens assume that the propaganda the state issues must at least reflect the state's confidence in its messages. Citizens tend to defer, without alternative evidence to the contrary.[73] Relatedly, Putin has instituted monopoly control of media sources particularly when they impinge on electoral campaigns. In 2021 he closed down Navalny's app, one designed to mobilize opposition votes. He did so by threatening to arrest the local employees of Google and Apple, which had hitherto hosted the app.[74]

The effects of autocratic government on foreign policy vary by the kind of autocracy. The great German eighteenth-century philosopher Immanuel Kant outlined the general challenges to responsible governance that characterized monarchical regimes. Autocrats lack two key constraints on public policy. The first is institutionalized deliberation that can come from institutions such as separation of powers—executive, legislative, and judicial—that require persuasion to form an authoritative governmental decision. Instead the unchallenged whims, passions, preconceptions, or interests of the single ruler rule. Advisors totally dependent on the ruler become unlikely to offer critical or objective information when their careers—or lives—are at stake. As the historian Lawrence Freedman has argued, authoritarian states thus tend to suffer from a dearth of candid strategic advice.[75]

Second, the state lacks a responsible link to its citizen-subjects that can require it to justify policy in the public interest. Instead, the personal interests of the autocrat shape policy as Kant memorably indicted in his 1795 essay, "Perpetual Peace":

> But under a constitution where the subject is not a citizen, and which is therefore not republican, it is the simplest thing in the world to go to war. For the head of state is not a fellow citizen, but the owner of the state, and war will not force him to make the slightest sacrifice so far as his banquets, hunts, pleasure palaces and court festivals are concerned. He can thus decide on war, without any significant reason, as a kind of amusement, and unconcernedly leave it to the diplomatic corps (who are always ready for such purposes) to justify the war for the sake of propriety.[76]

Not all autocratic, nonrepublican or nondemocratic regimes are the same. Some, as Jessica Weeks has argued, are personalist (like Kant's monarchs above), but others are military regimes, party regimes, or oligarchies. There, constraints do operate, and "selectorates" (the military or party bureaucracy) in place of "electorates" can correct many of the personalist faults noted above by insisting on deliberation and attention to the wider interests of the military or the party, though rarely or reliably to the interests of the wider public.[77]

Indeed, China has long displayed a trait exceptional to most authoritarian systems. As noted by political scientist Andrew Nathan, authoritarian systems tend to be fragile because of weak legitimacy, overreliance on coercion, over-centralization of decision making, and the predominance of personal power over institutional norms. He observed: "Few authoritarian regimes—be they communist, fascist, corporatist, or personalist—have managed to conduct orderly, peaceful, timely, and stable successions." The Chinese Communist Party, however, was unusually resilient among authoritarian regimes, because of (1) "the increasingly norm-bound nature of its succession politics"; (2) "the increase in merito-cratic as opposed to factional considerations in the promotion of political elites"; (3) "the differentiation and functional specialization of institu-tions within the regime"; and (4) "the establishment of institutions for political participation and appeal that strengthen the CCP's legitimacy among the public at large."[78]

Each of those exceptional characteristics began to change with Xi's "third revolution" starting in 2013. Following Mao's Communist Revo-lution of 1949, and Deng Xiaoping's turn to the market in 1978, Xi has effected a "third revolution" since 2013 in which the Communist Party and Xi's personal control are central and unmatched since the days of Mao. Xi has declared himself chairman without term limits, returning to a pattern set by Mao. His campaign against corruption has reinforced his factional control. The state moreover has retaken control of society by establishing a "virtual wall of regulations and restrictions that more tightly controls the flow of ideas, culture and capital into and out of the country."[79] This includes control over the public media, permitting the party to shape what the public sees and hears, as evidenced in the highly critical account of the democracy protesters in Hong Kong in 2019, por-trayed in mainland media as a narrow gang of foreign agents of the United States and violent criminals.[80]

As a result, in China, the state ruled by the Communist Party domi-nates the oligarchs who control the economy. Moreover, under Xi, China has established an "unmatched policing regime"[81] in Xinjiang in order to control Uighurs. Chen Quanguo, the governor, has installed thousands of neighborhood police posts and data surveillance. He sent in 1 million Han (ethnically Chinese) to monitor and live with Uighur families. The regime collects facial-recognition data and biometric data, including blood samples from all persons, ages twelve to sixty-five—a model being touted for elsewhere in China and as a model for other developing coun-try dictatorships.

As inequality grows and the old party control of labor disappears, a new way to control populations has emerged called "social credit." It offers comprehensive social control through light means. Like US and other financial credit score monitoring approaches, it tracks behavior, but unlike them it covers legal and educational records, antisocial acts, and even shopping preferences (in cooperation with Alibaba, Tencent, and Baidu). High scorers receive preferences in air travel and securing loans. "Debtors" are banned from air and rail travel.[82]

Foreign Policies

The foreign policy implications of Russian and Chinese corporatist, nationalist authoritarianism are significant. Neither Russia nor China faces a cross-border threat of armed attack. Both rely on the suppression of potential dissent for domestic security. The security threats to these regimes are thus predominantly internal, not external.[83] They arise from disgruntled and empowered citizens, not armies threatening to cross their borders.[84] Thus the memory of Tiananmen Square for Beijing and the experience of the 2012 demonstrations for Moscow shape policy. The foreign policy of each externalizes the threat of internal instability. At the same time, both Russia and China perceive that the international liberal order treats their firms with suspicion (as with Nord Stream 2 as agents of the state) and imposes barriers to technological competition (Huawei and 5G).

As noted earlier, China may be driven by aggressive confidence in the evolving relative decline of the United States or by defensive concern that a global liberal order poses an existential threat to an authoritarian state. Or by both. Aggressive confidence may make compromises difficult—time is on China's side as the naval and economic balance shifts. Defensive concern may also limit the willingness to cooperate in that interdependence is seen as destabilizing, potentially empowering dissidents.

China, for example, asserts control of the South China Sea to placate its military and hyper-nationalists. It has shown that it will not tolerate a fully democratic Hong Kong in order to avoid the example it would set.

The official spokesperson of the Chinese Foreign Ministry blames the summer 2019 protesters in Hong Kong on the United States: "It is, after all, the work of the United States."[85]

Beijing's self-presentation is radically different. Xi is said to promote a strategy of "harmony and diversity" that is based on mutual benefit through economic growth and noninterference in each others' self-determination. "All countries," Xi has declared, "should respect each other's sovereignty, dignity, and territorial integrity, each other's development paths and social systems, and each other's core interests and major concerns."[86]

Xi sees this as distinctly different from the human rights, rule of law, market and poverty reduction conditions and democratization incentives imposed by the Bretton Woods institutions. "Harmony and diversity" imposes no Chinese model, but it offers a world safe from the pressure of liberalization and thus a safe harbor for authoritarian and corporatist modes of governance.[87] It also offers a set of institutions that are free from the influence exercised by the United States and Western Europe over the World Bank (whose president is always American) and the IMF (whose president is European and over whose loans the United States exercises a veto).[88]

The Asian Infrastructure Investment Bank and the Belt and Road Initiative are the two prongs of harmony and diversity. The first is open to all and offers finance for infrastructure desperately needed in Asia, and the second offers a concerted plan to create land and sea links that will tie Asia and Africa in an ever-expanding transportation network to China. While open to all, most of the funding of the Asian Infrastructure Investment Bank is Chinese.

The Belt and Road Initiative (BRI), Chinese president Xi Jinping's signature foreign policy undertaking and the world's largest infrastructure program, poses a significant challenge to US economic, political, climate change, security, and global health interests. Since BRI's launch in 2013, Chinese banks and companies have financed and built everything from power plants, railways, highways, and ports to telecommunications infrastructure, fiber-optic cables, and smart cities around the world. If implemented sustainably and responsibly, BRI has the potential to meet long-standing developing country needs and spur global economic growth. To date, however, the risks for both the United States and recipient countries raised by BRI's implementation considerably outweigh its benefits.

BRI was initially designed to connect China's modern coastal cities to its underdeveloped interior and to its Southeast, Central, and South Asian neighbors, cementing China's position at the center of a more connected world. The initiative has since outgrown its original regional corridors, expanding to all corners of the globe. Its scope now includes a Digital Silk Road intended to improve recipients' telecommunications networks, artificial intelligence capabilities, cloud computing, e-commerce and mobile payment systems, surveillance technology, and other high-tech areas, along with a Health Silk Road designed to operationalize China's vision of global health governance. Hundreds of projects around the world now fall under the BRI umbrella.[89]

Beijing has made it clear that it plans to assist its companies in "dominat[ing] the industries of the future, from artificial intelligence and supercomputers to aerospace equipment. Its policies have sought to replace imports of high-tech products with Chinese-made goods, pressuring multinationals to move factories from the United States and resulting in the loss of American jobs." China asserts that these measures are necessary for its future growth and are thus, in the words of Liu He, China's top negotiator, "major matters of principle" on which China was unlikely to bend.[90]

An early and famous example of this was China's policy toward Sudan during the campaign Khartoum was waging against Darfur. In a policy motivated to ensure a steady flow of oil to China, the Chinese government supplied the Sudanese government with a grant of $2.5 million for "any project" deemed worthy by the government, smuggled arms sought by the government, and promised to shield the regime from external multilateral sanctions.[91] China was not crusading for authoritarianism and, even less, for the crimes against humanity the Sudanese authorities were inflicting on Darfur. But its policies made Sudanese crimes nearly costless, made the Sudanese authoritarian government dependent on Beijing, and helped divide the world into a clash between human rights and sovereignty, between the United States and its liberal allies and China and Russia and the Sudans of the world.

This pattern has been repeated again and again, up to and including China's (and Russia's) policy toward the Syrian civil war. There Russia and China provide a shelter from international sanctions for Syrian president Bashar al-Assad. With the significant exception of the use of chemical weapons, Chinese and Russia vetoes shield Assad, and Russian arms prop him up.

Another example is China's relations with Australia. Australia's lobster exports to China became the latest casualty of mounting tension between China and the democracies. China accounted for around 96 percent of Australian exports of southern rock lobster, trade worth over half a billion US dollars a year.[92] Relations declined sharply when Australian prime minister Scott Morrison attended the G7 summit in Cornwall (June 2021), and the G7 issued a statement chastising Beijing for repression of its Uighur minority and other human rights abuses, as well as "nonmarket policies and practices" that undermine the global economy. This followed Australian criticisms of the treatment of Uighurs, the decline of democracy in Hong Kong, and China's policies in the South China Sea and toward Taiwan, as well as curbs on Huawei and questions about the origin of COVID-19 (all policies that have become a leitmotif in G7 reaction to China). The complicating factor is that China accounts for nearly 40 percent of Australia's total exports, and China has curbed Australian beef imports and levied tariffs totaling 80 percent on barley and over 200 percent on wine imports. Exports to China fell by approximately $2.3 billion in US dollars in 2020.

A 2021 task force of the Council on Foreign Relations concluded that the BRI served China by helping to close the gap between the country's affluent coastal cities and its impoverished interior, thus boosting domestic political stability. It absorbed excess manufacturing capacity, putting its accumulated savings to work, and secured a consistent source of inputs for its manufacturing sector while reorienting global commerce away from the United States and Western Europe toward China. For other countries, including recipients, the BRI increased the likelihood that debt crises would materialize over the coming years by funding economically questionable projects in heavily indebted countries and subsidizing privileged market entry for state-owned and non-market-oriented Chinese companies. All this enabled China to lock countries in to "Chinese ecosystems by pressing its technology and preferred technical standards on BRI recipients." This, in turn, increased dependence on carbon-intensive power through its export of coal-fired power plants and made it harder for the World Bank to insist on rigorous environmental and social-impact assessments while tolerating corruption. Countries thus become susceptible to Chinese political pressure, and China gains a greater ability to project its power.[93]

Thus the particular advantages of the BRI to Xi's China are significant. By eliminating the Bretton Woods multilateral monopoly, Xi creates the foundations for a world safe for authoritarianism, a world in which reform pressure for liberalization on China and all other authoritarians declines. The Belt and Road Initiative employs China's surplus capacity in state-owned enterprises focused on construction and materials. China creates the lines of trade and transport that will ensure its favorable access to the world's raw materials and ports, free from the constraints of relying on Western corporations or navies. And, time and again, projects such as the Pakistani port of Gwadar or the new port in Sri Lanka or road projects in Africa become dependent on Chinese subvention and control.

Not surprisingly, the BRI has faced backlash, including competition from the United States and the G7. An AidData study looked at China-backed projects in 165 countries over 18 years, worth $843 billion in total, and noted that Beijing's annual international development finance commitments were double those of the United States. But it observed that "[a] growing number of policymakers in low- and middle-income countries are mothballing high profile BRI projects because of overpricing, corruption and debt sustainability concerns." And in June 2021, the Biden administration announced a rival G7 initiative known as Build Back Better World (B3W) to provide financial support for developing nations to build infrastructure.[94]

Chinese cyber policies are another distinct challenge. Attribution problems complicate deterrence in cyberspace because malicious code can be written by state or non-state actors, and knowing the location of the machine that perpetrated an attack is not the same as knowing the ultimate instigator. However, deterrence is not impossible when there is enough evidence available.[95] Also provoking conflict is the weakness of global norms and law on cyberspace. China seeks to become a "cyber superpower," which includes increasing China's role in governing the Internet globally and particularly with a focus on multilateral fora developing new rules respecting sovereign control of national cyberspace.[96] The United States, in contradistinction, has focused on bilateral engagement with China to prevent commercial espionage and separately worked through the UN Group of Government Experts forum to develop international agreement that existing bodies of law should be applied to cyberspace.[97]

Liberal democracies may be at a disadvantage in cyber competition by free-expression concerns that arise when mitigating dangers on a communications network. On the one hand, the very openness of liberal democracies may make them vulnerable to misinformation.[98] On the other, great powers like the United States continue to maintain control over Internet exchange points and technology firms that can be wielded to gain bargaining advantages as choke points.[99]

The roots of the China challenge are both structural (in Chinese corporatism, nationalism, and authoritarianism) and also historical. Sulmaan Wasif Khan, a scholar of China's foreign policy, noted the sources of China's "wolf warrior" diplomacy, a blend of resentful nationalism and autocratic vulnerability: "The most persuasive explanation is that China has poisoned itself through its own rhetoric. In the aftermath of the 1989 Tiananmen Square massacre, nationalism was seen as a way to get citizens on the same page as the party. It was not really meant to inform practical foreign policy. But as the United States discovered in the Donald Trump years, one cannot stoke nationalistic fires without their eventually blazing beyond control. Over the years, rhetoric about how the Taiwanese needed to be made grateful, about the protests in Hong Kong being a product of Western influence, about Western aggression, about Japan never apologizing for World War II, about the righteousness of the party and the infallibility of the Chinese government and the hurt feelings of the Chinese people—all this seeped in and took hold."[100]

Putin's foreign policy reflects both similarities to and differences from China's. It was eerily previewed in the famous "Just Kidding" speech of 1992 by Russian foreign minister Andrei V. Kozyrev. In what he immediately after described as a "wake-up call," he shocked European foreign ministers with a Cold War–era diatribe. In it he threatened to force former Soviet republics to join a Russian-dominated federation and demanded an end to Western interference in Yugoslavia. Russia, he said, would denounce Western sanctions on Serbia and would take control of the entire territory of the former Soviet Union, "using all available means, including military and economic means," insisting that "the former U.S.S.R. republics join without delay a new federation or confederation" dominated by Moscow. Half an hour later, Kozyrev explained to the shocked US and European foreign ministers of the Conference on Security and Cooperation that his speech was meant as a demonstration of the policies the world will face if right-wing nationalist factions some day take power in Moscow. US secretary of state Lawrence S. Eagleburger remarked that Kozyrev's forceful message "brought home . . . that, should reform fail in Russia, we could well be faced with what we heard from Mr. Kozyrev this morning but in a far more serious vein . . . that would leave Russia totally isolated from the rest of Europe."[101]

Thirty years later, much of that vision is in place. Hostility between Putin and the West is evident, and Russia has seized parts of Georgia and Ukraine, intervened in Syria, and forcibly mediated the war between Armenia and Azerbaijan and now has invaded Ukraine (2022) with still unclear aims in mind. Putin claims to be "denazifying" the country ruled by a freely elected, Jewish former comedian and reuniting the country as part of the "Russian" people (within whom—contrary to Putin—the Ukrainians do not place themselves). The people have risen in opposition to the invasion, the army resisting by all the means it has and civilians facing down tanks while casualties and destruction mount and a million and more flee as refugees. The clear aim is to crush its independence.

Political economist Chris Blattman nicely summarized the forces that produced Putin's gamble of invading Ukraine in 2022:

> Despite Ukraine's weakness, recent trends alarmed Mr. Putin and his inner circle. The Ukrainian people had twice tossed out Russia-leaning leaders in revolutions in the past 20 years. Ukraine was a society with which many Russian citizens identified and a powerful example for an uprising against Mr. Putin's regime. Mr. Putin could wield his leverage to extinguish the threat, but war would be expensive and risky, so he first tried other means. He spent years influencing Ukrainian politics with money, propaganda, assassinations and support for separatists. These risky investments didn't pay off—and might have pushed Ukrainians closer to the West and democratic government. This was a worrisome trend for Mr. Putin. As Ukraine entrenched its freedoms, regime change there became more difficult. As Kyiv obtained more missiles and drones, the costs of invasion grew. Mr. Putin's leverage over Ukraine was reaching its peak. Russia had one last tool, invasion, and a closing window to use it.[102]

Putin has long regarded the collapse of the Soviet Union as a catastrophe. With the latest aggression against Ukraine, he seems bent on turning the clock back to 1980. Whether he plans on—and can succeed in—annexing the entire country or the eastern half, he hopes to so dominate the country that it will remain subservient to Moscow henceforth. The Ukrainians, so far (spring 2022), are successfully resisting those fates, determined to maintain both their territorial integrity and political independence.

Putin supports Alexander Lukashenko, the Belarusian strongman to his west, and to the south will not stand for a Ukraine that would join the European Union. If Russia's client in Ukraine, Viktor Yanukovych, could not be propped up, better a Ukraine stripped of Crimea with a restive and newly vulnerable Russian minority in constant need of potential rescue: all this to keep Ukraine divided and crisis-ridden and a lesson to all who might seek democracy within or autonomy outside the Russian orbit.

Each also has oligarchs with corporations whose profits must be ensured with state support, subsidies, and sometimes industrial espionage.

The 2020 election crisis in Belarus illustrated these forces at work. After Lukashenko's alleged rigging of the elections, demonstrations broke out across the country demanding a fair election as Ms. Sviatlana Tsikhanouskaya, the "losing" candidate, fled to nearby Lithuania. Lukashenko appealed to Putin, stressing a threat to either of them was a threat to both, and both reaffirmed, despite earlier spats, the "union state" of the two. Both then accused the demonstrations of being expressions of unspecified "foreign meddling" and asserted that no "outside meddling" will be permitted to succeed in toppling their regimes. Lithuania's foreign minister Linas Linkevičius summed up the situation in a tweet: "Former president of #Belarus now asks Putin for help. Against whom? Against own people carrying flowers on the streets?"[103]

Even more significant than the direct foreign action each power takes are their indirect effects. Both Russia and China serve as alternatives to US and European sanctions on regimes that are violating human rights or trashing the environment. Russia and China teamed up to prevent discussion of human rights abuses in Syria at the UN Security Council in 2018.[104] Russian arms are a substitute for US arms; Chinese markets replace European threats of sanctions against environmental degradations. Brazil's populist president, Jair Bolsonaro, responded to threats of EU boycotts by saying that China would take whatever quantities of Brazilian soybeans or cattle that the Europeans were threatening to boycott over Bolsonaro's encouragement of ranchers burning the Amazon.

Retired Gen. David Petraeus and US senator Sheldon Whitehouse see a new cold war in the confrontation between the rule of law and Putin's corruption. The authoritarian rulers have worked assiduously to "weaponize corruption as an instrument of foreign policy, using money in opaque and illicit ways to gain influence over other countries, subvert the rule of law and otherwise remake foreign governments in their own kleptocratic image." And they acknowledge that: "For figures such as Putin, the existence of America's rule-of-law world is intrinsically threatening. Having enriched themselves on a staggering scale—exploiting positions of public trust for personal gain—they live in fear that the full extent of their thievery could be publicly exposed, and that the U.S. example might inspire their people to demand better."[105]

These views are mirrored in China. "The Cold War mentality has come back to drive the security strategy and policy of a major power," China's disarmament ambassador Li Song told the Conference on Disarmament in Geneva.[106] Li went on to compare the United States to Don Quixote, searching for windmills (imaginary security threats) to destroy, and making all other states unsafe in the process.

The result is reciprocal escalations of insecurities and threats. For the Americans, this is just what a declining hegemon would expect in hegemonic transition for the challenger to say, when the challenger benefits from existing rules of international trade and investment as China does. Significantly, China is also linking more closely with Russia in military cooperation. This is portrayed as not mere convenience. These are deeper ties, but also "partnerships, not alliances" in the words of the official Chinese military spokesperson.[107] But for the Chinese and the Russians, the true threats are domestic, and US and Western charges seem provocative and aggressive rather than defensive.[108]

CHAPTER FIVE

Liberal, Capitalist Democracies

The drivers of tension and conflict in Cold War II are not all coming from China and Russia. Liberals in the West decry and want to impose additional sanctions on the authoritarians for their widespread violations of human rights. At the extreme end, the United States has launched destabilizing aggressions as with the Bush administration's invasion against Saddam Hussein in 2003—partly inspired by Bush's "Freedom Agenda" and thus setting authoritarians everywhere on edge. And multinational corporate elites sound the alarm at having to compete with Chinese and Russian state-controlled or state-owned enterprises. Liberal democratic capitalism in just about any form will find cooperation with the corporatist, nationalist autocracies (CNAs) difficult.

But more destabilizing still, an aggressive new right-wing nationalist ("America First") populism grips formerly liberal democracies. Foreign policy, as almost never before, is rhetorical, driven by sensationalism and tailored to the psychological fears and aggressive drives of domestic political factions who are its almost sole intended audiences.

Liberalism, Capitalism, and Democracy

Liberal, capitalist democracy shapes how the ideas and ideals individuals espouse (such as human rights, liberty, and democracy) affect social forces (capitalism, markets) and political institutions (democracy, representation) and vice versa: how social forces and institutions shape individual aspirations. It contrasts with the assumptions built into the model of nationalist, corporatist autocracies. It also differs from "structural realists" regarding the determinative role of system structure (unipolar, bipolar, or multipolar) and the consequent assumption of state homogeneity (rational, material, and unitary actors). By opening the box of state action and allowing for the effects of varying liberal ideas, capitalist interests, and democratic institutions, liberal, capitalist democracy (LCD) helps us understand foreign policy behavior.

Liberal, capitalist democracy is identified with an essential principle—the importance of the freedom of the individual. Above all, this is a belief in the importance of moral freedom—of the right to be treated and a duty to treat others as ethical subjects and ends, and not as objects or means only. A concern for this principle generates rights and institutions. The challenge within liberalism is how to reconcile the three sets of liberal rights. The right to private property, for example, can conflict with equality of opportunity, and both rights can be violated by democratic legislation. The liberal tradition has evolved two high roads to individual freedom and social order: one is laissez-faire or "neo-conservative" liberalism, and the other is social welfare or social democratic (or in US terms, "liberal") liberalism. Both reconcile these conflicting rights (though in differing ways) by successfully organizing free individuals into a political order.

A commitment to a threefold set of rights forms the foundation of liberalism. Liberalism calls for freedom from arbitrary authority, often called "negative freedom," which includes freedom of conscience, a free press and free speech, equality under the law, and the right to hold, and therefore to exchange, property without fear of arbitrary seizure. Liberalism also calls for those rights necessary to protect and promote the capacity and opportunity for freedom—the "positive freedoms." Thus such social and economic rights as equality of opportunity in education and rights to health care and employment, necessary for effective self-expression and participation, are among liberal rights.[1] A third liberal right, democratic participation or representation, is necessary to guarantee the other two. To ensure that morally autonomous individuals remain free in those areas of social action where public authority is needed, public legislation has to express the will of the citizens making laws for their own community.

The democratic political order *combining* laissez-faire and social welfare liberals is marked by a shared commitment to four institutions.[2] First, citizens possess juridical equality and other civic rights such as freedom of religion and the press. Second, the effective sovereigns of the state are representative legislatures deriving their authority from the consent of the electorate and exercising their authority free from all restraint apart from the requirement that basic civic rights be preserved. Most pertinently for the impact of liberalism on foreign affairs, the state is subject to neither the external authority of other states nor the internal authority of special prerogatives held, for example, by monarchs or military castes over foreign policy. Third, the economy rests on the recognition of the rights of private property, including the ownership of means of production. Property is justified as a stimulus to productivity and a limit on the monopoly of state authority. The institution of private property excludes state socialism or state capitalism, but it need not exclude market socialism or various forms of the mixed economy. Fourth, economic decisions are predominantly shaped by the forces of supply and demand, domestically and internationally, and are free from strict control by bureaucracies.

In order to protect the opportunity of the citizen to exercise freedom, laissez-faire liberalism has leaned toward a highly constrained role for the state and a much wider role for private property and the market. In pursuit of the same goal of freedom, welfare liberalism reverses that approach, and instead has expanded the role of the state and constricted the role of the market. However, both perspectives accept the four institutional requirements and as a result contrast markedly with the monarchical regimes, military dictatorships, and single-party governments, including Communist and Fascist dictatorships, with which they have shared the political governance of the modern world. Not even overwhelmingly liberal countries are purely liberal. Liberal principles and institutions sometimes vie with autocratic or racist rivals for the allegiance of the public.[3] There are also domestic variations within liberal regimes. For example, Switzerland was liberal only in certain cantons; the United States was liberal only north of the Mason-Dixon Line until 1865, when it became (minimally) liberal throughout ("Jim Crow" and other discriminations persisted until the mid-twentieth century). These lists also exclude ancient "republics," because none appear to fit modern liberal criteria of individualism.[4]

This is obviously an ideal theoretical model. Like democracy itself and human rights, none exist in pure practice. Not even overwhelmingly liberal countries are purely liberal. As noted above, liberal principles and institutions sometimes vie with autocratic or racist rivals for the allegiance of the public as they did throughout the nineteenth century and some of the twentieth century. Rights are never comprehensively respected (and only partly because they sometimes conflict), and no country guarantees an equal voice on all issues to all of its inhabitants. But it is possible to compare degrees of democratic participation and implementation of rights, and the more countries incorporate democratic practice and respect rights, the more likely they are to maintain peace with each other.

The domestic successes of liberalism are apparent. After the defeat of the Fascist challenge in World War II and the collapse of the Communist Soviet Union and spread of market democracies in the 1990s, liberal, capitalist democracy appeared to some as the "end of history."[5] Never had so many people been included in, and accepted the domestic hegemony of, the liberal order; never had so many of the world's leading states been liberal, whether as republics or as constitutional monarchies. Indeed, the success of liberalism as an answer to the problem of masterless men in modern society was reflected in the growth in the number of liberal regimes from the handful of semi-liberal regimes that existed in the first half of the nineteenth century (for example, Britain, France, and the United States) to more than a hundred that existed at the end of the twentieth century.

But we should not be complacent about the domestic affairs of liberal states. Significant practical problems endure, including enhancing citizen participation in large democracies, distributing "positional goods" (for example, prestigious jobs), controlling bureaucracy, reducing unemployment, paying for a growing demand for social services, and achieving large-scale restructuring of industries in response to growing foreign competition.[6] The eminent liberal philosopher John Rawls highlighted the absence of public funding of elections and of the state's role as the employer of last resort. He also noted the weakness of the social safety net (especially national health care) as barriers to the effective exercise of genuine liberal equality.[7]

Nor should we be complacent about liberal, democratic control of foreign affairs. Even in the best of times, foreign policy raises problems of democratic accountability. Robert Dahl's influential analysis of democratic control of foreign policy noted (1) public opinion tends to be poorly informed of international issues; (2) the public's views are too diverse to constitute a steady guide; and (3) parties have many and diverse constituencies. As a result, elites decide foreign policy primarily by bargaining among themselves.

There remain two important sources of liberal, democratic grounding of foreign policy. In Dahl's "Revised" version, he shows that the public can be mobilized by big events to demand change, such as in the course of World War II, the Vietnam War, 9/11, and the travails of the Iraq War after 2006.[8] Liberal principles were widely shared between the elite and the public during much of the Cold War. As Michael Tomz and Jessica Weeks have shown with survey evidence, when the public operates from a script favoring liberal principles, they tend to give foreign democratic states the benefit of respect not accorded to nonliberal autocratic states.[9]

But the current challenges extend beyond these normal limitations. Democracy itself, in recent years, has entered a "recession." In 2019, Freedom House noted the trends, as Table 5 illustrates.[10]

More significant than the numbers in Table 5, large and influential countries have experienced large declines in civil rights and democratic governance, among them Turkey, Venezuela, Poland, and Hungary. Of

Table 5. A Democratic Recession?

Year	Percent of Countries (%)		
	Free	Partly Free	Not Free
1986	34	34	32
1996	41	31	28
2006	47	30	23
2019	44	30	26

course, since 2012, Russian autocracy has deepened, and Putin is now nearly permanently in charge. Xi Jinping abolished term limits and has targeted civil society and any dissent.

We are not in the decade of the 1930s and its collapse of liberal democracy in Italy, Japan, Germany, and Spain. Moreover, there is some good news. Cautioning about excess pessimism, political scientist Sheri Berman has countered that "today's democratic troubles don't seem so profound." More democracies exist today than at any previous point in history: There were 11 in 1900, 20 in 1920, 32 in 1970, 77 in 2000, and 116 in 2018. Democracies have suffered less backsliding in recent years than after the previous waves of democratization that began in 1848, 1918, and 1945.[11] Moreover, the long-supposed cultural limits to liberal democracy continued to fall. In the nineteenth and early twentieth centuries, liberalism was said to be only for northern European Protestants, then after World War II spread to cover southern European Catholics and Latin Americans and Japanese. In the 1990s, popular government emerged in the East European Spring, reaching an Arab-Muslim Spring in 2011; only to collapse in Egypt and elsewhere with the exception of Tunisia, where democratic government (very shakily) persists.

In the United States itself, democracy is under threat. The "new authoritarian populism" and "America First-ism" has meant that the United States has walked away from its long-standing role as the self-proclaimed leader of the "free world." We recently had a US president who talked about torturing the families of alleged terrorists and invading countries to seize oil resources. Today, US democracy appears increasingly dysfunctional. The January 6, 2021, Trump putsch sent a shock wave through the polity. In 2021, partisanship stalled administrative appointments in unprecedented ways, and even on infrastructure, the most traditionally bipartisan legislation, only thirteen Republicans voted for the 2021 bipartisan infrastructure bill—and they were then roundly condemned by their Trumpist party. All these pose large challenges to which I return in the last chapter when I describe the reforms, both international and domestic, needed to achieve a cold peace.

Yet the tradition of liberal, capitalist democratic international relations is notable, distinct, and displays regular patterns.

Liberal World Politics

The two previous World Wars all ended with re-constitutionalized international orders, embodied in the postwar settlements of the League of Nations and the United Nations (including the Bretton Woods institutions).[12] But a new peace after the Cold War that would recognize the potentially cooperative roles of a democratizing Russia and a globalizing China did not inaugurate a post–Cold War era. Instead, Russia received second-class observer status in NATO. China was admitted into the WTO. Neither was accorded more of a role or (failing that) status as a comanager of the international order whether in the World Bank or the IMF. This contrasts strikingly to the equal status assumed by each of the Permanent Five (United States, USSR, France, United Kingdom, and China) in the UN Security Council in 1945. Instead, Western drivers of distrust and conflict continue to threaten Russia and China. Distrust (in the end, validated) precluded change.

The first source of distrust and conflict is US concern over a declining yet militarist Russia and, even more, a rising China, the so-called Thucydides Trap. Discussed earlier, the once dominant, now relatively declining power experiences deep insecurity and sometimes chooses to strike preventively to preclude a future dominated by its rising rival.[13] This logic makes even accommodations offered by the rising power seem suspect, perceived by the declining power as stratagems to lull the declining power until the rising power achieves clear dominance.

The second source of immediate relevance is two drivers within liberalism itself. The first driver is the aggressive internationalizing of human rights. Even benign advocacy of freedom of expression and assembly can appear destabilizing to Russian or Chinese autocrats. The "color revolutions" that toppled autocrats in Eastern Europe clearly alarmed Putin. When the West adds aggressive strategies akin to the George W. Bush "Freedom Agenda" of forcible regime change of the sort launched against Iraq, autocrats everywhere cringe.[14] The second driver is Western private corporations calling out for state assistance when they are required to compete with state-owned enterprises.

Liberalism has dual effects. The first is a separate peace among liberal republics. Within liberalism, the combination of representative institutions, human rights principles, and economic and social interdependence has given rise to a well-established democratic peace among fellow democratic republics.[15] This separate peace provides a solid foundation for the crucial alliances of the United States with the liberal powers (NATO, the US-Japanese alliance, the alliance with Australia and New Zealand). It also offers the optimistic promise of a continuing peace among liberal states, and with increasing numbers of liberal states, it announces the possibility of a self-enforcing global peace without establishing a world state.

The reasoning is threefold:

1. Liberal republics are constrained by deliberation among executives, legislatures, and courts in the government, and with societal actors enjoying freedom of speech. Together, this increases the probability of prudent decisions. It also encourages responsibility to the majority of electors, who, unlike monarchs and dictators, cannot regularly displace the costs of going to war on others.

2. If, moreover, those elected or their electors respect liberal principles, governments will respect the rights of other peoples similarly free to

express their rights and will negotiate rather than fight over differences of interest.

3. Respect for rights of property, transnational social ties, and the benefits of commercial exchange will encourage multiple societal contacts that can encourage mutual understanding and reinforce these moral commitments with the material advantages of commercial and other exchanges that can flourish when they are not constrained by security concerns.

No one of these factors is itself sufficient to produce a peace among liberal states. But together they work to make a liberal peace likely.

Unfortunately, and as a second effect, the same respect and self-interest that generate a self-enforcing peace among liberal republics produce distrust of states that oppress their subjects and compound conflicts of interest between liberal republics and nonliberal autocracies that neglect property rights and restrict trade and other contacts. This is what makes for a peace among liberals, but not between liberal and nonliberal states.

But if democracies still have staying power, so do their pathologies. Unfortunately, liberal democratic republics tend to distrust countries that are neither liberal nor democratic nor capitalist. Peaceful restraint seems to work only in liberals' relations with other liberals; liberal states have fought numerous wars with nonliberal states.

Many of these wars have been defensive, and thus prudent by necessity. Liberal states have been attacked and threatened by nonliberal states that do not exercise restraint in their dealings with liberal states. Authoritarian rulers both stimulate and respond to an international political environment in which conflicts of prestige, of interest, and of pure fear all lead states toward war. Thus, war and conquest have characterized the careers of many authoritarian rulers and ruling parties—from Louis XIV and Napoleon to Mussolini's Fascists, Hitler's Nazis, Stalin's Communists, and Putin's nationalists.

But imprudent aggression by the liberal states—liberal imprudence—has also characterized many of these wars.[16] Both liberal France and liberal Britain fought costly expansionist colonial wars throughout the nineteenth century. The United States fought a similar war with Mexico in 1846–1848, waged a war of annihilation against the Native Americans, and intervened militarily against sovereign states many times before and after World War II. Liberal states invade weak nonliberal states and display exceptional degrees of distrust in their foreign policy relations with powerful nonliberal states.

The liberal record as pacifiers is also problematic in interstate war. Liberal states acted as initiators in 24 of the 56 (43 percent) interstate wars in which they participated between 1816 and 1980, while nonliberals were on the initiating side in 91 of the 187 (48 percent) times in which they participated in interstate wars.[17] But the liberal imperial centers were the overwhelming participators in "extrasystemic" wars, colonial wars, which we can assume to have been by and large initiated by the imperial center. Furthermore, the United States intervened in the then "Third World" more than twice as often in the period 1946–1976 as the Soviet Union did between 1946 and 1979.[18] Further, the United States devoted one-quarter and the Soviet Union one-tenth of their respective defense budgets to forces designed for Third World interventions, where responding to perceived threats would presumably have a less than purely defensive character.[19]

In relations with powerful nonliberal states, liberal states have missed opportunities to pursue the negotiation of arms reduction and arms control when it has been in their mutual strategic interest, and they have failed to construct wider schemes of accommodation that are needed to supplement arms control.

Consider this example: Deeply held suspicion appears to have characterized US diplomacy toward the Soviet Union. In a fascinating memorandum to President Wilson written in 1919, Herbert Hoover (then one of Wilson's advisors) recommended that the president speak out against the danger of "world domination" that the "Bolsheviki"—a "tyranny that is the negation of democracy"—posed to free peoples. Rejecting military intervention as excessively costly and likely to "make us a party in re-establishing the reactionary classes in their economic domination over the lower classes," Hoover proposed a "relief program" designed to undercut some of the popular appeal that the Bolsheviks were garnering in both the Soviet Union and abroad. Although acknowledging that the evidence was not yet clear, he concluded: "If the militant features of Bolshevism were drawn in colors with their true parallel with Prussianism as an attempt at world domination that we do not stand for, it would check the fears that today haunt all men's minds."[20]

In the post–World War II period, and particularly after the outbreak of the Korean War, US foreign policy equated the "International Communist Movement" (all Communist states and parties) with "Communist imperialism" and with a domestic tyranny in the Soviet Union that required a Cold War contest in order to legitimize Soviet control at home. Secretary of State John Foster Dulles most clearly expressed this conviction, together with his own commitment to a strategy of "liberation," when he declared: "[W]e shall never have a secure peace or a happy world so long as Soviet communism dominates one-third of all the peoples that there are, and is in the process of trying at least to extend its rule to many others."[21]

Imprudent vehemence is also associated with liberal foreign policy toward weak nonliberal states, such as many in the Third World. This problem affects both conservative liberals and welfare liberals, but the two can be distinguished by differing styles of interventions.

Protecting "native rights" from "native" oppressors and protecting universal rights of property and settlement from local transgressions introduced especially liberal motives for imperial aggression. Ending the slave trade and encouraging "legitimate trade" (while protecting the property of European merchants) destabilized nineteenth-century West African oligarchies. Declaring the illegitimacy of suttee (self-immolation as practiced by widowed women in India) and domestic slavery also attacked local cultural traditions that had sustained the stability of indigenous political authority. Europeans settling in sparsely populated areas destroyed the livelihood of tribes that relied on hunting. When the locals retaliated defensively in force, the settlers called for imperial protection.[22] In practice, once the exigencies of ruling an empire came into play, liberal imperialism resulted in the oppression of "native" liberals seeking self-determination in order to maintain imperial security, avoid local chaos, and preclude international interference by another imperial power attempting to take advantage of local disaffection. Thus nineteenth-century liberals, such as British prime minister William Gladstone, pondered whether Egypt's proto-nationalist rebellion (1881–1882) was truly liberal-nationalist (they discovered that it was not) before intervening to protect strategic lifelines to India, commerce, and investment. These dilemmas of liberal imperialism are also reflected in US imperialism in the Caribbean where, for example, after the Spanish-American War of 1898, Article III of the Platt Amendment gave the United States the "right to intervene for the preservation of Cuban independence, the maintenance of a government adequate for the protection of life, property, and individual liberty."[23]

Elsewhere in the post–World War II period, when the United States sought to protect liberals in the Third World from the "Communist threat," the consequences of liberal foreign policy on the nonliberal society often became far removed from the promotion of individual rights or national security. In Vietnam and elsewhere, intervening against "armed minorities" and "enemies of free enterprise" meant intervening for other "armed minorities," some sustained by oligarchies and others resting on little more than US foreign aid and troops. Indigenous liberals simply had too narrow a base of domestic support. These interventions did not advance liberal rights, and to the extent that they were driven by ideological motives, they were not necessary for national security.

To the conservative liberals, the alternatives were starkly cast: Third World authoritarians with allegiance to the liberal capitalist West or "Communists" subject to the totalitarian East (or Leftist nationalists who, even if elected, were seen as but a slippery stepping stone to totalitarianism).[24] Conservative liberals were prepared to support the allied authoritarians. The Communists attacked property in addition to liberty, thereby provoking conservative liberals to covert or overt intervention, or "dollar-diplomacy" imperialism. The interventions against Mohammad Mosaddegh in Iran, Jacobo Arbenz in Guatemala, Salvador Allende in Chile, and the Sandinistas in Nicaragua appear to fall into this pattern.[25]

President Ronald Reagan's simultaneous support for the military in El Salvador and guerrilla "freedom-fighters" in Nicaragua also tracked this pattern, whose common thread was a rhetorical commitment to freedom and operational support for conservative free enterprise.

To the social welfare liberals, the choice was never so clear. Aware of the need for state action to democratize the distribution of social power and resources, they tended to have more sympathy for social reform. This could produce, on the part of "radical" welfare liberals, a more tolerant policy toward the attempts by reforming autocracies to redress inegalitarian distributions of property in the Third World. This more complicated welfare-liberal assessment could itself be a recipe for more extensive intervention. The conservative oligarchs or military bureaucrats with whom the conservative liberal was well at home were not so congenial to the social welfare liberal, yet the Communists were still seen as enemies of liberty.

In their foreign policy, Leftist liberals have justified extensive intervention first to encourage, and then to sustain, Third World democracy in a political environment that is either barely participatory or highly polarized. Thus, Arthur Schlesinger recalled President Kennedy musing shortly after the assassination of President Rafael Trujillo (former dictator of the Dominican Republic): "There are three possibilities in descending order of preference, a decent democratic regime, a continuation of the Trujillo regime [by his followers] or a Castro regime. We ought to aim at the first, but we can't really renounce the second until we are sure we can avoid the third."[26] Another instance of this approach was President Jimmy Carter's support for the land reforms in El Salvador, which one US official explained in the following analogy: "There is no one more conservative than a small farmer. We're going to be breeding capitalists like rabbits."[27] President Bill Clinton's administration seems to have succumbed to a similar dose of optimistic interventionism in its conviction that friendly nations could be rebuilt democratically in both Somalia and Haiti, although democracy had never existed in the first and was led in the second by Jean-Bertrand Aristide, a charismatic Socialist and an eloquent critic of American imperialism.

This is a disturbing record of imprudent confrontation, but not a necessary one. There is nothing in basic liberal principles of equal respect for fellow human beings that calls for armed intervention. Indeed, just the opposite inference, a respect for self-determination, is the more natural conclusion. Liberal philosophers such as John Stuart Mill offered one of the earliest and most profound condemnations of armed intervention as lacking respect for authentic self-determination and for generally producing counterproductive results.[28] Mill included many colonialist exceptions, none of which would be acceptable today. But his key message holds, especially for those who subscribe to the centrality of human freedom: each country must discover and pursue its own route to freedom.

Yet, in circumstances of state capture by special property interests, ignorance of or widespread prejudice against other peoples, or geopolitical insecurity, then liberalism can become part of the ideological gloss that exaggerates threats and justifies intervention. And that too has unfortunately been part of its historical record.

Liberal Globalization

Within the liberal capitalist world, the post–World War II economy flourished. The allied leaders successfully rebuilt liberal interdependence, constructing a new way to mix together democracy and social stability.[29] They developed a series of safety nets that would make people less vulnerable to the vagaries of the market both domestically and internationally. Rather than adjusting to a world of intense national competition among closed economies (as in the 1930s) or letting trade and finance flow freely in response to market incentives (the nineteenth century), the capitalist democracies in the postwar period constructed the International Monetary Fund (IMF), the General Agreement of Trade and Tariffs, and the World Bank to help regulate and consciously politically manage the shape of the world market economy. Trade was opened on a regulated basis, and currencies were made convertible when economies could sustain the convertibility and cushioned with financing to help maintain parities. Long-term financing, a form of global Keynesianism, was provided first to Europe and then (in lesser amounts) to the developing countries in order to spread opportunity and reduce the conflicts between the "haves" and "have nots" that had wracked the Interwar period. All this helped promote stability, cooperation, and solidarity in the Cold War struggle against the Soviet Union. Thus with a set of political-economic policies that have been called "embedded liberalism," the postwar leaders of the West found a way to manage the tensions that Polanyi had described, the dangers of marketization.[30]

It was good while it lasted, but by the 1980s, frustration with overregulation, falling productivity, and the oil shock, together with a demand for ever more profit and cheap goods, produced a move back to marketization, the Thatcher-Reagan "magic of the marketplace." Reacting to the welfare state's restrictions on consumption and profit (and seeking a more dynamic spur to industrial reallocation and profits), many of the protections embedded in the postwar political economy were relaxed. Increasing trade, floating exchange rates, opening of financial markets, and privatization became the "Washington consensus," the watchword of international economic orthodoxy and the standard prescription of the IMF for countries in balance-of-payment difficulties.

As the barriers to global marketization fell, the forces that propelled ever closer interdependence accelerated. One force accelerating the effects of global marketization was advances in communication and transportation technology. The costs of transportation and communication began to fall radically in the postwar period. In 1930, the cost of a telephone call between New York and London was (in 1990 dollars) $245 for three minutes. By 1998, the same call cost 35¢: a vast reduction in the cost of communications. That and the related twenty-first-century expansion of the Internet are what makes much of global banking—and all of global academia—possible.

The second force was trade, a near revolution in the amount of trade tying the countries of the world together. Even the United States, which because of its continental scale is one of the less interdependent economies, has experienced a large change in the impact of trade. In 1910 (that is, during Globalization I), 11 percent of US gross domestic product

(GDP) was in trade (exports and imports). By 1950, this fell to 9 percent. That is what the Globalization I crisis—the Great Depression and the two World Wars—was all about. But by 1995, trade had risen to 24 percent. This is more than double the extent of trade interdependence in the previous era of globalization. In the Germany of 1910, 38 percent of its GDP was in exports and imports. By 1950, this fell to 27 percent; by 1995, up to 46 percent. The United Kingdom, the leader of the first wave of globalization and the most globalized economy at the time, in 1910 had 44 percent of its GDP in trade. In 1950, this dropped to 30 percent. By 1995, 57 percent was again in exchangeables. Among the highly developed industrial economies, only Japan is less dependent upon trade and investment income than it was in 1910. It is the only major industrialized economy that is less globalized now than it was in 1910.

Foreign direct investment and portfolio flows of finance had an even more dramatic effect in deepening globalization. Between 1980 and 1994, the volume of global trade doubled; but in that same period, foreign direct investment grew by six times, and portfolio flows of finance grew by nine times.

As in the earlier age of globalization, these flows of trade and finance changed the operation of the world's political economy—altering what was profitable, what was politically sustainable, and what was not. Perhaps most strikingly from an economic point of view, the world appeared to be one large market, a single division of labor. From the standpoint of the multinational company, production strategies became genuinely global, as parts of the production process were allocated to subsidiaries and contractors in countries or regions around the world where they were most cost-effective, forming a global process of production and marketing that was a highly interdependent whole at the global level. In the old global interdependence, companies made cars or shoes and they were traded among many countries; under globalization, a company made cars or shoes globally with component factories spread around the world.[31]

The new market interdependence posed deep challenges to the liberal scheme of democratic peace and interdependence. In addition to the widely noted effects of transboundary "collective bads," such as cross-border pollution, that are tying national fates together, three challenges have emerged.[32]

The first was and still is a combination of commodification and mobility. The 2000 World Trade Organization meeting, and demonstrations in Seattle against it, demonstrated the first trade-off, the trade-off between globally regulated market prosperity and democracy. Another was the flow of migrants and refugees into Western Europe and the United States. The trade-offs became more politically costly as interdependence increased. Politically, the democratic challenge was well put by Edward Mortimer (then *Financial Times* foreign editor) when he said that too much democracy kills the market (that's Polanyi's account of national and social democracy in reaction to the pre–World War I era of globalization) and, on the other hand, too much market kills democracy (this was the threat some saw posed by the post-1970s deepening of globalization). Commodities seem to rule citizens. And borders, the traditional bulwark of sovereignty, seem to be dissolving.

The second challenge to democratization and fuel for populism concerns both intranational and international equality. Globalization allows for those who are most efficient to earn the most. That is what markets usually do. And as the barriers fall to global sales, production, and investment, inequality—at least in the short to middle run—also tends to rise. Globalization did not appear to exacerbate poverty and may indeed contribute toward its reduction. Instances can be found in which global pressures, as in those to resolve the East Asian financial crisis of 1997, hurt the poor in a variety of countries, most noticeably Indonesia. But, worldwide, the proportion of those in extreme poverty ($1 a day) was falling, although this was largely a product of growth in China and India, while elsewhere in Africa, Eastern Europe, and Central Asia, the proportions of those in poverty was increasing. Moreover, the absolute number of those in poverty did not appear to be increasing—and may have been falling— from the 1.2 billion of 1990.[33]

Inequality, not growth, appears to have been the problem. Domestically in the United States, beginning about 1975, the economic fates of the top 5 percent and bottom 20 percent of the US population substantially diverged. By 1995, the real family income of the top 5 percent stood at 130 percent of the 1973 level, but over the same period, the real family income of the bottom 20 percent stayed at the 1973 level. This has played itself out in the United States by fueling partisanship. Former president Donald Trump has stoked those concerns by animating the grievances of the white middle class against minorities and the educated elite, with significant effects on both US domestic and international politics (discussed later).

Internationally, we can see what appear to be significant differences in a comparison of the Organization of Economic Co-operation and Development (OECD; the rich industrial economies) to the rest of the world and the 1970s to the 1990s and the 2000s. In 1970, the OECD enjoyed 66 percent of global GDP. By 1978, its share was up to 68 percent; in 1989, to 71 percent; and in 1995, to 78 percent.[34] But in the 2000s, the OECD share fell to 50 percent, the BRICS (Brazil, Russia, India, China, and South Africa) nations and Indonesia rose to 30 percent, and the rest of the world rose to 20 percent.[35]

In per capita terms, while the real per capita GDP of the developing countries increased from \$936 to \$1,417 from 1980 to 2000, in the developed countries it soared from \$20,397 to \$30,557.[36] The most famous evocation of global income shares inequality among globally measured quintiles was the "Elephant Chart" advanced by Christoph Lakner and Branko Milanovic of the World Bank.[37] It showed that the global extreme poor had low rates of income growth (the "tail"); the global middle class (the "body"—India and China) had high rates; the global bottom of the "trunk" (the OECD middle class) had very low rates; and the global high end of the "trunk" (top OECD 10 percent) had very high rates—all together making the "Elephant" in profile. But Homi Kharas and Brina Seidel (also of the World Bank) have shown with updated (2011) data and more nuanced methods of comparison that the "Elephant" is an exaggeration. The global poorest have done quite well, the global middle class still very well, the global low trunk better than previously thought, and the global high trunk less well. Inequalities abound, but they are less extreme.[38] But within the global elite, the global top 2 percent may have indeed done very well, holding approximately half the world's wealth.[39]

Whatever the deep sources and potential cures, the most productive states are winning, accumulating wealth in their own hands. The consequences of globalization appear to be favoring some over others—the rising tide is not lifting all the boats at the same rate. Not surprisingly, demands for accountable control rise.[40]

The third challenge is security. Liberalism produces security and peace (among the liberal republics). But globalization challenges the stability of liberal geopolitics in two ways. On the one hand, what Americans call globalization is what many others call Americanization. That is, the US leading role within the world economy, which to Americans appears as an economic issue of dollars and cents, is to other countries a power issue, one fraught with control and guns. The other hand is that global rules for trade and investment have allowed China to benefit from its high savings rate and labor productivity, becoming one of the fastest-growing economies in the world (as discussed in Chapter Three). If you add rapid growth to a large population (and if the World Bank projections are correct and if China continues to grow at recent past rates), then soon after the year 2020, China will have a GDP that is larger than that of the United States or Europe. From an economic point of view, the prospect of many more Chinese consumers and producers should make everyone content. But from a geopolitical point of view, China's growth entails a massive shift of world political power eastward. That makes the statesmen of the United States and Europe nervous, especially if, referring again to the liberal peace argument, China has not democratized.

Post–Cold War US Foreign Policy

With the end of the Cold War and the collapse of the Soviet Union, the US State Department drafted in 1992 a new doctrine to replace "containment" of the Soviet Union. Prepared under the auspices of Under Secretary of State Paul Wolfowitz, it declared (once leaked to the *New York Times*):

> Our first objective is to prevent the re-emergence of a new rival, either on the territory of the former Soviet Union or elsewhere, that

poses a threat on the order of that posed formerly by the Soviet Union. This is a dominant consideration underlying the new regional defense strategy and requires that we endeavor to prevent any hostile power from dominating a region whose resources would, under consolidated control, be sufficient to generate global power.[41]

An uproar followed, focused on its blatant imperial pretension and its apparent determination to dominate any and all other states. Defense secretary Dick Cheney and chairman of the Joint Chiefs of Staff Gen. Colin Powell redrafted the doctrine to make it clear that, while imperial in ambition, it reaffirmed the significance of a "democratic security community," staying within liberal foreign policy doctrine:

> ... to strengthen and extend the system of defense arrangements that binds democratic and like-minded nations together in cooperation on defense against aggression, builds habits of cooperation, avoids the renationalization of security policies, and provides security at lower costs and with lower risks for all.[42]

NATO Expansion and Ukraine

One large and problematic measure was the spread of NATO into Eastern Europe, which alarmed the Soviet-Russian establishment as a signal of their decline and potential isolation and an apparent betrayal of informal promises made by the George H. W. Bush administration consequent on the reunification of Germany.[43] Indeed, Gorbachev was "led to believe" that NATO would not be expanded as he sought to create "a common European home" that would include a democratic Russia.[44]

Much more sensible as a way to address both Russian and East European security concerns would have been to create a new "collective security" system to replace both NATO and the Warsaw Pact. Rather than the collective defense commitment espoused by NATO and the Warsaw Pact against external aggression, in a collective security organization both the United States and Russia would have been equal members united in a mutual commitment to resist aggression against any member by any state, whether in or outside the organization. In such a collective system, unanimity rules or vetoes are replaced by supermajority (two-thirds or three-quarters) decision rules in order to ensure action against egregious aggressions. Unfortunately, the appetite for radical change was limited as both the United States and the USSR sought to understand the complexities of the "post–cold war" that they were entering.[45]

It has been suggested that NATO expansion is the root of Putin's aggression against Ukraine in 2022. But the claim is both normatively and causally problematic. Normatively, states have legally enshrined sovereign rights to join defensive alliances that will have them as members. Great powers have no authority to dictate the foreign polices of their neighbors. The US 1961 invasion of Cuba in the Bay of Pigs incident, as an example, was not an instance of a great power "legitimately" protecting its sphere of influence. Today, Cuba, Venezuela, North Korea, Myanmar, and others have a complete legal right to ally with or align with Russia and China in an anti-Western grouping.

States have legitimate discretion over their foreign trade and investment and do use both to influence other states. The United States thus uses embargoes to pressure its unfriendly neighbors in Cuba and Venezuela. Russia uses oil and gas to create international dependencies, as in Germany and in Ukraine. Painful to the Ukrainians as it would have been, Putin could have legitimately used natural gas embargoes to pressure it to renounce NATO. (He also could have offered to return the Donbas and Crimea in return for Ukraine rejecting NATO.) On top of that, Putin allegedly rejected an offer from Ukraine to pledge to stay out of NATO on the eve of Russia's invasion of Ukraine.[46] But Putin's invasion of Ukraine in 2022 has neither legal nor normative foundations.

Analytically, to portray the NATO expansion as an "existential threat" to Russian national interests and as the causal driver is to neglect Russian efforts to join NATO's Partnership for Peace in 1994, the establishment of the Permanent Joint Council with NATO, joint air exercises between the air forces, and Russian supply assistance to the United States in the post-9/11 US attack on Afghanistan in 2001. NATO was not an existential threat to the Russia of the 1990s when it was relatively weak. Importantly, the implied condition of NATO nonexpansion was the successful democratization of Russia. There is thus an inherently circular dynamic in play: Russian failure to democratize legitimizes (in East European and US eyes) NATO expansion; NATO expansion legitimizes (in Russian eyes) aggressive regional domination.[47]

The decisive root causes appear to be later.[48] Putin's policy of restoring superpower status and hegemonic prestige are key. Putin's rolling reversal of Russian democratization, his aggressive campaigns against Georgia (2008), and his assumption of dictatorial authority in 2012 (discussed earlier) are deeper roots of the change in Russia, leading to a policy of external aggression as a justification of a garrison state and an appeal to aggrieved Russian prestige. The result was a spiral of suspicion, the United States and Russia reacting to each perceived threat, and growing animosity between them.

Putin and his apologists have said that NATO somehow poses an existential threat to the international order of sovereign states. Putin clearly advances this line, and he has persuaded Xi and other allies to repeat it. NATO is a defensive alliance. There is no evidence that a NATO member, new or old, has articulated a cross-border threat of invasion against Russia. The insanity of such an attack on a nuclear power is obvious. The various aggressions on Russia's borders, Georgia, Crimea, and now Ukraine, have all been the other way: Russia attacking its non-nuclear and much weaker neighbors. NATO did attack Serbia, without legal authorization from the UN Security Council, in a poorly managed attempt to stop the slaughter of Kosovars by Slobodan Milošević. An international commission led by Justice Richard Goldstone deemed the intervention "illegal but legitimate."[49] But it nonetheless resonated deeply in the Russian political consciousness as an illegitimate act.

If, moreover, fear of NATO expansion was indeed the key driver of the Russian invasion, it is difficult to imagine a more counterproductive measure than the invasion that mobilized the Ukrainian public around its charismatic democratic leader Zelensky, giving him the standing to address Ukraine's long-standing corruption, and won for Ukraine a vast improvement in the quality of its military forces and thus greatly advanced its prospects for actual NATO membership. The only way Putin could have succeeded in his strategy was to have easily installed a compliant puppet regime in Kyiv. Winning the Donbas and the landbridge to Crimea would not have been enough. Ukraine was until recently a poor candidate for rapid NATO membership with its corruption and weak military forces; no longer. Putin has mobilized a greatly strengthened and expanded NATO (with Finland and Sweden) and earned Ukraine, a country deep in the former Soviet space, a strong claim on membership.[50]

Putin's alleged fear of NATO is thus either disingenuous or misplaced. Disingenuous in that his aim appears to be not the defense of the territorial integrity and political independence of Russia but the domination of neighbors, either re-creating the former Soviet Union as a restored and glorious imperial power or preventing his neighbors from having the security that would permit independence at home and abroad. It is also misplaced in that waving the flag of NATO appears to successfully mobilize the manipulated Russian public to rally around Putin.[51] Indeed, opposition to NATO appears to be the existential prop of his military regime.

On the other hand, the European Union, with its democratic principles and enormous prosperity, has and does pose an existential threat . . . not to Russia, but to Putin's regime of autocratic corruption. Putin's regime would not pass muster as an acceptable democratic, rule-of-law, market society (the Copenhagen principles of membership outlined in the European Union's *acquis communitaire*). If the Russian public wants to join Europe, Putin will need to be dis-elected. And, ironically, in 2022, Putin's invasion of Ukraine appears to have motivated the Finnish and Swedish applications to join NATO and to have strengthened Ukraine's case for accelerated membership in the European Union—exactly the threat that should most concern Putin.[52]

Nonetheless, Russians, with some justification, have charged that American missile defenses (ten radars and air defense interceptors) in Poland and the Czech Republic threaten Russian security. They dismiss as far-fetched the excuse that they are targeted only against possible Iranian missile attacks. They are, the Russians claim, designed to undermine a Russian nuclear deterrent threat that offsets its conventional military inferiority to the NATO alliance, and thus erode Russian security. There is thus substantial room, if both sides are prepared to negotiate, to improve mutual security through mutual arms control measures in a cold peace, despite the current tensions, as the last chapter will argue.

Liberal doctrine provided inspiration for the Clinton administration policy of "engagement" in the 1990s. And it was one among the many justifications offered by the George W. Bush administration for the invasion of Iraq. It continued to shape policy under President Barack Obama—at least rhetorically, as when he reiterated the special pacific feature of liberal democratic alliances in his famous (seemingly premature—seven months into his presidency) Nobel Peace Prize acceptance speech and declared: "I believe that peace is unstable where citizens are denied the right to speak freely or worship as they please; choose their own leaders or assemble without fear." And Obama added: "Only when Europe became free did it find peace. America has never fought a war against a democracy."

The 2017 National Security Strategy announced a change of course: "These competitions require the United States to rethink the policies of the past two decades—policies based on the assumption that engagement with rivals and their inclusion in international institutions and global commerce would turn them into benign actors and trustworthy partners. For the most part, this premise turned out to be false."[53]

Thus when we look to current US foreign policy, it is not at all unusual to see a "new Red Scare" emerging in Washington in 2019.[54] With warnings sounding like the original "Cold War," the Committee on the Present Danger, "a long-defunct group that campaigned against the dangers of the Soviet Union in the 1970s and 1980s, has recently been revived." Their views resonated in "President Trump's Washington, where skepticism and mistrust of China readily took hold . . . Beijing's rise was unquestioningly viewed as an economic and national security threat and the defining challenge of the 21st century." Stephen Bannon, one of the group's new leaders, opines: "These are two systems [US and China] that are incompatible. . . . One side is going to win, and one side is going to lose." Larry Kudlow, the White House chief economic advisor, cautioned, "They're not the Soviet Union. But this kind of government control, statism, never works for long," and the possibility that China could collapse like the Soviet Union has "always been an undercurrent" in the trade war.

The United States and the Rise of China

The US strategy of trying to manage the rise of China had two strands in the 1990s. Some liberals optimistically hoped that the successful integration of China into globalization through the WTO would lead to a democratization and liberalization of China.[55] The 1989 suppression of the democracy movement at Tiananmen Square cautioned against and the later rise of Xi's powerful autocracy refuted those ideas. The opposite view of containing the rise of China arose in US "structural realist" academic circles, which urged that the United States "make sure that China does not become a peer competitor."[56] The problem with that strategy was that much of Chinese economic growth was domestically driven. But to the extent that trade and investment barriers would contain China, they would also harm, as Thomas Christensen has argued, US trade and that of the many allies in Japan, Australia, South Korea, Germany, and others that the United States needed to balance Chinese power.[57] Moreover, to the extent it was successful in curbing Chinese economic growth, it risked the creation of a deeply resentful and hostile power—a North Korea at Chinese scale.[58]

When we look at the specifically capitalist economic sources of tension, we see a looming industrial clash of historic proportions, particularly with China. US tariffs have been ratcheted up to 25 percent, and Chinese firms have been placed on Cold War–style "entity lists" that cut them off from essential technology, trade inputs (as with Huawei), and investment. Much of this is in response to China's long record of restricting trade, wholly or in part, to certain non-strategic sectors, to its state subsidies that undermine market-based competition, and to its required technology transfers in foreign investments. But equally important is a looming conflict over the future of the world economy. China's announcement of the "Made in China 2025" plan directly targets for competition the robotics, pharmaceutical, aerospace, and artificial intelligence sectors that are the leading sectors of current and hoped for US economic growth.

A striking example of this emerged in 2019 with the Chinese-owned video app TikTok, especially popular with American teenagers, who downloaded it 110 million times. As noted in Chapter 1, the app was considered an element of cold war confrontation. In 2019, US senators Charles Schumer, Tom Cotton, and Marco Rubio wanted a US national security investigation of the threat it allegedly posed to US counterintelligence and cybersecurity. The app gathers information on its users (including location), and this information would be made available to Chinese intelligence agencies. It could be used to manipulate information available in US elections and provide blackmailable information linked to individuals. Its growth crowded out Western information sources that could report on issues not acceptable within the Chinese "Great Firewall." (TikTok carried fewer videos of Hong Kong protests than did other apps.) All of this was seen as warranting a national security investigation. TikTok denied that it was controlled by the Chinese government, but the US senators working on the supposition that there is no effective independence for Chinese firms insisted on an investigation. But it is clearly difficult to separate the national security dimension from the commercial rival dimension, and it is significant that Mark Zuckerberg, CEO of rival Facebook, also sounded the alarm and noted TikTok's threat to US business.[59]

The Trump Factor

Russian or Chinese national corporatist authoritarianism interacting with aggressive liberalism would be a challenge to the international order even if democratic liberalism were flourishing. But this is manifestly not the case. Elected leaders such as Viktor Orbán in Hungary explicitly reject the premises of liberal democracy in favor of what he praises as the "illiberal state." Similar trends appeared in the Philippines under Rodrigo

Duterte, Poland under the Law and Justice Party, in Italy, Slovakia, Serbia, and as (so far) minority movements in Austria, Germany, Greece, France, and Britain. The mismanagement of the Greek financial collapse, the Syrian refugee crisis, and Brexit illustrate regional-level dysfunctions in what hitherto had been the deepening and widening of the European Union.

Even more striking has been the rise of Donald Trump in the Republican Party and his election to the US presidency. Not since Charles Lindbergh's pre–World War II and similarly styled "America First" movement has the United States seen so forthright a rejection of international engagement and embrace of xenophobic nationalism. During his campaign, Trump endorsed torture, the targeting of civilians, and wars for looting (seizing Iraqi oil). The right-wing populists flirt with the dictators: as Lindbergh did with Hitler, Trump does with Putin. Unlike Lindbergh, Trump was actually elected. Trump moreover sounds more like Putin than he does the other democratic leaders of the G7 or OECD, who now articulate and defend the international liberal order in ways that he did not.

Trumpian populism reflects the long-term forces described earlier: domestic inequality in the United States that has helped polarize the US electorate by eroding the middle class; challenges from highly competitive producers such as China and the European Union that have stimulated a deep suspicion of globalization; and then the 2008 recession, which revealed government's inability to reach the most forgotten classes (while rescuing Wall Street). The new information technology of Facebook and its competitors rather than uniting the public or promoting national communication has facilitated the fracturing of the marketplace of ideas into a myriad of specialized audiences rife with suspicion and conspiracy theories. Together they produced a fertile field for the Trumpian politics of resentment.

Trump's "Make America Great Again" defended traditional hierarchies with revolutionary rhetoric. He seemed to be making a promise to "weaken America's commitment to principles of fairness and equality to strengthen privileges of race, gender and wealth." While his personal life trumpeted "hedonism, excess and contempt for conservative moral-ity, . . . he pitched himself as a bulwark against cultural and demographic change, a symbol of white patriarchal manhood aligned against immigrants, feminists, and racial minorities."[60]

Trump embraced "nationalism" as a simultaneous attack on domestic elites (with their politically correct language) and on perfidious foreigners. When asked what it meant, he said: "I love our country. And our country has taken second fiddle. ... We're giving all of our wealth, all of our money, to other countries. And then they don't treat us properly."

The essence of "America Firstism" is not isolationism, but unilateralism. Trump and his team believed that bilateral bargaining that permits the direct exercise of US bargaining leverage is better than multilateral institution building. The logic of America First was that every relationship should be squeezed for maximum profit. The traditional liberal multilateral order promise was that restraint produced more value from an expanding pie, produced by the openness that secure and more equal multilateral arrangements could foster.[61]

Whether Trump's rhetoric will shape US policy in the long run remains obscure (and dependent on the policies that are adopted by the traditional Democrat president Joe Biden and whether Trumpism continues to dominate the Republican Party). Trump faced an entrenched democratic and liberal order at home and abroad, which resisted his brand of white nationalism. US liberal democracy was headed to a rivalry with the corporatist nationalisms of Russia and China irrespective of Trump. Indeed, the election of Hillary Clinton might have exacerbated the confrontation. A white nationalist with authoritarian predilections like Trump might thus have seemed a mollifying influence. But instead the only sure effect was greatly exacerbated insecurity and confusion, domestic politicization, and the straining on historic alignment among liberal democracies that grew out of the Cold War.

The multilateral trade negotiations across the Pacific were trashed in favor of bilateral standoffs with China; NAFTA has been repackaged as the US-Mexico-Canada Trade Agreement. A nuclear standoff with North Korea turned into a strange (unproductive) bromance between Trump and Kim. It began with puerile posing by both Kim Jong-un and Donald Trump. Juvenile bellicosity—a willingness to threaten war (the threat itself is illegal under UN Charter Article 2.4)—merged into personalistic photo ops (including ones on the inter-Korean DMZ).

Alliances came under deep strain. NATO was still in place, but its arms control regime with Iran was trashed by Trump. NATO was newly divided, and no one in the Trump administration seemed capable of designing stable arrangements that would control the nuclear standoffs with both Iran and North Korea. The failure to consult NATO before the retreat of US forces from northern Syria (exposing US allies to Assad's attack) and the failure to warn of the assassination of Iran's Gen. Qasem Soleimani left Europeans stunned and face to face with the prospect of Assad driving his opposition into Turkey and then Europe as refugees. But the deeper sources of disarray were Trump's approaches to alliances in general. As with trade, alliances were transactional. The United States would provide troops if the Europeans would make trade concessions. This weakened the credibility of mutual defense, created significant uncertainty, and sent Italians, Greeks, and the French scrambling to establish ties and perhaps even appease Russia.[62]

Even the alliances with Japan and South Korea came under strain. Trump praised Kim and extorted and insulted old ally South Korea, bragging at a Hamptons fund-raiser: "It was easier to get a billion dollars from South Korea than to get $114.13 from a rent-controlled apartment in Brooklyn."[63] Trump's abandonment of the TransPacific Partnership, designed to create a multilateral democratic front to deepen trade and avoid dependence on China, left the region scrambling to come to terms with China in bilateral deals.

There was no better exemplar of the domestic politicization of Trumpian foreign policy than the decision to move the US embassy to Jerusalem. The move undercut a wide multilateral consensus that the ultimate status of Jerusalem should be decided by negotiation between the Palestinians and the Israelis, serving as an incentive for a two-state peace. But its real purpose was more than fulfilled as a campaign promise to very wealthy, Far Right, Jewish Republican donors (Sheldon Adelson most prominent among them). At the same time, in the choice of pastors Robert

Jeffress and John Hagee for the welcoming prayers at the new American Embassy, Trump rewarded Far Right, Christian Evangelical Fundamentalists who believe that Israeli sovereignty over Jerusalem is a step toward the second coming of Christ. Only the Trump administration could have made this pairing complete with the two pastors who are reported to preach that all Jews are going to hell and that Hitler's Holocaust was part of God's plan to return the Jews to Israel.[64]

The apotheosis of Trumpism arrived on January 6, 2021, with the attack on the US Capitol encouraged by President Trump in a fiery address to his supporters in which he denounced the certification of the election by Congress. Counterintelligence officials from NATO allies speculated that Trump had actually planned the events as a putsch. One went on to note:

> The broader damage around the world will be extensive in terms of reputation, and that's why Putin doesn't mind at all that Trump lost. He's got to be happy to take his chips and count his winnings, which from the Trump era will be a shockingly quick decline in American prestige and moral high ground. Every moment the Americans spend on their own self-inflicted chaos helps China, it helps Putin, and, to a lesser extent, it helps the mini-dictators like [Turkish President Recep Tayyip] Erdogan and [Hungarian Prime Minister Viktor] Orban, who breathe cynicism about politics, human rights, and democracy as their air. They won't miss Trump; they'll be glad to see his drama leave so they can enjoy the poisoned political climate.[65]

The Trump effect has yet to disappear. Despite the invasion of Ukraine by Russia, former president Donald Trump described Mr. Putin as "smart" and "savvy." A Yahoo News/YouGov poll from January 2022 found that 62 percent of Republicans and Republican-leaning independents consider Vladimir Putin a stronger leader than Joe Biden. Trump's allies chimed in with similar sentiments. Conservative commentator Rod Dreher wrote, "I adamantly oppose risking the lives of boys from Louisiana and Alabama to make the Donbas safe for genderqueers and migrants."

The white nationalist Richard Spencer has referred to Russia as "the sole white power in the world."[66]

The roots of these populist upheavals are deeper than the antics of Trump. They lie in a combination of increasing domestic inequalities in some places (such as the United States) with seeming loss of control of borders and economy in others (as in Europe). Both have rocked the foundations of stable liberal democracy. Political polarization strains the governability, and white nationalist xenophobia erodes the values, of all liberal democracies. And it is not yet clear how many more Orbáns or Trumps are likely to prevail and unite in transnational political coalitions.[67]

In the United States, perhaps the most dangerous trend is searching for foreign scapegoats for the de-industrialization and erosion of skilled labor jobs caused by automation and globalization. We saw this in Trump's attacks on trade with China, with the "national security" tariffs on steel and even washing machines. China was alleged to be driving down the price of those products to undermine basic US manufacturing capacity (even though much of the direct competition was coming from others, such as Indonesia, Vietnam, Mexico, and India). And it was not clear whether the WTO would accept the national security escape clause (it requires evidence-based justification). In any case China retaliated, targeting the retaliation carefully, politically, against soybeans in order to cause maximum political pain.

Domestic Strategic Vulnerability

The root of the emerging national security problem that the United States faces is a polarization that has two insidious effects. First, it makes the country vulnerable to foreign subversion, as in 2016, and, second, it renders the polity less able to mount a sustained national defense that requires significant investment in material and social infrastructure.

Political polarization has reached levels unseen for more than a century. The January 6 Trump putsch and the refusal of a majority of the Republican voters to accept the legitimacy of the 2020 election of Joe

Biden is the emblem of a deeply divided polity. Trump "MAGA" voters are alienated and reflect a core aggrieved identity. Overwhelmingly a combination of white, rural, Evangelical Protestant, not college educated, and working middle class, they divide from the minorities, poor and middle class, urban, and college educated who form the core of the current Democratic Party.[68]

The distinctions carry deep grievances. The Democrats have long demanded recognition and political equality including racial equality and feminist equal treatment. Trump followers express grievances over disrespect from the educated elites, globalization and its loss of blue-collar union work, and "replacement" fears by non-whites and women. These divides made the US public an easy target for Putin's negative messaging and anti–Hillary Clinton manipulation.

These divides also make it difficult to mobilize the national will to innovate and invest in infrastructure that will be needed to compete with China and rebuild a political center that can pursue coherent global strategy. Only thirteen Republicans voted for the "bipartisan" infrastructure bill that passed the US House of Representatives in 2021, despite the Republican senators who helped craft it.

The New Cold War Crux Is in the Combination

Liberal, capitalist democracies clearly accommodate each other, despite economic competition and large differences in power status, without embroiling each other in national security competition. It is also possible to imagine a liberal, capitalist democracy managing its relations in a largely cooperative way with an authoritarian state. The United States in the Cold War welcomed friendly (and less powerful) authoritarians, such as Francisco Franco of Spain and António de Oliveira Salazar of Portugal, and the dictators of many Central American and Caribbean states, as long as they were anti-Communist and capitalist and committed to aligning with the United States against the USSR. Liberal, Democratic Socialist corporatisms, such as Sweden and Norway and other European states, have (at least until recently) gotten along well with the United

States throughout the Cold War and post–Cold War period. Rising global powers have been accommodated by (relatively) declining ones, as the rising liberal United States was by the liberal United Kingdom at the turn of the twentieth century.[69]

The emerging cold war we now face is thus a product of a contentious combination: a clash of domestic structures and ideological affinities—such as corporatist, nationalist authoritarians and liberal, capitalist democracies—with rising and declining power dynamics.

What we see is a spiral of hostile perception and corresponding escalation in which deep concerns about legitimacy translate into exaggerated ideas of threat and consequent retaliation setting off a further escalation.

Putin repeatedly permits cyberattacks on the United States, as the SolarWinds attack on the US government was followed by the 2021 hack of human rights and other organizations. He passed up the opportunity to jointly address the private ransomware hijack of the Colonial Pipeline or to criticize Lukashenko's hijacking of the airliner over Belarus. The West has thus kept sanctions in place and refuses to extend a Cold War–era safeguarding mechanism that involved a military-to-military information-sharing arrangement (seen to reduce the risk of accidental war).

China's approach to investigations of the origins of COVID-19 in 2020 fueled suspicions of cover-up. It could have permitted an open scientific investigation and embraced the genuine uncertainty in the scientific community and the then scientific consensus that, if the virus had escaped from a lab, it was an accident. The cover-up then fueled Western conspiracy theories and, more important, governmental perceptions of Xi's hostile strategic ambitions.

These suspicions and Chinese overreactions set up another conflict spiral in Europe. China's extensive trade and investment treaty with the European Union ran afoul of very modest EU criticism and very minor sanctions targeted on four local officials in response to Chinese actions in Xinjiang (after the European Union refused to endorse the US characterization of the oppression of the Uighurs as a "genocide"). China went ballistic. It imposed sanctions on the entire EU Political and Security

Committee, as well as the parliamentary subcommittee on human rights, five leading European parliamentarians, and even academic experts who study China. The trade deal is now on the rocks. After Canberra called for an independent inquiry into the origins of COVID-19, China decreed trade restrictions and accused Australia of "poisoning bilateral relations" and demanded that the country's media and think tanks stop writing negative reports about China. The Australian government canceled Belt and Road agreements made with China. After minor border confrontations in the Himalayas, India in 2020 joined the United States, Australia, and Japan in their largest naval exercises in over a decade.[70]

These spirals of confrontation are a large step away from the cooperative relations of the 1990s and early 2000s when China pursued a strategy of "peaceful rise" and the West pursued "engagement." Today, Xi Jinping has consolidated political power in one-man rule and heavily invested in the bedrock state economic sector. The West is experiencing fragile polarized democracy, encouraging populist xenophobia. And China's so-called wolf warrior (rhetorically aggressive) diplomacy is confronting a "new cold war," and a dangerous set of spirals is the result.

Worlds Safe for Democracy or Autocracy

The United States, Russia, and China are very unlikely to establish a "warm" peace, such as that enjoyed within Western Europe or between Europe and the United States and its other allies. Yet none of the powers are particularly aggressive. The United States did invade Afghanistan and Iraq (the latter on the basis of very faulty intelligence) and intervened with allies in Libya and Syria. Russia invaded Georgia and Ukraine. China asserts territorial claims over the South China Sea and Taiwan.

The deeper source of conflict, as this chapter has shown, is defensive. The United States and its allies do not want to impose democracy by force.[71] They want to make "a world safe for democracy" in which national security is affordable, elections are secure, markets are free, and in which human rights remain an ideal. China and Russia, correspondingly, seek "a world safe for autocracy" in which governments are free to have or not have elections, the state exerts control over the economy, and no one outside the government questions state policy. Both sides are threatened because those two systemic visions are incompatible.

Before we turn in Part Four to what can be done to head off a new cold war, I turn in Part Three to a distant mirror of how a liberal, capitalist democratic United States managed its relations with two other corporatist, nationalist authoritarians—Mussolini's Italy and post-Taisho Japan in the 1930s. I do so in order to illustrate how their relations evolved from cooperation in the 1920s to the growing confrontation in the 1930s that contributed to the onslaught of World War II.

Part Three

DISTANT
MIRRORS

Italy, Japan, and the United States

from the 1920s to the 1930s

■ THE LOOMING NEW COLD WAR
has important historical analogues. We have no crystal ball to discover
how current tensions will or will not resolve. Thus it is worthwhile to look
back at a distant mirror of previous US engagement and rivalry with corporatist, nationalist autocracies. US relations with Italian Fascism and
Japanese militarism in the 1930s will not be repeated in a world war (we
can reasonably hope). Still, there is much to learn from the similarities to
and differences from US relations with the two powerful autocracies of
Italy and Japan for current relations with Russia and China.

Though Putin is not Stalin, Xi is not Mao, and no one today is Hitler,
there are important parallels between twenty-first-century national corporatist autocracy and twentieth-century Italian Fascism and Japanese
militarism. There are fascinating parallels between the ideology and policies of Putinism, the ideas of the Fascists of the 1920s and 1930s, and the
policies of Benito Mussolini in his attacks on Libya, Ethiopia, and into
the Balkans. Like Putin today, Mussolini tried to seize military glory and
expand his foreign control in order to support his program to secure a
domestic autocratic state.

Although the divided polity of 1920s and 1930s Japan has no obvious
parallel in modern China, there are important similarities between the
strategic environment and choices made by the Japanese military regime
of the 1930s and the environment confronted and policies chosen by
Xi in China today. Parallels resonate between Japanese rapid economic
growth and Japan's plans for a "Greater East Asia Co-Prosperity Sphere"
and Chinese claims today over the South China Sea, as well as its Belt
and Road Initiative.

What is equally, if not more, important is that there are analogies between how the United States treated its historical rivals and US policy toward China and Russia today. The United States both appeased and confronted its rivals. The United States was both fascinated by and suspicious of the dictatorship it saw in Mussolini. The United States patronized liberal Japan in the 1920s. It relied on and reacted against Japan's 1930s militarism. Before Japan turned against key US interests in China and Southeast Asia, it was a useful counterweight to the radical Chinese nationalism of Chiang Kai-shek. Americans also saw the threat posed by corporatism to free competition idealized in capitalist markets.

It is also important to learn from the past that differences between autocratic corporatism and liberal capitalism did not and do not make a cold war automatic. Mussolini was welcomed by many in the United States in the 1920s. And even the military takeover in Japan in 1931 did not escalate into a strategic crisis until later in the 1930s.

The differences are equally important. Unlike the current reaction to Chinese and Russian corporatism and autocracy, the United States was not only fascinated by the successful parts of the Fascist response to the Great Depression but also sought to imitate it in parts of New Deal policy. Fascism was seen as attractive in part because it was the alternative to the threat posed by Socialist revolution and because it catered to and reflected widespread anti-Semitism.

Japanese militarism, too, had its virtues in US eyes: it helped contain rising Chinese nationalism and joined in the partnership with the United States and Britain in exploiting China. Neither Russia nor China has the political draw that Fascism did in the 1920s and 1930s. Fascism became popular in the United States in a way that Putinism has not (except among extreme elements of the Trumpian right). China has some of that efficiency attractiveness but not the breadth or depth of emulation in the United States that was seen in Mussolini's regime. China today plays no role for the United States akin to Japan's in the 1920s in helping to police East Asian instability. Neither Italy nor Japan were peer competitors the way China is seen as being. But both Japan in the Pacific and Italy (and its Nazi partner) in Europe posed ever more pressing strategic threats in the 1930s, leading up to the crises that escalated to World War II.

Fortunately, we are not about to replay World War II. Nuclear deterrence alongside other differences are vitally significant. We still, however, have much to learn from the driving forces underlying the actions of the 1920s and 1930s statesmen and the mistakes they made.

CHAPTER SIX

Italian Fascism and American Politics

Fascists were once popular and, indeed, admired in the United States. In 1933, as the United States descended into the depths of the Depression, Italo Balbo, a heroic pilot as well as Benito Mussolini's son in law and minister of aviation, landed in America. Under the editorship of Henry Luce, *Time* was laudatory of Balbo and his fellow pilots. Balbo was "accompanied by US Army planes in formation spelling *Italia*." The then secretary of the navy, Claude Swanson, commended Balbo for his "enviable reputation" and "remarkable capacity for organization and leadership." The US ambassador to Italy, Breckinridge Long, told Mussolini of Roosevelt's "admiration for the flight of General Italo Balbo to America." Long also remarked how "the American people had acclaimed them with enthusiasm and admiration."[1]

The reception was remarkable given Italian Fascism's assault on democracy and the particular role Balbo played in that assault as the violent boss for Mussolini's party in Ferrara. But in another sense, it reflected the popular disdain for involvement in foreign affairs following the diplomatic squabbling that emerged in the Paris Peace Conference. The "war to end all wars" led to the reemergence of the long-standing American mood of isolationism.[2] Some in the public also displayed wider skepticism toward and disparagement of liberal capitalism caused by World War I, the world economic crisis, and the failure of democratic governments to adequately address those two catastrophes. Many of the sentiments at play then are all too familiar now. Prefiguring the democratic pessimism that resonates today, Henry R. Spencer of Ohio State University took to the pages of the *American Political Science Review* in 1927 to remark upon the dictatorships of Mussolini, Miguel Primo de Rivera, and Joseph Stalin. He noted "an apparent reversal of the supposed universal progress toward democracy that he had been taking for granted."[3] Another scholar, in 1928, William Kilborne Stewart, expressed the "tragic irony of history that the World War, which was said to be waged 'to make the world safe for democracy,' has been followed by a general disillusionment regarding democracy, and in some cases, notably in Russia and in Italy, by a definite repudiation of it."[4]

These trying times drove numerous liberals into sympathy with Fascism. In 1933, FDR as president even contemplated including in his first radio address to the American Legion a problematic and questionably constitutional appeal to veterans to protect—with force if need be—the New Deal from potential opponents.[5] And Charles Merriam, a distinguished political scientist, in the same year praised Mussolini's Italy for its "experimental nature, antidogmatic temperament, and moral *élan*" and in 1936 led a mission to Italy for Roosevelt to take home lessons for the New Deal.[6] Merriam subsequently defended New Deal planning proposals (especially the National Resources Board), arguing that

> [o]ur democratic system is based upon the principle that the gains of civilization are essentially mass gains and should be diffused throughout the people as promptly and equitably as possible. With this end in view, there is reason to believe that systematic, forward-looking planning would facilitate the adoption of such policies regarding our natural and human resources as would best serve

this basic purpose of our system, increasing our output and providing for sounder distribution.[7]

As late as 1936 (after Mussolini's brutal invasion of Ethiopia), Bishop Thomas O'Reilly of the Diocese of Scranton, Pennsylvania, returning from vacation in Italy, said that he had not heard any American tourists find fault with the country. He added: "Under Mussolini there is not a city in Italy that has not made a hundred years progress in ten years. We talk about the slum problem, but he just tears them down and then rebuilds."[8]

Among the most enthusiastic advocates of Fascism was the former US ambassador to Italy and Mussolini biographer, Richard Washburn Child. He took "dictation" from the Duce and edited Mussolini's English-language *My Autobiography*. He also authored his own account of America, *The Writings on the Wall: Who Shall Govern Next*. Warning in the latter book that Bolshevism is like a "cuckoo" stealing the nests of others, he urged "realist statesmen" to take cognizance of two facts: Communism does not need a majority to win, and it will win if parliamentary machineries are not reformed.[9] There is, he added, "an ideal nation," objectively waiting to be freed from politics, parties, minorities, and special interests by "strong leadership" prepared to "seize the reins by general approval" and implement a corporatist economy that will curb the special interests and manage the economy as it was by the War Board (during World War I).[10]

Fascism appealed beyond progressives and enthusiasts like Child, to genuinely reactionary voices.[11] Walter J. Shepard used his 1934 presidential address to the American Political Science Association to voice his concern that New Deal "[d]ictatorship stalks across the state naked and unashamed, and openly casts its covetous eye upon the White House." At the same time, he argued that elements of Fascism ought to be appropriated, especially "the dogma of universal suffrage must give way to a system of educational and other tests which will exclude the ignorant, the uninformed, and the anti-social elements which hitherto have so frequently controlled elections."[12]

By 1939, however, liberals changed their minds. Merriam, for instance, called Fascism "the new despotism" and attacked Italian theorists for their elitist conception of politics. Illustrative of this new anti-Fascist position, he argued that: "It may be said very broadly that the Soviets attempt a form of equality but destroy liberty; that Fascism and Naziism [*sic*] destroy both liberty and equality; but that the democratic state may protect and develop both equality and liberty."[13]

This end point in the US fascination with Italian Fascism is well expressed in FDR's "Declaration of War on Germany" speech, in which he identified German Nazism as the main threat: "The movement of world conquest, accompanied by methods of enslavement, barbaric lawlessness, general destruction, and fiendish cruelty without a parallel."[14] Earlier, in his famous "Stab in the Back Speech" on June 10, 1940, at the University of Virginia where he was addressing the students (among whom was his son, graduating from law school), FDR had assessed the wider significance of the contest between the "system of force" (exemplified by Italy's recent declaration of war on France and Britain) and the democracies:

It is understandable, to all of us that they [American youth] should ask this question. They read the words of those who are telling them that the ideal of individual liberty, the ideal of free franchise, the ideal of peace through justice, are decadent ideals. They read the word and hear the boast of those who say that a belief in force— force directed by self-chosen leaders—is the new and vigorous system which will overrun the earth. They have seen the ascendancy of this philosophy of force in nation after nation where free institutions and individual liberties were once maintained. . . .

But in this new system of force the mastery of the machine is not in the hands of mankind. It is in the control of infinitely small groups of individuals who rule without a single one of the democratic sanctions that we have known. The machine in hands of irresponsible conquerors becomes the master; mankind is not only the servant; it is the victim, too. . . .

Some indeed still hold to the now somewhat obvious delusion that we of the United States can safely permit the United States to become a lone island, a lone island in a world dominated by the philosophy of force.

Such an island may be the dream of those who still talk and vote as isolationists. Such an island represents to me and to the overwhelming majority of Americans today a helpless nightmare of a people without freedom—the nightmare of a people lodged in prison, handcuffed, hungry, and fed through the bars from day to day by the contemptuous, unpitying masters of other continents.[15]

Today, a new spirit of isolationism stalks both the Democratic Party and the Republican Party in the United States. Progressives and conservatives are rightly saying that the United States needs to abandon militarism, but some seem prepared to drop human rights and a commitment to assist democratic states facing aggressive threats.[16] Following their lead will, I suggest, have severe and harmful consequences on US security and global civility. Understanding the appeal of Fascism in the Interwar period, and how its appeal eroded to eventually become a denunciation of Fascism as being nearly equivalent to Nazism, is the mirror we need to illuminate.

Mussolini's Fascism

In Italy, Fascism's appeal rested directly on discrediting liberal republicanism, seen as responsible both for Italy's entrance into World War I and the dreadful way in which the war was managed, which resulted in hundreds of thousands of casualties and embarrassing defeat after defeat.[17] Balbo himself memorably and colorfully (if obscurely) denounced the liberal state as "rotten to the bone, lying and false," a "nest of owls."[18] Fascism's success also rested on a fear of revolutionary Socialism experienced by the traditional conservative (landowner and Catholic) and formerly liberal (capitalist and urban) elite.

The only "official" definition of Fascism comes from Mussolini, who outlined three principles of a Fascist philosophy.

1. "Everything in the state." The government is supreme and all-encompassing, and all within it must conform to the ruling body, often a dictator.

2. "Nothing outside the state." The country must grow, and the implied goal of any Fascist nation is to rule the world and have every human submit to the government.
3. "Nothing against the state." Any type of questioning the government is not to be tolerated.[19]

As Mussolini elaborated: "We are, in other words, a state which controls all forces acting in nature. We control political forces, we control moral forces[,] we control economic forces, therefore we are a full-blown Corporative state."[20]

Totalitarianism was a Fascist ambition. Unlike Nazi Germany, Stalinist Russia, and Maoist China where totalitarianism was close to reality, Fascist reality was more complicated.

Antonio Gramsci, the leader of Italian Communism and an influential Marxist philosopher, came to grips with the meaning of Italian Fascism in his *Prison Notebooks*. From his prison cell, Gramsci thought through the forces that had both sidelined Italian Communism after its failed revolutionary uprising and imprisoned him. He rejected the simple Marxist notion that Mussolini was a direct agent of the capitalist bourgeoisie. The large industrialists, he argued, still preferred the bankrupt liberalism of Giovanni Giolitti's government, which shortly predated Mussolini. He also rejected the more sophisticated idea that Mussolini was a new "Caesar" or "Bonapartist," like Louis Napoleon. For a Marxist, Caesarism was a militaristic solution to "who governs" that resulted when the capitalist classes and the working class were in a revolutionary deadlock.[21] Fascism, for Gramsci, was wholly capitalist, but it also reflected the failure of the capitalist bourgeoisie to achieve "hegemony" (cultural domination and legitimacy). Instead, it was a product of contradictory bourgeois forces, and especially of the rivalry between two factions of the bourgeoisie—the petty bourgeois radicals, who followed the ebullient poet of Fascism, Gabriele D'Annunzio; and the industrialists, who lined up behind Mussolini.

Fascism was a coalition. The Fascist coalition was sustained by the urban industrialists' fear of proletarian revolution (stimulated by the threat of a general strike in 1921) but also drew on semiautonomous, non-economic forces. One force was the anger and resentment of the unemployed former shopkeepers and veterans outraged by Italy's defeats in World War I, who aligned behind D'Annunzio. The other was the Catholic Church and rural landowners, who combined behind Mussolini.[22]

In 1922, Mussolini seized all the strings and "Marched on Rome."

A nuanced, political and historically sensitive definition of the wider phenomenon of twentieth-century Fascism is found in Robert Paxton's magisterial study, *The Anatomy of Fascism*:

> A form of political behavior marked by obsessive preoccupation with community decline, or victimhood and by compensatory cults of unity, energy, and purity, in which a mass-based party of committed nationalist militants, working in uneasy but effective collaboration with traditional elites, abandons democratic liberties and pursues with redemptive violence and without ethical or legal restraints goals of internal cleansing and external expansion.[23]

Nine key features are stressed above: "obsession with decline," "cults of unity," "mass-based party," "nationalist militants," "with traditional elites," "abandons democratic liberties," "redemptive violence," "internal cleansing," and "external expansion." In the real world, no movement is likely to have them all, but having most of them is what makes for Fascism.

These regimes, like their twenty-first-century counterparts such as Russia, China, Venezuela, and others, were nationalist, corporatist, and autocratic. They also included distinct features that account for similarities to and differences from the current realities of autocratic nationalism.

Fascist Nationalism

As does Putin's, Mussolini's nationalism seethed with resentment at Italy's lack of a "place in the sun." As he paraded in front of a 1935 mass meeting, which he promptly called the "greatest demonstration in world history," he declaimed: "When in 1915 Italy threw in her fate with that of the Allies [against Germany and Austria in World War I], how many cried of admiration, how many promises were heard? But after the common victory, which cost Italy six hundred thousand dead, four hundred thousand lost, one million wounded, when peace was being discussed around the table only the crumbs of a rich colonial booty were left for us to pick up. For thirteen years we have been patient while the circle tightened around us at the hands of those who wish to suffocate us."[24]

Mussolini's totalist form of nationalism was clear from his core principles of "everything in," "nothing outside," and "nothing against." He rejected both liberal individualism and Socialist egalitarianism. "We were the first to state," he elaborated, "in the face of demo[cratic] liberal individualism, that the individual exists only in so far as he is within the State and subjected to the requirements of the state and that, as civilization assumes aspects which grow more and more complicated, individual freedom becomes more and more restricted."[25] He also proclaimed, "Fascism is . . . opposed to Socialism to which unity within the State (which amalgamates classes into a single economic and ethical reality) is unknown, and which sees in history nothing but the class struggle."[26]

Fascism, moreover, claimed the totality of all the Italian people, expressed in the will of the few (if not one) along lines that can best be called spiritual or religious in their claims. Mussolini claimed his government was the "conscience and the will of the mass, of the whole group ethnically molded by natural and historical conditions into a nation, advancing, as one conscience and one will, along the self-same line of development and spiritual formation. . . . Not a race, nor a geographically defined region, but a people, historically perpetuating itself; a multitude unified by an idea and imbued with the will to live, the will to power, self-consciousness, personality."[27]

The distinctive features worth noting are that Fascist nationalism was not just a norm-setting, public lawgiver, but "an educator and a promoter of spiritual life." It is not just shared obligation, not shared history or culture, but a "spiritual force" rooted in the past and present. Neither is it defined by majority will, but definable by the few or, even, one who claims its complete authority. This means the self-appointed leader can define its content, claim its total authority, without reference to what the majority of the people, constitutional procedures, or set standards or principles might determine. This makes both the aggressive content and the unaccountability of Fascist nationalism a splendid resource for a dictator's political toolbox.

Here we can see distant echoes of Putin's conversion to Orthodox religiosity (odd for a former KGB agent), scorn for his dissenting opponents as "scum," advocates of "gender freedoms," and elite "oyster-eaters."[28] He claims to be speaking with the voice of a scorned Russia, slighted by the West in general and the US superpower in particular. These attitudes were bolstered by the increasingly autocratic and closed decision-making of the Russian polity after 2012.

Mussolini rejected democratic constraints and the "absurd conventional lie of political equalitarianism, the habit of collective irresponsibility, the myth of felicity and indefinite progress."[29] He instead glorified the Fascist state as an exercise in power and command, drawing on its Roman roots (the "fasces" represented official power in Rome). Imperial power for the Fascist was "not only territorial, or military, or commercial; it is spiritual and ethical." After lying fallow "during centuries of foreign servitude," Italy was now experiencing "an imperialistic spirit—a tendency of nations to expand—a manifestation of vitality." Those who limited their interests to their home country, he added, were experiencing a symptom of decadence.

Fascist nationalism should not be read or systematized as a coherent philosophy. Mussolini, a former editor of *Avanti*, the Socialists' youth magazine, was a brilliant polemicist. (Despite his authorial credentials, the "Doctrine of Fascism" was probably ghost-written by Giovanni Gentile.) Fascism contradicted itself in every other paragraph (and sometimes in the same paragraph). Nonetheless, it did then and has (later) displayed common rhetorical and political traits, an "Ur-Fascism" in Umberto Ecco's telling label.[30] Those include an utter rejection of modern rationalism; an affinity toward violence and action for action's sake; a deep sense of historical humiliations; an affiliation with a frustrated middle class fearing its collapse into the lower classes; a populism that finds refuge in a common identity in one nation; and a nation whose unity and familiarity is then defined by and against internal and external enemies, in the voice of a self-appointed leader.

Fascist Corporatism

The "Constitution of Carnaro," was designed by D'Annunzio for the revolutionary regime he brought to Fiume (modern Rijeka in Croatia) in a transnational coup in 1919. In it he outlined an ideal of corporatist syndicalism. The constitution established a corporatist state with nine "corporations" to represent the different sectors of the economy. Membership was mandatory. It included a symbolic tenth corporation devised by D'Annunzio, to represent "superior individuals" (for example, poets, "heroes," and "supermen"), among whom he seemed to include himself. The more prosaic other nine corporations were: industrial and agricultural workers; seafarers; employers; industrial and agricultural technicians; private bureaucrats and administrators; teachers and students; lawyers and doctors; civil servants; and co-operative workers.[31]

Mussolini borrowed the corporatist idea, contrasting it to both the owner domination (or union-management hard bargaining) of capitalism and the worker domination of Socialism. "When brought within the orbit of the State," Mussolini explained, "Fascism recognizes the real needs which gave rise to socialism and trade unionism, giving them due weight in the guild or corporative system in which divergent interests are coordinated and harmonized in the unity of the State."[32]

For Italy, the corporatist state was more rhetorical than actual. It was neither as communal as its Fascist advocates claimed nor as effective. Later, it became more effective (and coercive) as the pressures of the Great Depression and then the conflicts over Ethiopia required extensive centralization and government control of production, as food and raw materials (especially oil) became in very short supply. In 1934, with the global depression deepening, the government took on more power. Twenty-two corporations were created to represent Italy's industry. These bodies included representatives of management and workers. They allocated scarce inputs and set production targets. They acted as a kind of parliament, with nominal powers to set wages and conditions of employment. After the lower house of the Italian parliament (the chamber of deputies) was abolished in 1938, Mussolini replaced it with "The Chamber of Fasces and Corporations," where 800 people represented 22 corporations. But in practice, this body was merely advisory.[33]

Like Putin's crony capitalism that erects a face of market relations and a claim of national prosperity through coordinated production, neither then nor before were Fascism's communal or quasi-socialist claims met. Louis Franck diagnosed its false front in a perceptive article published as early as 1935.[34] He found that the corporations elaborated norms for contracts between employers and laborers. They called for "unitary discipline of production," drew up "agreements between producers in the same group, between producers belonging to different groups (e.g., between smelters and mine owners, between sugar refiners and producers of beet)"; and they attempted to fix prices for every product and economic service.[35] But it only tried to exercise these functions when they advantaged the industrial owners and when directed to do so by the relevant governmental minister and, only then, when authorized by Mussolini.

Fascist Authoritarianism

In his 1932 "Doctrine of Fascism," Mussolini provocatively described Fascism as "organized, centralized, authoritarian democracy."[36] It was certainly organized, centralized, and authoritarian, but "democratic" only in two senses: the Fascists (like Putin) claimed to represent the true interests of the people, and they sometimes enjoyed (successfully cultivated) widespread popularity.

The Fascists were the dominating second choice. The nationalistic ex-servicemen and small shopkeepers made Fascism their party of first choice. But financiers and industrial owners preferred the liberals (but feared the Socialists); the large landowners and the Catholic Church preferred the traditional and monarchist parties (but feared the secular Socialists); and workers preferred the Socialists (but were eager for jobs and security).

The famous 1922 "March on Rome" was a legalized military coup. But its success rested less on armed might or revolutionary ardor than on the collapse of the previous regime. In 1919, national elections produced a progressive front in the assembly, with the Socialists and the Popular Party (Catholics) together forming a large majority. But they were deeply divided over religious issues and crumpled politically. The old liberal war horse, Giolitti, assembled an electoral coalition for the 1921 elections with the conservatives, and included Mussolini's Fascists. Luigi Facta, a Giolitti lieutenant, became the new coalition prime minister, but soon lost his majority. In that context, sensing opportunity, in 1922 the Fascists launched demonstrations and takeovers across the Po Valley and announced a "March on Rome." The government in Rome had the elite military resources that could have stopped the march (which was dissolving of its own lack of accord as it neared Rome). Instead, King Victor Emmanuel refused Prime Minister Facta's request to declare martial law, rejected a conservative effort to form a new government without Mussolini's party members, and then invited Mussolini to become prime minister and form a government, ratifying the Duce's blustering bluff.[37]

Mussolini's Fascist revolution came after, not before or during, his coup, and it emerged in steps. From 1922 until 1924, Mussolini ruled in a conventional fashion in a coalition government with nationalists, liberals, and other conservatives. Nonetheless, he enlisted *squadristi* (cohorts of armed Fascist activists) to engage in violent acts to intimidate regional voting and pressure the lower house of parliament into accepting a strange electoral rule that awarded two-thirds of the seats to the leading party (the Fascists) as long as it received one-quarter of the vote.

The turning point arrived with the murder of a Socialist deputy, Matteoti, in 1924, apparently by associates of Mussolini. Rather than defending the rule of law, the king and the military dithered. Starting in 1925, Fascist militias shut down opposition newspapers and proceeded to arrest opposition leaders. The Fascist-dominated parliament then passed a series of "Laws for the Defense of the State" that strengthened the power of the administration, replaced the elected mayors with appointed officials (*podesta*), subjected the press and radio to censorship, reinstituted the death penalty, gave Fascist unions a monopoly of labor representation, and dissolved all parties but the Partita Nazionale Fascista (PNF).[38]

With assassinations, armed intimidation, and press censorship, it is easy to see how Mussolini's Fascists dominated Italy. It is also easy to see parallels to Putin's emergence to power. Putin was not the product of a coup. He came to power through legal channels, first as Yeltsin's deputy and then through formal elections. But, as the previous part noted, asset seizures (first of Mikhail Khodorkovsky's Yukos) and convenient assassinations (starting with, in 2006, Anna Politkovskaya, the critic of Putin's crushing of Chechnya, and then Boris Nemtsov in 2015 and through to the attempted poisoning of Alexei Navalny, the leader of democratic opposition to Putin) have drawn a firm line against opposition to the regime. Control of the media after 2012 and manipulation of polls reinforce the dictatorship.

But it would be a mistake to neglect how much popular support they mobilized. Putin's United Russia Party has repeatedly "won" elections and clearly draws support from nationalists and even, on occasion, approval from moderates such as Mikhail Gorbachev for stemming the collapse of the Russian state at the end of the 1990s. So, too, Mussolini's nationalist coalition of conservatives, some liberals, populists, and church leaders orchestrated by Mussolini's Fascists garnered 64 percent of the vote for parliament in 1924. But even more strikingly, Fascism consciously set about creating a "culture of consent," described in Victoria de Grazia's pathbreaking analysis. It centered on the charismatic strongman that Mussolini presented to the nation as he assumed credit for every positive step and blessed every act of public policy. It focused on the *dopolavoro*, or Fascist leisure-time organizations. De Grazia traces their spread through thousands of local clubs into every domain of urban and rural life. She demonstrates their overwhelming impact on the distribution, consumption, and character of all kinds of recreational pursuits—from sports and adult education to movies, traveling theaters, radio, and tourism.[39]

Mussolini's Grand Strategy

In 1915, at the onset of World War I, Italy abandoned its German ally, and in 1919, as part of the victoriously restored European order negotiated in Paris, sought tokens of colonial spoil in Libya and the former German colonies. Mussolini took these dreams of colonial imperialism that Italian liberals had seen as a complementary sideshow of Italy's effort to obtain recognition as a major power within the European international order and turned them into a destiny that Italy would shape as it overturned the European order.

His grand strategy had two prongs. Mussolini mounted a double gamble for greatness: He imposed internal unity in the cause of imperial expansion and imperial expansion in the cause of internal unity. He would make Italy strong in order to solve its strategic dependence and encirclement. And imperial Italy, a new Rome, would make Fascism domestically supreme and him the new emperor.

The Fascist domestic revolution after 1925 was a step-by-step seizure of the domestic reins of power. Once in control, the Fascists set about a program of public works and regulation that increased employment and built needed public infrastructure such as roads and railways. But the Fascists saw Italy as internationally vulnerable. British and French naval bases in Toulon, Bizerte (Tunisia), and Malta were the tight inner ring; dependence on foreign coal, oil, iron ore, grain, and fertilizer and above all capital were the chains; and the British bases at Suez and Gibraltar were the outer walls of Italian subservience.[40] Nationalist nostalgia for the Roman Empire partly inspired the combined strategy of domestic autocracy and international empire. The navy's influence was clear in the emphasis on sea power. But the domestic political drive was paramount, as was evident in Mussolini's speech on October 2, 1935, rallying support behind the invasion of Ethiopia. "It is not only the army marching toward its goal," he announced, "but it is forty-four million Italians marching in unity behind this army." And, further, he intoned: "This manifestation signifies that the tie between Italy and Fascism is perfect." But at the same time, he assured the wary public that the "authentic" (free from their politicians) people of Britain will not want to "spill blood and send Europe into a catastrophe for the sake of a barbarian country [Ethiopia], unworthy of ranking among the civilized nations."[41]

Mussolini regularly assured his domestic audience that the military moves in Libya, Albania, Ethiopia, and Spain would not provoke a Europewide war. He claimed to stand as a force for peace between Germany and the liberal states. Moreover, with the help of the traditional bureaucrats in the foreign ministry who wanted just such a moderate diplomacy under the umbrella of Britain,[42] Mussolini successfully persuaded the French, British, and American foreign ministries of that, while in private describing his diplomacy as a "formula to put [the] democracies to sleep."[43] He well recognized, after 1933, that his geopolitical aims and his domestic dominance rested on an alliance—what Mussolini called a "community of destiny"—with a Nazi overturning of the European order.

The Democracies and Fascism

This chapter began with the expressions of enthusiasm for Fascist dynamism coming from scholars, officials, and democratic politicians. Praising the dynamism, welcoming the alternative to the democratic stalemate or capitalist dysfunction (depending on political leanings), they cheered Balbo and welcomed Mussolini. But the deeper roots were hard-headed assessments of economic interest and political views on what the alternative to a Mussolini would be both in Italy and Europe. Here we see roots of accommodation that were present then and are not present in the US-Russia confrontation.

US economic ties to Italy slowly shifted from cooperation in the 1920s to reluctant conflict in the 1930s when Italy invaded Ethiopia and Roosevelt imposed economic sanctions on Italy.[44] Economic relations between the parties primarily dealt with trade between Italy and the United States and US investment in Italy, reflecting Italy's relative impoverishment and scarcity of capital compared to the United States.[45]

Before the rise of Fascism in Italy, relations between it and the United States were disturbed by restrictive US immigration laws beginning in

1922.[46] Italy had relied on emigration to reduce stress on its economy from its unemployed and on remittances from the United States to stimulate economic activity.[47] With Mussolini's seizure of power in 1925, he quickly moved to court the American business class, recognizing the significant power of the United States and that it was the only major power with which Italy could affect a significant diplomatic breakthrough.[48] American business then, as American business is now, was interested in making deals. It was thus generally receptive to Mussolini and greeted his rise to power with cautious optimism.[49]

Economic relations between Italy and the United States in the 1920s centered around the Morgan bank, which at that time had become one of the primary financial intermediaries between the United States and European powers. Before the settlement of Italy's war debt in 1925, Italy had a rocky relationship with the New York financial market. With the settlement of this debt and the signing of the Locarno Pact, however, Italy gained access to significant capital from American markets, with loans totaling $316 million made from 1925 to 1928. The Italian government sought to attract international investment, including American, in the country's growing economy.[50] The corporatist government required approval for foreign ownership to operate in the country, and with the onslaught of the Great Depression, Italy began increasing capital controls and regulation of foreign-owned firms.[51] This affected American investments, focused as they were on large capital projects such as dams, providing necessary financial resources to the capital-scarce Italian economy.[52] US business then began to sour on Italian state corporatism (just as it did the New Deal at home).

The 1935 attack on Ethiopia came with new currency and trade controls, which further increased government control over the Italian market.[53] Cooperating with the League of Nations that the United States had refused to join, Roosevelt quickly declared a moral embargo to prevent exports of oil and other materials above "normal peacetime levels" to Italy in response to its invasion.[54] American financial institutions significantly reduced trade-financing activity and lending to the Italian government.[55] However, exporting businesses were much less willing to follow the lead of Roosevelt's government and worked hard to both maintain trade volumes and evade restrictions on export of raw materials, contributing significantly to the failure of the League of Nations' attempt to use economic sanctions to stop Mussolini's aggression against Ethiopia.[56] And automobile manufacturers and oil companies both found it useful to take advantage of other nations' sanctions against Italy to increase their own exports during the conflict.[57]

However, the Italian invasion of Ethiopia did set off a reevaluation of Fascist Italy within the Roosevelt administration.[58] In particular, the war weakened the financial relationship between banks in the United States and Italy. In addition, the Italian move toward a policy of autarky naturally weakened trade ties between the two nations, and Italy sought to reduce dependence on foreign countries.[59] But it was not until the repeal of the Neutrality Acts in 1939 that the United States had the institutional means to limit economic ties to Italian Fascism.

The political calculations behind US-Italian Interwar diplomacy were well summed up by Victor Berger, a tough congressman from Wisconsin: "Both Communism and Fascism are war babies, the result of the great war. One of the babies came into the world red-headed. . . . The Italian has black hair. Otherwise, there is little difference between the two—on the surface at least. The reason why the ruling classes dislike the red-haired baby so, is because the Bolsheviki laid violent hands on the sacred rights of property—while the Fascisti just as violently are protecting the vested rights of those who have vested rights."[60]

Although they shared a fear of international Socialism, the views of the democratic publics and elites, and those in the United States in particular, were deeply divided on Mussolini's Fascism. In the 1920s and well into the 1930s, neither the public nor the governments had a clear assessment of whether the Fascists would be reliable and effective partners against "Socialism" (and later against Nazism). Both clearly underestimated how radical Mussolini's aims were and how unlikely it would be that he would split from his Nazi allies.

Italian Americans and Catholics leaned toward Italy, though Italian labor and Socialist refugees from Fascism made their critical views known.[61] And by the later 1930s, the anti-UK sentiments of Irish Americans sometimes translated into pro-Mussolini feelings.[62] But the true leaders of the pro-Mussolini constituency were the bankers, for Italy was an exceptional customer for British and US loans.[63]

At the US banking forefront was Thomas W. Lamont of J. P. Morgan, to whom much of US foreign economic policy management seems to have been delegated during the isolationist normalcy of the 1920s. In 1925, Lamont lobbied the US government to support a reduction of Italy's interest rate on its wartime debt at the same time as Morgan was floating a new $100 million long-term bond. The Morgan bank soon acquired a large unsold position in the Italian bonds it had issued and, as it did for its other clients, lobbied the US public vigorously on its client's behalf.[64] Lamont seems to have been a genuine cultural Italophile and, in a public debate with William Y. Elliott of Harvard, he praised Mussolini for restoring order after the chaos that followed World War I and for eliminating unemployment and strikes. He further asked whether we shouldn't allow Italy to have "the sort of government they apparently want?" The New York *World* called him out the next day: "But with parliamentary institutions suppressed, free speech muzzled, a free press no longer in existence and a dictator in complete control of every avenue of act and expression, how is Mr. Lamont or anyone else to know what sort of government Italy does want?"[65]

If the intellectuals were anti-Fascists, and the bankers were pro-Fascists, the public was growing increasingly suspicious. Elliott may have been among the most philosophical, but he was not the only US critic of Italian Fascism.[66] Hardened in part by Mussolini's aggression against Ethiopia, a poll of "friendliness" attitudes of Americans put Italy among the top three of countries to which Americans felt least friendly (Table 6).

By 1938, in US congressional hearings, Congressman Charles Plumley countered the view that emphasized the Fascists as anti-Socialists and guarantors-of-order.[67] He identified the sources of growing international tension in both debts (debtors resent lenders) and trade (imports steal jobs). "Do not," he declared, "forget for a minute that Italy, Germany and Japan and the other totalitarian states will organize at the expense of the

Table 6. Roper Poll of "Friendliness" Attitudes of Americans (Fall 1935)

"What foreign country do you feel least/most friendly toward?"[68]

Country	Least Friendly (%)	Most Friendly (%)
Germany	17.3	4.4
Japan	11.2	0.1
Italy	6.7	1.2
Russia	5.8	0.8
France	4.5	4.7
England	1.2	28.6
China	0.7	0.5
Finland	0.1	2.3

American producer. Do not overlook that fact that their conception of international trade under their dictatorships differs entirely from ours. So I say these trade treaties will throw us right into the center of that gigantic conflict between the totalitarian state and our democratic republican ideals."[69]

In perhaps the largest difference between then and now, in a remarkable memorandum written to brief the investor, eminent diplomat, and Roosevelt advisor, Norman H. Davis, the State Department offered a contrary and official view of the dynamics of global world politics. It highlighted security threats and portrayed appeasement and trade as solutions bolstering peace.

> Germany, most of all; Italy, due to the Abyssinian [Ethiopian] palliative, less; Japan, because of the acquisition of Manchuria which is difficult to absorb, least, are suffering from the same complaint: their natural resources are inadequate to support their expanding populations at a decent level. Without action on their part, or on the part of others, suffering must ensue. When there is suffering, the dissatisfied masses, with the example of the Russian revolution before them, swing to the Left. The rich and middle classes, in self-defense, turn to Fascism or personal government. Fascism,

which repudiates democratic institutions and ideologies, looks to force to achieve its aims. It must succeed or the masses, this time reinforced by the disillusioned middle classes, will again turn to the Left. If Fascism cannot succeed by persuasion, it must succeed by force. Japanese nationalism has "exploded" into Manchuria; Italian Fascism has "exploded" into Abyssinia. Germany, the most dynamic of all, has so far not "exploded." However, unless it is aided, in adjusting economic conditions as a "have not" nation by the "haves," Germany must "explode," possibly down the Danube.[70]

Equally remarkably, the State Department officials seemed confident that arms control agreements (especially naval limitations) and trade agreements would satisfy the "have nots." But the State Department also advanced back-up measures (reflecting the US national mood). These contemplated US withdrawals (they would a few years later be called appeasement), offered the "Danube" to Germany, and planned a US withdrawal in the Pacific to the Panama-Hawaii-Alaskan "triangle," ceding China and the Philippines to Japan. It is worth recalling how much isolationist sentiments bolstered appeasement. A 1937 Gallup Poll revealed that two-thirds of Americans thought that participation in World War I had been a mistake.[71]

Similar views appeared in British Cabinet discussions. They illustrated a dual assessment: Fascism was both dangerous and weak, casting doubt on the hitherto vaunted efficiency of Fascist economic and political management.[72]

It must be admitted that the laws of economics must tell in the end. The countries which have deliberately ignored them in order to push on with military policies must eventually pay for what they have wasted. The allocation of national capital to unproductive enterprises must result in national impoverishment and eventual weakness. Japan and Italy have, it is thought, wasted more proportionally of their economic strength than Germany. Italy is probably nearer to overstrain than Japan. But the examples of the USSR and Germany have shown that centralised control within a closed economy can do marvels in organising resources and controlling discontent; so it is too early to count on an economic smash in Italy. On the other hand, the greater the economic stress the more necessary will Signor Mussolini find it to divert popular attention abroad and to produce foreign scapegoats to bear the blame for the difficulties in which his people may find themselves.[73]

Warning about additional sources of foreign conflict, the Cabinet paper continues:

The crash will not, of course, come in the immediate future—indeed the day of reckoning may be deferred for a considerable time by focusing on export trade at the expense of the home market with the help of such expedients as a new devaluation or export subsidies.[74]

It is impossible to neglect three other factors that seemed to support isolationism and made both Hitler and Mussolini of little concern to Americans (and others in the democracies). Fortunately, none of these attitudes are prevalent today in US-Russian foreign relations. The first was a pervasive anti-Semitism that made the Nazis less consequential. To give a flavor of what it sounded like in the words of a privileged member of the US upper class, consider the words Joseph P. Kennedy, Jr. (JFK's older brother), penned in a letter to his father (soon to be Roosevelt's ambassador to the United Kingdom):

Hitler came in [to power]. He saw the need of a common enemy. Someone of whom to make the goat. Someone, by whose riddance the Germans would feel they had cast out the cause of their predicament. It was excellent psychology, and it was too bad that it had to be done to the Jews. This dislike of the Jews, however, was well-founded. They were at the heads of all big business, in law, etc.

It's all to their credit for them to get so far, but their methods had
been quite unscrupulous. . . . As far as brutality [by the Nazis] is
concerned, it must have been necessary to use some, to secure the
wholehearted support of the people, which was necessary to put
through this present program.[75]

These views were amplified by the private ownership of the British and
US press. Lords Beaverbrook and Rothermere in the United Kingdom and
William Randolph Hearst in the United States were hostile to Socialism
(unsurprisingly), flirted with Fascism and anti-Semitism, and, above all,
were fully committed to isolationism and appeasement of the Fascist
great powers.[76]

Those sentiments seemed to prevail past the Munich Agreement's
"peace with honor" and "peace for our time," hailed by Neville Chamberlain and echoed by Joe Jr.'s father, Ambassador Kennedy. They persisted,
at least until Kristallnacht, the Nazi rampage against Jews in November 1938, after which denials of Nazi brutality seemed both clueless
and cruel.[77]

Second, of equal import was US anti-Black racism. As documented by
Ira Katznelson, southern segregation was the second pillar of the Democratic Party in these years. Minor concern for the national rights of
Haile Selassie's Abyssinia should hardly be surprising. Combining anti-
Semitism with racism, Charles Lindbergh took to the airwaves as Hitler
invaded Poland and denounced potential US intervention: "It is the European race we must preserve; political progress will follow. Racial strength
is vital—politics, a luxury. If the white race is ever seriously threatened, it
may then be time for us to take our part in its protection, to fight side by
side with the English, French and Germans, but not with one against the
other for our mutual destruction."[78]

And, third, the most significant factor was the persistent fear of Socialism noted at the beginning of this chapter. Even the exuberant and youth-
ful JFK, in a letter home during a summer 1937 trip to Italy, opined:
"What are the evils of Fascism compared to Communism?"[79]

Comparisons

The corporatist, nationalist, and authoritarian roots of tension with the liberal West link Mussolini and Putin. Government by assassination, corruption, and armed adventuring made stable relations exceptionally difficult in Mussolini's time and engendered—and now engender—suspicions that led, and now lead, to constant tension. The inability to separate the state from commercial or financial relations also eroded stable cooperation and seemed to make business dealings inherently political.

Still, what we saw in the US-Italian relationship was both tension (that eventually contributed to war) and much more persistent accommodation. US-Italian relations were caught in the cross-currents described earlier. There was no single, powerful inflection point that turned the United States and Italy on a path to war. The Italian invasion of Ethiopia, in the view of the US ambassador to Italy, William Phillips, turned Mussolini from a popular strongman into a ruthless dictator.[80] The mix of US attitudes and policy choices became more confrontational, but there was no inevitable slide to war. And the rollercoaster of liberal attitudes toward Mussolini's Italy did not of course cause the war in which Mussolini found himself engaged in 1939. Mussolini chose the Nazis because only they could overturn the Mediterranean order dominated by Britain and France and help make Italy the great Roman Empire he sought. But their evolution traces how liberal and democratic publics tried to both cooperate with and then reject the opportunity and threat Fascism came to represent.

The United States and the United Kingdom responded to these threats with appeasement. Beginning in 1935, a series of legislative acts barred US arms exports (1935) and loans to all belligerents (1936) and required "cash and carry" provisions that limited belligerents to cash transactions and goods to be carried in their own ships. All were designed to avoid entangling the United States in war. The US and European response to Mussolini's aggression against Ethiopia offered token sanctions; none (as oil sanctions would have) constituted significant deterrent pressure. UK prime minister Chamberlain was prepared to appease Hitler, conceding territorial demands to Germany and the erosion of the Treaty of Versailles (which many on the left and the right judged inequitable to begin with). Chamberlain did build up British fighter plane resources, and Roosevelt's 1937 "Quarantine Speech" (designed to isolate aggressors) signaled a new appreciation of global danger. But the publics of neither country were prepared to be led toward engagement or preparation.[81]

Many isolationists shared the view of Ambassador Joe Kennedy expressed in a widely circulated Trafalgar Day speech on October 19, 1938, in which he claimed there was no sense in emphasizing the difference between dictatorships and democracies because, "after all, we have to live together in the same world, whether we like it or not"[82] (when Kennedy was heavily criticized in the press, he attributed the criticism to a Jewish conspiracy against him). Moreover, in 1938, Hitler was not about to attack the United States, nor was he necessarily bad for business. Many thus asked: "Why should the US care?" Today, as Part Two of this book argued, the world is much more closely integrated—economically, politically, and institutionally—making isolationism much less appealing and even less convincing.

Yet there are many differences between Italy in the 1920s and 1930s and Russia today. Together they make the likelihood of a repeat of Word War II extremely unlikely. Nuclear weapons offer existential deterrence, despite imprudent leaders and policies. Mussolini and his later ally Hitler, when combined, constituted an enormous concentration of military power and posed a deep threat to the security of Western Europe and, when Japan joined the Axis, the rest of the world. Putin's Russia has nuclear parity with the United States and possesses a formidable conventional military arsenal, but the latter is far less capable than that of the United States and NATO and poses a threat mostly to its immediate neighbors—Ukraine, Eastern Europe, and the Baltic states—and little direct military threat beyond.

Mussolini placed himself at the head of a populist movement determined to remake the liberal and conservative Italian state. Putin is a product of the KGB determined to use the resources of the Russian state to protect him and his associates from democratic populist upheavals (such as toppled his allies in Ukraine and in 2020 threatened his client in Belarus). And, as importantly stressed by Nolte and other scholars, the alternative to Mussolini was "International Socialism," seen as a vital threat by the liberals and conservatives in Italy, by Italy's foreign allies and rivals in Western Europe, and by the United States. Mussolini thus became a de facto transnational political ally against "Socialism." It took years of aggression and Mussolini's own strategic choices to make Italy into an enemy of the democracies in World War II. Putin benefits from no global fear of "International Socialism." And counterterrorism as a link between Washington and Moscow after 9/11 proved feeble.

As important, the democracies had deep aversion toward deterrent policy against Mussolini or Hitler. Scarred by World War I, defending empire in the United Kingdom and Jim Crow segregation in the United States, neither country was prepared to acknowledge the moral, political, and strategic challenge to liberal democracy posed by Fascism. And to the limited extent it was, Mussolini's Italy was seen as potential counter to, not ally of, Hitler's deeper threat. These illusions would not be fully shattered until Hitler, not satisfied with the Sudetenland, invaded Czechoslovakia in March 1939 and then threatened Poland, and Mussolini and Japan aligned with him.

CHAPTER SEVEN

Japanese Militarism and American Policy

United States relations with Japan started from different assumptions.[1] Some were amicable, for, unlike Italy, Japan was a fellow liberal democracy throughout the 1920s, taking an authoritarian turn only beginning in 1929. Their relations thus included significant periods of extensive cooperation, displayed in the Washington Conference negotiations in 1920–1922. Other relations were inimical. Japan-US relations, unlike Italy-US relations, had been marred by acts of racism and targeted economic restrictions, all of which experienced their notorious nadir in the internment of Japanese Americans during World War II (a fate not inflicted on either Italian or German Americans).[2]

There were additional significant sources of long-term, direct tension. Unlike Italy (a European problem), Japan was a direct rival across the Pacific. Some tensions reflected commercial and financial rivalry, shaped especially by the US perception of the corporatist character of the Japanese economy. Others centered on competition over access and influence in China: the "Open Door" controversies. And still others focused on naval competition for dominance of the western Pacific.

Just as US relations with Italy in the Interwar period previewed US relations with Putin's Russia, so the mix of positive and negative relations between the United States and Japan in the 1920s and 1930s serves as a mirror for the cooperative and conflictual US relationship with China over the past thirty years. The rising power of an autocratic Japan in the Pacific produced World War II. No World War III is in the offing with China, but tensions may be equally severe as autocratic China continues to rise.

The Lodge Corollary and Corporatist Threats

Woodrow Wilson conceived of Asia as "the market for which statesmen as well as merchants must plan and play their game of competition, the market to which diplomacy, and if need be power, must make an open way."[3] But these ambitious trade aims were complicated by an impression that Japan could not be a normal, arm's-length capitalist trade or investment partner.

As an early example of US concern, consider Senator Henry Cabot Lodge's addition of the "Lodge Corollary" to the Monroe Doctrine in 1912. Like the Monroe Doctrine, it was designed to protect the hemisphere from foreign conquest. Unlike the Monroe Doctrine, it defined foreign conquest as a commercial investment: a purchase of land around Magdalena Bay in Baja California (Mexico) by a Japanese corporation. As Lodge explained before the US Senate prior to the passage of his resolution, in "modern conditions" any corporation "found[ed] by a foreign government or by persons under foreign control" would threaten the "safety or the communications of the" United States.[4] Lodge summed up his feelings toward Japan, stating in Congress that Japan was "the coming danger of the world" and "the Prussia of the Far East."[5] Reflecting similar views as well as directly racial prejudices, the California state legislature passed legislation barring Japanese citizens from owning land in the state.[6] Significantly, both these measures were introduced before the period, starting in 1912, of Taisho democratic reform in Japan. Relations with Japan improved thereafter in cooperative schemes to manage East Asia and regulate naval armaments, until Japanese militarism took over in the late 1920s.

The "Open Door": China-Centric or Japan-Centric?

There was no greater potential commercial or financial prize in Asia than the China market. In January 1915, Japanese foreign minister Kato Takaaiki presented the northern Chinese revolutionary leader Yuan Shi-kai with Japan's secret "Twenty-One Demands" that would govern the terms of Japanese penetration into Chinese territory.[7] Wilson responded by insisting on the reestablishment of the four-power consortium—United States, United Kingdom, France, and Japan—as means to control Japan's unilateral encroachment in China, preserving China for the multinational "open door." In September 1917, Viscount Ishii Kikujiro, a Japanese envoy, traveled to Washington to try to persuade the United States to recognize Japan's paramount interests in China, akin to US claims to special interests over the Americas with the Monroe Doctrine. US secretary of state Robert Lansing eventually agreed to an exchange of notes recognizing Japanese "special interests" in those parts of China contiguous to its territories (Manchuria preeminent among them) in return for Ishii acknowledging the principle of "Open Door" for all in China.[8] Complicating relations further, both the United States and Japan sought German possessions in the Far East (Shantung for Japan and various islands for the United States), and both intervened in Siberia in the turmoil produced by the Bolshevik Revolution.

Foreshadowing strife to come, controversy erupted at the Paris Peace Conference over geopolitically infused racial equality. Japanese prime minister Hara Takashi attempted to introduce a "racial equality clause" into the draft of the Covenant of the League of Nations out of concern, as Walter LaFeber says in his influential history of the period, that Wilson's proposed League of Nations would seek to diminish Japanese influence in East Asia.[9] Wilson (himself a Jim Crow southern Democrat) mobilized British, French, and Italian opposition to the clause. The colonial powers were worried that the League of Nations would then become a platform for interference in their colonial holdings. In the end, as a condition for its agreement to ratify the covenant, Japan eventually won the inclusion in the covenant preamble of the "equality of Nations" phrase and possession rights over formerly German Shantung and various German islands.

US foreign policy views on how to engage with Japan divided into China-centric and Japan-centric approaches that would remain both rival and together dominant throughout the Interwar period.

The China-centric view (as articulated by Wilson's secretary of state Lansing) stressed the territorial integrity of China under a multilateral umbrella of the Open Door that would preserve equal access for the great powers (and contain Japan). One vulnerability of this approach was whether the other powers had the weight in East Asia to counter Japan and whether China, beginning to develop its own nationalist movement, would tolerate the foreign domination the Open Door trade and investment regime presupposed.

The Japan-centric group (including Wilson advisor Col. Edward House, secretary of state Charles Evans Hughes and other Republican secretaries of state of the 1920s) saw Japan as an ally and the "civilizing" anchor that would carve up China using methods similar to the ones employed by the European and American empires and yet in ways profitable to the other empires. Japan's trade boom (exports quadrupled between 1914 and 1917) and industrial expansion (the industrial population nearly doubled during those years) gave grounds for anchoring interests on Japan.[10] The US vulnerability in this approach, however, was whether Japan's dependence on US oil and steel imports and financing was enough to guarantee that, in fact, Japan would remain a useful agent and ally in keeping China "open."

With the return of Republicans to the presidency in the Harding administration from 1921 and the isolationist mood of the country,[11] the Japan-centric view moved to center stage, ceding much of US diplomacy to the bankers (Thomas W. Lamont of Morgan in particular) and paving the way for an important naval accommodation in the Washington Conference treaties. Indeed, as discussed below, the banking and naval agreements developed in parallel. The Washington Naval Treaty among the key naval powers and the Lamont-Kajiwara Agreement among the key private US and Japanese banking powers became the two pillars of the 1920s accommodation.

Accommodation in the 1920s: The Washington Conference Treaties and the Lamont-Kajiwara Agreement

The treaties made among the United States, Japan, the United Kingdom (and then France and Italy) at the Washington Conference between 1921 and 1922 were a triumph for US diplomacy. They simultaneously contained pressures from US isolationists to unilaterally disarm by cutting the military budget by 50 percent, sidestepped a League of Nations arms control initiative unacceptable to the United States (because it was led by the League), and dissolved the Anglo-Japanese Alliance that had kept the United States in an inferior position in the Far East.

The treaties would solidify a cooperative arrangement that rested on an expectation of a liberal constitutional monarchy in Japan and a Japan that played a key partnering role in exploiting China. Neither of these are replicated in the modern US-China relationship. Despite Chinese late twentieth-century market capitalist reforms and hopes that China would soon democratize, the expectation of continued democratization was not realistic after the crushing of democratic dissent at Tiananmen Square in 1989. And China played no equivalent role in containing a mutual threat, despite its on and off again cooperation in seeking to contain North Korea's emergence as a nuclear power. Still, the globalizing measures that China took in the 1990s and early 2000s opened a door for a cooperative relationship in which China emerged as a global manufacturing hub, a steadying force in international finance and monetary relations, and a cooperating good citizen in multilateral governance at the United Nations and elsewhere.

The accommodation with Japan was composed of three linked treaties. The Washington Naval Treaty (also known as the Five-Power Treaty)
set the naval forces of the United States, United Kingdom, Japan, France,
and Italy at 10-10-6-3.4-3.4. These ratios allowed for a large cutback
in planned battleship building while assuring the United States and
United Kingdom of equal global preeminence and Japan of predominance in the western Pacific. Japan had sought a "7" ration, but the
United States had penetrated its secret communications and knew that
"6" was its red line—sweetened by the permission for the *Matsu*, a new
battleship funded by popular subscription, to continue construction.
The Four-Power Treaty replaced the Anglo-Japanese Alliance of collective defense by the much weaker agreement among the United States,
United Kingdom, Japan, and France to consult in the event of a crisis.
The Nine-Power Treaty offered formal recognition of the Open Door for
nonexclusive economic development in China (China was not included
as a signatory) while recognizing special Japanese interests in Manchuria and Mongolia.[12]

The Japanese delegation was led by three elder statesmen (Adm. Kato
Tomosaburo, leader of the delegation; Shidehara Kijuro, Japan's ambassador to the United States; and Viscount Shibusawa Eiichi, Japan's leading
financier) who sought to preserve Japanese influence over Manchuria and
China but recognized "the need for cooperation with the West and using
instruments of trade, rather than going-it-alone with the instruments of
war."[13] Both the Japanese leadership, including the financiers, and their
cooperative attitude of the 1920s reflected the financial diplomacy that
preceded and followed the Washington Conference.[14]

Thomas W. Lamont, the "Ambassador from Wall Street" and president
of J. P. Morgan & Co., was the key US figure behind the second pillar of
the US-Japanese accommodation of the 1920s.[15] That pillar was finance.
As early as the Paris Peace Conference, Lamont began the design of a
financial consortium that would require British, French, US, and Japanese bankers to work together and share lending opportunities. Lamont
assured President Wilson that the consortium would be "the one practical thing left which is going to prevent Japan from having a free hand in

China. . . . I have had any number of people say to me that unless the Consortium actually functioned as outlined, our hope for any kind of square deal in the Far East was gone."[16]

In the face of direct opposition from the US government, which refused to recognize any infringement on the principle of the Open Door, Lamont worked out a compromise whereby in return for Japanese bankers' agreement to join the consortium, the American bankers would recognize Japan's economic interests in Manchuria and Mongolia, even though the American government would not. Lamont's agreement was with Kajiwara Nakaji, president of the Yokohama Specie Bank, Japan's central overseas banking institution. In an exchange of letters on May 11, 1920, the American bankers agreed not to interfere with Japanese-owned railroads in the Manchurian region, which effectively ceded control of the region's affairs to the Japanese.[17]

Illustrating the productive interplay of finance and diplomacy, Japan agreed to the Nine-Power Treaty's legal recognition of the Open Door in China largely because the United States agreed to incorporate into the treaty the line from the 1920 Lamont-Kajiwara deal that exempted Manchuria from Open Door principles. The Japanese then also conceded to withdrawing from Siberia, while retaining control over the region's key railway. The Japanese even agreed to "throw open" to the financial consortium options on loans, including to railways, in Manchuria and Inner Mongolia, thus surrendering much of the point that had nearly destroyed the first financial consortium and had set the US and Japan at loggerheads in 1919–1920. They could do so now, however, because the Washington Conference treaties were in place, giving them naval superiority in the western Pacific. The Nine-Power Treaty recognized their hold on Manchuria. The Japanese now seemed safe from American attack across the central Pacific.[18]

The head of the Japanese delegation, Adm. Kato Tomosaburo, summed up the financial foundations of the accommodation: "The answer is that there is no country other than America that could oblige Japan with the foreign credit required—and this would obviously not be forthcoming if America were the enemy. . . . At all costs Japan should avoid war with America."[19]

In a 1924 speech, Japanese foreign minister Shidehara Kijuro underscored the importance of peace with the United States and penetration of the China market, both being essential to help Japan cope with its rapid population growth and economic crises:

> [On] our restricted islands we suffer from a population increase of 700,000–800,000 annually. There is, therefore, no alternative but to proceed with our industrialization. It follows from this that it is essential to secure overseas markets and this can only be done by adopting an economic diplomacy. If we try to cure our economic problems by territorial expansion, we will merely destroy international cooperation. Japan, being closest to China, has an advantage by way of transportation costs and she has also the greatest competitive power because of her wages. It must therefore be a priority for Japan to maintain the great market of China.[20]

But relations were not altogether smooth. Like the twenty-first-century expectation that China would liberalize under the stimulus of globalization, the expectation that a consortium would neatly manage US-Japan-China relations did not work. The consortium failed to establish a collective approach to managing China's economic development. Instead, Japan stepped in and soon became the dominant economic power in China. American officials, furthermore, became concerned by Japan's willingness to cooperate with the Soviet Union, particularly along a China-Soviet-Japan axis. By 1925, Japan had restored its diplomatic recognition of Moscow and withdrawn its forces from the northern area of Sakhalin, the largest island off the coast of the Soviet Union just north of Japan. These moves led one US official to warn about a China-Soviet-Japan axis, stating, "that there is a menace to the entire West in such a combination seems self-evident." Moreover, the US State Department's hostility toward the Soviet Union made it impossible for Washington to use Moscow to contain Japanese expansion, and Tokyo's reluctance to join a possible military intervention by Western powers to halt Chinese attacks on foreigners deepened American frustration with Japan.

There are parallels here to US-China relations from the 1990s until the early 2000s. First, the United States was the key sponsor of China's accession to the WTO, and an exceptionally productive relationship developed in which US multinationals outsourced manufacturing to the low wages and disciplined labor they found in China. Second, China in return walked gingerly in avoiding challenging the United States and cooperating financially by holding dollars and not revaluing its currency in order to mute the 2008 financial crisis. But, there was no third power that China assisted the United States in managing (unlike the role Japan played for the United States in managing the Open Door in China in the 1920s and 1930s). And 1990s China despite its steady marketization took no steps toward democracy or liberalism that would have helped cement the kind of positive relations the United States enjoyed with Taisho Japan in the 1920s.

The Japan-centric approach prevailed in US policy toward East Asia, at least until the Manchurian Incident of 1931 when Japanese officers staged a military confrontation with Chinese nationalists and (with militarist allies in the homeland) began a rolling coup against constitutional government. This was the trigger for the United States to declare a fundamental interest in preserving both China and the Open Door. The United States did so with the Stimson Doctrine's refusal to recognize Japan's conquest of Manchuria. Nonetheless, no more stringent sanctions were imposed until 1939 when Japan set about the conquest of China. In the meantime, the United States continued to keep a line open to Japan, relying largely on the efficacy of financial diplomacy and Japan's underlying dependence on US capital and markets. In the 1920s, the United States accounted for 40 percent of Japan's exports, which mostly consisted of silk goods. At the same time, China became Japan's largest market for industrial exports, for which it exchanged vital foodstuffs and raw materials. Moreover, World War I had dramatized how Japan now depended on the wider world for its existence, not least in that the war had demonstrated that naval power was driven by oil, not coal—and Japan had no oil.

Taisho Democracy and the Emergence
of Showa Autocracy

The accommodation also reflected deeper transformations within Japan occurring during the reign of Emperor Taisho (1912–1926).[21] After industrialization, first among them was emerging democratization. Japan expanded the franchise in March 1919, but pressure to democratize further only increased. The economic recession following World War I generated rice riots, as farmers reacted to the steep decline in demand for wartime provisions. As many as 700,000 protesters flowed into the streets. Modernizing norms and mass media spurred new political parties and opposition to traditional *genro* ruling-class politics. The Japanese government also experienced pressure from a coalition of urban social forces— the *zaibatsus* (the large conglomerates in industry, commerce and finance) and smaller businesses—to cut back on military spending as draft evasion reached record highs and allegations of corruption rankled the cabinet. Moreover, labor unions started large-scale strikes to protest labor inequities and political injustices. A movement for women's suffrage and participation in the workforce soon followed.[22]

The great earthquake of 1923 put a temporary halt to these liberalizing movements as the nation reeled in shock and repressive martial law measures increased. Order was firmly restored when a more conservative arm of the government gained influence and passed the Peace Preservation Law of 1925. Besides threatening up to ten years' imprisonment for anyone attempting to alter the *kokutai* (rule by the emperor and imperial government, as opposed to popular sovereignty), this law severely curtailed individual freedom in Japan and attempted to eliminate any public dissent.[23]

The transition in the emperor's role to one of greater power began with the death of Emperor Taisho on December 18, 1926. Following tradition, his son Hirohito ascended to the throne and chose the name Showa, meaning "peace and enlightenment." Hirohito was a stronger character and more autocratic personality. He began his reign by performing all the ceremonial duties flawlessly but appearing in public only for highly orchestrated formal state occasions. As the political climate within Japan evolved to a more militaristic stance, so did the role of the emperor. One specific gesture is emblematic: When Emperor Hirohito first appeared in public in the early years of his reign, commoners would always remain dutifully seated to avoid appearing above the emperor, but they were permitted to look at him. By 1936 it was illegal for any ordinary Japanese citizen to even look at the emperor.

More significant was the gradual political shift in the later 1920s from a more liberal and democratic formation to a more militaristic and autocratic one. But this occurred simultaneously with, and partly in reaction to, the collapse of the world economy and the emergence of military factionalism that produced a near coup as the Japanese Imperial Army in Manchuria rebelled against the central Japanese government. From there a cycle of militarism and imperialism set Japan on a course of conflict with the United States and conquest in East Asia.

Japanese Imperialism in Manchuria: Corporatism, Militarism, and Nationalism

The two forces driving Japanese imperialism were the South Manchuria Railway Company (*Mantetsu*) and the officers of the Japanese Imperial Army (Kwantung Army). The railway resembled China's current Belt and Road Initiative. The army staged the Manchurian Incident in 1931 that reshaped both Japanese imperial administration and the government at home.

Japanese infrastructure-led expansion produced imperial power on steroids. Japan acquired railway concessions in Manchuria directly from China, following Japan's defeat of China in the First Sino-Japanese War of 1894. Japan then acquired Russian railway and port concessions following its defeat of Russia in the Russo-Japanese War of 1895. The Japanese railway, initially capitalized at 200 million yen, was chartered by the Japanese state not only to operate the railroad and to develop settlements and industries along its route (as many railroads were) but also to serve as the directing agent of both economic development and political control. In this respect, it resembled not just the classic imperial companies such as the British South Africa and British West Africa companies but more closely still the British East India Company, which governed India until 1858.

As early as 1907, *Mantetsu* employed 9,000 Japanese and 4,000 Chinese. By 1910, those numbers had increased to 35,000 and 25,000, respectively. Relying on imports of US-made rails and locomotives, the company developed coal mines and harbor facilities, hotels for travelers, and warehouses for goods. Japanese settlers were persuaded to immigrate through the construction of schools, libraries, and hospitals. *Mantetsu* initiated soybean farming on a massive scale. Indeed, the key to profitability came from soybean exports, both to Japan and to Europe. By 1927, half of the world's supply of soybeans was from Manchuria. As early as 1916 *Mantetsu* diversified, creating subsidiaries that included steel works, ceramics, glass, oil and fat, as well as flour mills and sugar mills, and electric power plants.

The company's assets rose from 163 million yen in 1908 to over a billion yen in 1930, making it by far the largest corporation in Japan, and also its most profitable, averaging rates of return from 25 to 45 percent per year. During the 1920s, *Mantetsu* provided more than a quarter of the Japanese government's tax revenues.[24]

Even more significantly for Japanese expansion was the fact it both attracted 800,000 Japanese immigrants and managed the bulk of the Manchurian economy through its control of railways. By 1938, with seventy-two subsidiary companies, development projects in twenty-five urban areas, and lines that carried 17,515,000 passengers per year, *Mantetsu* ruled as much as it managed through the combination of tremendous profitability, its political power to seize property and silence opposition and dissent at will, and, most important, its connections to the military.

The officers of the Kwantung Army supplemented *Mantetsu*, creating a war machine of military corporatism.[25] Junior officers assassinated a Manchurian warlord in 1928. Senior officers responded with the Manchurian Incident in 1931 and the follow-up invasion and conquest of

Manchuria in clear violation of orders from Tokyo. Faced with a momentous fait accompli, Tokyo had little choice but to back them up and complete the pacification of the puppet state of Manchukuo.[26]

The Kwantung Army played a controlling role in the political administration of the new state as well as in its defense. With the Kwantung Army administering all aspects of the politics and economic development of the new state, its commanding officer was equivalent to an imperial governor with the authority to approve or countermand any command from Puyi, the nominal emperor of Manchukuo.[27] A testament to the Kwantung Army's control over the government of Manchukuo was the fact that the commander-in-chief of the Kwantung Army also doubled as the Japanese ambassador to Manchukuo.[28]

Throughout the 1920s and 1930s, the Kwantung Army was the home base for the radical *Kadoha*, the "Imperial Way Faction." *Kadoha* agitated for the violent overthrow of the constitutional government in Tokyo in order to effect what they called a Showa Restoration, making the emperor the effective and totalitarian ruler of the state, economy, and society. *Kadoha* resonated with many of the reactionary ideas of the European Fascists. It drew strength from the 1927 financial crisis, political polarization, and the increasing domination of the *zaibatsus* over economic policy making. Like Mussolini's Fascists and the contemporary Chinese military, their aim was to couple domestic autocracy with an active imperial strategy.[29] While *Kadoha* dominated military policy making from the late 1920s through the highwater mark of the Manchurian Incident, after that a rival faction, also militaristic but asserting Tokyo's control over the Kwantung Army, took the lead, purging *Kadoha* officers between 1934 and 1936.

The key trend of Japanese policy making in the period was creeping militarism challenging liberal democratic rule. But what made this possible was not the autocratic centralization of Japan, but rather the factional rivalry that was made possible through political stalemates best understood as products stemming from Japan's late industrial development and incomplete democratization.

The Roots of Japanese Militarism and Escalating Tension with the United States

The emerging collision between the United States and Japan was rooted not just in what they did but also in what they were. In addition, a rapidly rising Japan challenged Western dominance of East Asia, and all contributed to rivalry and conflict.

On the Japanese side, late industrialization produced a strong state geared toward competing with the strong economies of the United Kingdom and the United States, which led the Industrial Revolution.[30] Motivated by fear of succumbing as so many Asian societies had to European and American imperial aggression, Japan modeled both its military organization and its grand strategy of industrialization and military expansion on the Prussian model of militaristic autocracy leading an (another late) industrialization drive. But other features, special to Japanese history, shaped its divided and faction-ridden government.

One key factor was dependence on the United States for oil. Japanese industrial development relied on national supplies of coal. Appreciating its vital significance for industrial development and national security, the Japanese state assumed control of coal mining from the feudal *han* landlords, and coal became "the first business of the Japanese state,"[31] a model for corporatist control. Oil, however, was the fuel for future development and particularly for the development of a modern fleet and airpower. And for that Japan depended on the United States (80 percent) and the Netherlands East Indies (10 percent). Japan's 1934 Petroleum Industry Law imposed state control of domestic refining and marketing and tried to establish a six-month stockpiled reserve (to reduce the threat of foreign coercion).[32] The United States successfully blocked the emergency oil reserve, with serious long-run consequences for Japan-US relations when the US oil embargo left Japan no alternative but war or retreat (from China) and thus encouraged the government to choose war.

Japan's economy reflected its late industrializing condition in other profound ways. It faced the challenging competition of the then-advanced economies making direct and indirect state subsidies and direction a vital factor in growth. At the same time, it benefited from known production technologies that it borrowed or copied, allowing for rapid growth.

Japan's small, efficient, yarn and textile industries became geared toward exporting silk and other consumer goods to the United States, Asia, and Europe. Highly efficient industries with small returns to scale, such as light manufacturing, silk, knitted goods, bicycles, pottery, and toys, neither needed nor wanted tariffs. They could export to world markets, often relying on raw materials from elsewhere. Eighty percent of Japanese silk was exported to the United States, and 85 percent of cotton textiles went to China, India, and the Dutch East Indies. But its emerging capital goods industries faced a different set of production possibilities. Global industrial competition in the early twentieth century was dominated by the United States, which benefited from large technological advances, a large domestic market, and plentiful capital. Foreign competitors in the 1920s and 1930s, particularly Japan, the United Kingdom, and Germany, made two responses: Firms with low production volumes sought trade protection to compensate for high unit costs, and economies with small home markets led firms to campaign to "enlarge empires and form trading blocs."[33]

The heart of the drive for overseas expansion was in capital goods (machines and heavy industry). Firms with large returns to scale, especially in heavy capital goods, had the most to gain from state support. In alliance with farmers, heavy industry supported agricultural tariff increases in return for support for the post-1931 trading blocs and imperial expansion that produced the markets the heavy industrialists sought.

Japan possessed controlled markets in Taiwan (conquered in 1895), Manchuria and Kwantung (1906), and Korea (1910). But in the early 1920s, Japan followed Open Door policies for trade.[34] Beginning in 1923, Japan brought Korea inside its raised domestic tariffs and began to rely on Korea and Taiwan for needed food imports and on Manchuria for coal and iron. Controlling the Manchurian puppet state of Manchukuo ensured privileged access for Japanese products, through "open and disguised preferences."[35] Toshiyuki Mizoguchi has thus argued: "Because Japan's new

large-scale industries still had high unit costs of production those enterprises found it difficult to break into world markets. Therefore they had
to turn to the privileged markets in the formal Japanese empire to sell
their products."[36] Japan raised tariffs in 1926 and raised them again in
1931 by 35 percent in response to the worldwide Depression and proceeded to grow its trading bloc into the Co-Prosperity Sphere that arrived
with the war in 1940.[37] Kerry Chase then concludes: "Only through access
to an imperial market on privileged terms could producers overcome the
scale advantages of foreign firms."[38]

The Depression further deepened the role of the Japanese state.[39] The
1931 Control Law helped establish cartel monopolies. That, together with
dropping the gold standard and extensive fiscal stimulus, produced the
remarkable growth rates of the middle 1930s, seeing 10.1 percent in 1933
and 8.7 percent in 1934 while the rest of the world was descending deeper
into depression.[40]

The politics sustaining the imperial political economy centered on the
zaibatsu and the army. Originally, the Meiji state fostered the *zaibatsu*
as a means to organize and speed economic growth; unsurprisingly, the
zaibatsu were soon shaping state policy. Almost 30 percent of the upper
house and 12 percent of the lower house of the Japanese Diet were directly
connected to the leading *zaibatsu*.[41] *Zaibatsus* in finance had substantial
stakes in heavy industry and then joined with the *zaibatsu* invested in
chemicals and steel to lead the imperial faction. The weight of the *zaibatsu*
increased throughout the 1930s as the Big Four *zaibatsus* gained direct
control over more than 30 percent of Japan's mining, chemical, and metals industries and almost 50 percent control of the machinery and equipment market, a significant part of the foreign commercial merchant fleet,
and 70 percent of the commercial stock exchange.

After 1931, the military aligned with hyper-nationalist ideologies, and
small farmers were prepared to support them. The army grew rapidly in
size in the 1920s, reaching 300,000 men by 1927. As significant as its size
was its influence in the government. Under the Meiji Constitution, the
War Ministry reported directly to the emperor, not the cabinet, and the
minister was typically a serving officer. Military spending, not surpris-

ingly, grew steadily, and the army set its own polices, just as the Kwantung Army often operated independently of the high command in Tokyo.[42] Despite the limits set by the London Naval Conference of 1930, Japan initiated a series of Circle Plans in the 1930s to build up the navy beyond the international limits.

Together, the *zaibatsus* and the army combined to drive an imperial surge from Manchuria into China.[43] Both operated in the legal context of the Meiji Constitution, which gave the emperor the right to exercise executive authority and appoint and dismiss all government officials. The emperor also had the sole right to declare war, make peace, conclude treaties, dissolve the Diet, and issue ordinances in place of laws when the Diet was not in session. The Cabinet and both the army and the navy answered to the emperor, not to the Diet. An informal group of designated notables, the *genro*, exercised substantial influence. The upper house of the Diet included members of the Imperial family, hereditary peers, and appointees. The lower house of the Diet, elected by male suffrage, progressively democratized in the early twentieth century until, by 1925, universal adult male suffrage was in place.

In fact, policy was less a product of centralized direction, even by the emperor, than a logroll among competing factions. The heart of the matter, as Miles Kahler and Jack Snyder separately argue, was not an autocratic, centralized militarist state akin to Mussolini's Fascist state. Instead, in Kahler's phrasing: "The Japanese 'state' remained a set of unstable coalitions, with each of the principal actors—the military, the civilian bureaucrats, and the zaibatsu—divided internally."[44]

This means domestically driven militarism can have two sources. It can be a product of the interests and ideology of a dominant party or leader, such as Mussolini and the Fascists were, or it can originate in a polity with accommodationist-internationalist democratic factions that are incapable of maintaining control and indeed cede control to militarist interests and factions, such as happened in Japan in the late 1920s with the takeover by the military, and the local thrust into China by its Kwantung Army in the 1931 Manchurian Incident. In this respect, Putin's personalist control resonates with the Mussolini pattern; just as the party and emerging military politics of modern China (some fear) may resonate with the militaristic policy coalitions of 1930s Japan.

United States: The Other Determinant of the Escalation to War

In ways that reflect the multiple sources of the twenty-first-century new cold war, Japan alone was not the sole cause of the tensions with the United States that would later escalate into World War II in the Pacific. Nor does it suggest that the tensions and rivalry would inevitably lead to war. Many more mistakes were needed in the later 1930s to push the United States to institute crippling oil sanctions and the Japanese to attack Pearl Harbor in December 1941.

Prewar tensions however were real and growing, and in those the United States also played a role. The racism that the United States displayed toward Japanese immigrants in the United States in the 1920s was an ideological albatross about the neck of efforts to develop friendly commerce and strategic cooperation.

Economic ties might have helped sustain cooperative relations. US investments in Japan focused on finance, shipping, insurance, and trade more broadly.[45] Reflecting the relative economic strength of each country, Japan sought to export commodities to the United States, particularly silk, and import industrial goods deemed necessary for Japan's continued development. The primary organs financing and supporting this trade with the United States were Japanese trading companies and banks. These companies maintained offices in the United States in New York and other major cities to act as intermediaries between Japanese businesses and the American market.[46] Japan's primary export to the United States during this time was silk and involved large Japanese trading companies, particularly Mitsui & Co.[47] Indeed, at the peak of silk prices in 1925, exports from Japan to the United States had equaled 37 percent of all of Japan's exports.[48] On the other hand, most of the manufactured goods produced in Japan for export went to Asian markets.[49] Insofar as these exports interacted with the US market, it was primarily over concern that Japanese competition might push out American manufacturers in regions such as China.[50]

Before World War I, Japanese lending and trade moved primarily through London, where prior to the war, thirty-two of the forty Japanese foreign-currency denominated bonds were traded.[51] After World War I, Japanese foreign trade settlement and much of Japan's sovereign and quasi-sovereign lending moved to New York.[52]

The Great Depression significantly reduced demand for luxury goods, and as a result silk exports by Japan fell off dramatically after 1929.[53] Although trading companies attempted to diversify their sales in the United States, they were never able to build a significant market for Japanese manufactured goods, and most of these goods continued to flow to Asia.[54] "Japan-bashing," which had been rare in the 1920s, increased in the 1930s under the protectionist political forces unleashed by the Great Depression.[55] In an oft-repeated pattern of trade competition producing nativist animosity that we see in contemporary US-China relations, Japan was one of the largest buyers of cotton from the US market, and simultaneously exported significant quantities of manufactured clothing back to the United States. Unsurprisingly, this resulted in political concerns that Japanese exports could cost American workers their jobs or steal market share in other Asian nations.[56]

In addition, the Japanese invasion of Manchuria and its withdrawal from the League of Nations marked a significant change in its relationship with the United States that would echo in the trade relationship between the two nations. The Great Depression significantly decreased interest in funding Japanese government debt, and Japanese aggression in Manchuria further reduced the willingness of American banks to lend to the Japanese government and businesses.[57]

Other sources of mounting tension lay in policy perceptions. The US commitment to an Open Door in China looked like a policy to promote China's territorial integrity and political independence from Washington. From Tokyo, it looked like a policy to deny Japan the imperial control that the Europeans and Americans had claimed for themselves in Africa, the Middle East, and in South and Southeast Asia.[58] Some prominent American political scientists increasingly came to believe that the tension with Japan reflected deep ideological and constitutional differences. Harold Lasswell developed the concept of the "garrison state" in the fall of 1937 when he published "The Sino-Japanese Crisis: The Garrison State versus the Civilian State" in the *China Quarterly*, exploring the incompatibilities between centralized military states and constitutional democracies.[59] In another interpretation, Harold Quigley, the University of Minnesota's resident Japan scholar, argued in words then reminiscent of Mussolini, and now of Putin and even Xi, that the "Japanese official doctrine calls for a regionalized world; each region is to be self-sufficing and to refrain from interfering with the others; relations between the regions are to be slight; within each region a powerful state is to be free to dominate its lesser neighbors."[60] Japan in his view was attempting to undermine the newly inaugurated Kellogg-Briand Pact, which outlawed war as an instrument of national policy, and return world politics back toward an older order, in which states possessed the right to expand territorially and subjugate their neighbors.[61] Quigley was outlining, before the fact, the policies that Japan would later articulate as the Co-Prosperity Sphere.

The deep-seated ambiguity in US policy toward the western Pacific was also a factor. The United States in the 1920s never decided between policies that either designated Japan as the partner of American commercial, financial, and geopolitical interests in containing Chinese radical nationalism or that placed the defense of China's independence from Japan as the linchpin of US interests.[62] Nor did the United States ever decide whether its vital interests were contained in the West by the line enclosing Hawaii and the Philippines or whether they stretched to China and even Manchuria.

US secretary of state Henry Stimson thus was equally determined to punish Japan rhetorically with the "nonrecognition" of the Manchurian conquest as he was to undermine an effort by the League of Nations to impose material economic sanctions on Japan.[63] Japan thus had good reasons to believe that the United States could become neither a reliable ally nor a serious barrier to further imperial conquest in China and Southeast Asia. Both were fatal signals that made war more likely.

Table 7. GDP Comparisons (Billions, 1990 US Dollars):
United States and Japan and United States and Japanese Empire[64]

Year	United States	Japan	Japan plus Empire and Manchukuo
1920	594	95	111
(Percent of US GDP)		(15%)	(18%)
1930	769	119	143
(Percent of US GDP)		(15%)	(25%)
1940	931	210	302
(Percent of US GDP)		(23%)	(33%)

Comparisons

The current US-China relationship bears some of the hallmarks of the spiraling rivalry between the United States and Japan before World War II. Fortunately, the differences are equally important.

Like the contemporary US-China economic power balance, the United States clearly outweighed Japan in economic capacity, but in the 1920s and 1930s, Japan was catching up. The Japanese Empire increased from 18 percent to 33 percent of US GDP (Table 7), and equally noticeably the empire was contributing proportionately more than the homeland. (US attention, moreover, was divided; the Pacific being only half, and the rest focused on Europe.)

Japan's rapid industrial growth and the naval rivalry in the western Pacific made for tension. So, too, did Japan's national resentment of past and present indignities, both imperial and racial. The corporatist cartel-ization of the economy made Open Door cooperation in exploiting China especially difficult, when no business arrangement could be separated from the direct engagement of the Japanese army and the South Manchu-ria Railway Company.

Worrisomely, Chinese demographics and economic growth today are even more impressive, rapidly converging its economy with that of the United States in a way that Japan could not conceivably match. And China's Belt and Road Initiative has flavors of the South Manchuria Railway Company in its concerted measures of public and private investment designed to produce national economic value and strategic influence.

But the differences are decisive. The 1930s tensions followed on a decade of cooperation between constitutional liberal Taisho Japan and the capitalist liberal United States. Nuclear weapons provide an immense block to the steady spiral to war that characterized the later 1930s. None in the United States can think that economic coercion will contain China in the way the United States then thought the oil weapon would contain Japanese imperialism. No one in China can imagine that a preventive war strike on the US homeland would force the United States to a recognition of Chinese domination of the Pacific in the way that Japanese planners (very unwisely) did in 1941 with the attack on Pearl Harbor.

Moreover, while the United States, China, and Japan all benefited from growing economic interdependence—in the 1920s for Japan and 1990s and 2000s for China—the US direct investment in China today is much more substantial. Domestic politics also differ. While China did not benefit from the democratic accommodation Japan enjoyed in the 1920s, and the Chinese army is a hotbed of nationalist fervor, China appears to be a more coherent polity, one not as afflicted by the cartelized logrolling that shaped Japan's policies after the Manchurian Incident in 1931.

Altogether, and fortunately, this makes hot war much less likely. These economic interdependent conditions also make cold war much more costly, but not necessarily less likely. The growth of China and the systematic differences of corporatist and capitalist development and autocratic and democratic politics constitute a fertile ground for cold war tension, barring wise policy and concerted reform, to which we turn in the concluding chapters.

Part Four

❖

COLD PEACE

■ THE DANGERS OF A HOT WAR between the United States and Russia and China are immense and obvious. The United States has almost 5,500 and Russia almost 6,000 nuclear warheads; China has 350 and growing. Each of these arsenals is sufficiently destructive to provide existential deterrence. But the next war might well be fought predominantly through sabotage by cyber warfare. All three countries have extensive cyber capabilities that could wreak havoc on financial institutions, electrical grids, and hospitals.[1]

Moreover, we sometimes forget how costly the Cold War was. As noted in the Introduction, the financial cost to the United States in defense spending alone from 1948 to 1990 was $11 trillion (1990 dollars). And that was against the USSR, a declining economy one-third the size of that of the United States. China would be a much more formidable rival should a full-blown cold war emerge. In addition, the opportunity costs of what cannot be accomplished range from measures to address climate change, alleviate global poverty, and protect global public health—and these are just three of the indirect, consequential effects of a cold war between democracy and autocracy.

The United States and its allies—and indeed China and Russia, too—need to turn from cold war to a cold peace.[2] As discussed earlier, a cold war is war conducted without "hot" armed hostilities but directed toward undermining the other side's political independence or territorial integrity. Today we require a truce in which subversive transformation is taken off the table in the name of mutual survival and global prosperity. Persuasion and critical debate must remain legitimate. But subversive cyber warfare and covert operations directed against domestic political institutions and vital infrastructure need to be banned as a form of illicit force.

Speaking at the Munich Security Conference a full year before the Russian invasion of Ukraine, President Biden appeared to be aware of the scope of the challenge. "Democracy," he proclaimed, "doesn't happen by accident. We have to defend it, fight for it, strengthen it, renew it. We have to prove that our model isn't a relic of our history; it's the single best way to revitalize the promise of our future. And if we work together with our democratic partners, with strength and confidence, I know that we'll meet every challenge and outpace every challenger."[3]

He singled out competition with China, noting that:

> We have to push back against the Chinese government's economic abuses and coercion that undercut the foundations of the international economic system. Everyone—everyone—must play by the same rules. U.S. and European companies are required to publicly disclose corporate governance to corporate governance structures and abide by rules to deter corruption and monopolistic practices. Chinese companies should be held to the same standard. We must shape the rules that will govern the advance of technology and the norms of behavior in cyberspace, artificial intelligence, biotechnology so that they are used to lift people up, not used to pin them down. We must stand up for the democratic values that make it possible for us to accomplish any of this, pushing back against those who would monopolize and normalize repression.

He then called upon the United States and its allies to "meet the threat from Russia," stating that, "The Kremlin attacks our democracies and weaponizes corruption to try to undermine our system of governance. Russian leaders want people to think that our system is more corrupt or as corrupt as theirs. But the world knows that isn't true, including Russians—Russia's own citizens. Putin seeks to weaken the European project and our NATO Alliance. He wants to undermine the transatlantic unity and our resolve, because it's so much easier for the Kremlin to bully and threaten individual states than it is to negotiate with a strong and closely united transatlantic community."

In the aftermath of Russia's invasion of Ukraine and following the joint Russia-China declaration of an "unlimited partnership,"[4] Xi Jinping announced a "global security initiative" to implement the partnership. In a virtual address at the annual 2022 Boao Forum for Asia (China's version of Davos), Xi painted his preferred international order in which "We humanity are living in an indivisible security community," and added "that the Cold War mentality would only wreck the global peace framework, that hegemonism and power politics would only endanger world peace, and that bloc confrontation would only exacerbate security challenges in the 21st century." He claims instead to foster "sustainable security" that upholds sovereignty, territorial integrity, and non-interference in internal affairs, as well as a respect for the policy choices of every nation, based on a nation's unique sociopolitical system.[5] This vision rejects (in an apparent reference to NATO expansion) "the pursuit of one's own security at the cost of others' security" and (in a reference to US sanctions) equally rejects the "wanton use of unilateral sanctions and long-arm jurisdiction," as measures that decouple globalization and create cliques.

Xi's vision backs Putin and is clearly oblivious to the invasion of sovereign Ukraine. It denounces the kind of democratic alliance building the United States is constructing to block Putin's aggression and Xi's claims to sovereign control over Taiwan and the South China Sea and an effective hegemony over East Asia. Classically, it reflects the rising challenger's claim to defend the existing sovereign order while that order permits the accumulation of power it is steadily building. And it challenges any conception of human rights and democracy as universal values that all countries should endeavor to respect—unless, that is, that each country can define rights and democracy in purely national terms that preclude any international assessment.

Clearly the division of the world has deepened following the invasion of Ukraine. President Biden also seeks to avoid, as we should, a "return to the reflexive opposition and rigid blocs of the Cold War. Competition must not lock out cooperation on issues that affect us all." The world as a whole thus must cooperate to meet shared threats, like COVID-19, climate change, and nuclear proliferation. But the task has become even more difficult.

Perhaps Biden's most important lesson is that "international security will not be achieved without first rebuilding the economic foundations of liberal democracy at home."

So what can be done? What scenarios are seen as most likely from Washington and other capitals? What can be done to help make the West resilient against Chinese and Russian threats? How should the most pressing hot issues—Taiwan, Crimea, cybersecurity—be handled?

And, if the tensions across the divides will remain, what can be done to moderate them while mobilizing cooperation among democracies? What can be done to set rules of the game that assure each side that their vital interests are not at risk? In the end, the key message is: The threats to security are serious, but they are responsive to moderating measures. On top of that, in order to make a world safer for democracy, American democracy must be made not only safer from but also safer for the world.

CHAPTER EIGHT

Future Scenarios

US Scenarios

President Biden concluded his April 28, 2021, speech to Congress proposing a "blue-collar blueprint to build America" with just a few comments on foreign policy. The speech was overwhelmingly focused on education, jobs for a Green economy, and families. He spoke about the roots of US foreign policy as follows:

> Can our democracy deliver on its promise that all of us—created equal in the image of God—have a chance to lead lives of dignity, respect and possibility? . . . America's adversaries, the autocrats of the world, are betting we can't. And I promise you, they're betting we can't. They believe we are too full of anger and division and rage. They look at the images of the mob that assaulted this Capitol as proof that the sun is setting on American democracy. But they are wrong. You know it, I know it. But we have to prove them wrong. We have to prove democracy still works, that our government still works, and we can deliver for our people.[1]

A few weeks later, he promised that the new struggle will include a competition for the future of high tech as well:

> As new technologies reshape our world in fundamental ways, exposing vulnerabilities like ransomware attacks and creating threats such as invasive AI-driven surveillance, the democracies of the world must together ensure that our values govern the use and development of these innovations—not the interests of autocrats.[2]

In an equally defining speech on Memorial Day, 2021, President Biden proclaimed: "We're based on an idea: that we hold these truths to be self-evident that all men and women are created equal. We're unique in the world." Then he added: "I had a long conversation—for two hours—recently with President Xi, making it clear to him that we could do nothing but speak out for human rights around the world because that's who we are." And: "I'll be meeting with President Putin in a couple of weeks in Geneva, making it clear that we will not—we will not stand by and let him abuse those rights."[3]

The two points most worth emphasizing are that, first, most of the work must begin at home in our own democracy. Second, the autocrats are "adversaries" not "enemies." The implication is that while the democracies will differ from them on human rights, promote different rules of market competition, and support alliances with like-minded states, the democracies will also need to find common ground with them on climate change and arms control.

The US National Intelligence Council laid out the future options that defined the worldview of the new administration. *The Global Trends 2040* study noted:

> Western democratic governments probably will contend with more assertive challenges to the Western-led political order from China and Russia. Neither has felt secure in an international order designed for and dominated by democratic powers, . . . [they seek instead] a sovereignty-based international order that protects

their absolute authority within their borders and geographic areas of influence. China and Russia view the ideas and ideology space as opportunities to shape the competition without the need to use military force. Russia aims to engender cynicism among foreign audiences, diminish trust in institutions, promote conspiracy theories, and drive wedges in societies. As countries and nonstate actors jockey for ideological and narrative supremacy, control over digital communications platforms and other vehicles for dissemination of information will become more critical.[4]

The 2022 National Security Strategy summed up the US position by identifying an emerging world of "competition [that] is underway between the major powers to shape what comes next." The People's Republic of China (PRC)—"America's most consequential geopolitical challenge"—is the "only competitor with both the intent to reshape the international order and, increasingly, the economic, diplomatic, military, and technological power to do it . . . [in order] to become the world's leading power." Meanwhile, Russia is "an immediate and persistent threat to international peace and stability" but, given that it "lacks the across-the-spectrum capabilities of the PRC," the U.S., while competing with China, will "constrain" and manage the "acute threat posed by Russia." The U.S. will do both by relying heavily on NATO and by building new more flexible arrangements, like the Indo-Pacific Quad.[5]

Three geopolitical strategies that once may have seemed attractive are now unrealistic: One was transforming China and Russia through "engagement" into liberal democracies.[6] If successful, that would greatly reduce if not eliminate US national security concerns in those two key relationships, offering the prospects of a community of interests not unlike the relations with other liberal democracies such as the European Union. Both, however, have demonstrated that their autocratic institutions, rather than liberalizing, are deepening and hardening.[7] The second was to contain and cap Chinese power—to "make sure that China does not become a peer competitor."[8] There is little that the United States can do to limit Chinese growth without harming—as with embargoes and other measures—its own economy and those of its key allies in East Asia and Europe. Moreover, the very act of trying to limit the growth of a country still working to overcome historic poverty would be provocative in the extreme. The existence of Russian strategic might and Chinese long-run development cannot be wished away. Instead, the United States and its liberal allies need to develop strategies for the world that has emerged.

A third was isolationism. Isolationism has been a persistent temptation for democracies who generally prioritize the interests of citizens over foreigners and sometimes just wish the latter would go away. But today we live in an inescapably linked world—linked by climate change, pandemics, and geostrategic vulnerability. In the far past, the two oceans were bulwarks for America. Today, as since World War II, they serve no such protective purpose. FDR assessed in his 1945 State of the Union Address the prospects for US grand strategy in words that remain persuasive. He knew that despite the approach of victory, victory alone would not achieve the vital objectives for which the war had been fought. "In our disillusionment after the last war we preferred international anarchy to international cooperation with nations which did not see and think exactly as we did," he reminded the public. "We gave up the hope of gradually achieving a better peace because we had not the courage to fulfill our responsibilities in an admittedly imperfect world. We must not let that happen again, or we shall follow the same tragic road again." At the end of the Cold War, we assumed that because nations thought, or claimed to think, very much as we did, no effort to structure cooperation was needed. We now know that was a mistake. It is time to emulate the best plan proposed by FDR in 1945 and structure a world designed to achieve cooperation among rivals who might also be adversaries.

In that world of competitive geopolitics, US planners outlined five scenarios, only two of which appeared positive and viable. The three negative scenarios involved China as the leading state ("A World Adrift") as global cooperation deteriorates; a breakdown of globalization into rival regional blocs ("Separate Silos"); and revolutionary change consequent on global environmental crises, with likely leadership from a surviving China, the

European Union, and the United Nations ("Tragedy and Mobilization") and the decline of the United States. The two positive scenarios are a prosperity in a world led and divided by China and the United States ("Competitive Coexistence"); and the last, most favored by and resonating with the Biden administration's statements, is a world in which the United States leads a renaissance of democracies ("Renaissance of Democracies").

The "Renaissance of Democracies" rests on "rapid technological advancements fostered by public-private partnerships in the United States and other democratic societies" that transforms the "global economy, raising incomes, and improving the quality of life for millions around the globe." "In contrast, years of increasing societal controls and monitoring in China and Russia have stifled innovation."[9]

"Competitive Coexistence" presents a tolerable vision of bipolar stability, but also presupposes important transformations at home and a stabilization of global rivalry. It foresees a rapidly growing world economy led by the United States and China, who have restored "a robust trading relationship" but compete "over political influence, governance models, technological dominance, and strategic advantage. The risk of major war is low, and international cooperation and technological innovation make global problems manageable." In this connection, the United States and NATO condemned China's "malicious cyber activity" after the Microsoft Exchange hacking incident and called on China to respect "international commitments and obligations and to act responsibly in the international system, including in cyberspace."

"Competitive Coexistence" is the closest to the cold peace I advocate. In the next chapter, I outline what more is needed for it to be stable.

China's Scenarios

China's vision of the future has, since the Maoist period, become both accommodationist, encapsulated in the doctrine of "peaceful rise," and confrontational, labeled by commentators as "wolf warrior" diplomacy.[10] The post–World War II international rules-based order has been very good for China. It has included WTO multilateralism and global superpower equality embodied in China's veto-bearing permanent member-ship in the UN Security Council. The first offered the opening of trade opportunities with most-favored nation nondiscrimination that gave China all the trade opportunities offered to other WTO members, and the second gave China an equal claim to exercise the collective UN Security Council monopoly on the legal exercise of nondefensive force. But as argued before, China and Xi see the world as a hostile place. This derives in part from the "century of humiliation" and from internal drives that reward tension in domestic support. The hostility trope also resonates in a $10 billion investment in propaganda geared to promote "wolf warrior" rhetorically aggressive commentary.[11] But its deepest concern is that the United States and its allies regard Chinese corporatism with its industrial espionage and authoritarian rule and human rights abuses as sufficient to regard the Chinese regime as illegitimate. Wild statements like of that of former president Trump fueled these fears, as when he called for 100% tariffs on Chinese goods, debt cancellation, and $10 trillion in reparations for COVID-19.[12]

Xi himself, in an address to an international forum in 2021, proclaimed that China is committed to a "UN-centered multilateral system," one based on international law—as interpreted by each great power. "We must not let the rules set by one or a few countries be imposed on others." Openness and integration in an age of economic globalization is "an unstoppable historical trend." Cold war–style confrontation is anathema: "we must reject the cold war and zero-sum mentality and oppose a new 'cold war' and ideological confrontation in whatever forms." Instead, said Xi in his keynote address at the Boao Forum on April, 20, 2021, "Pulling Together Through Adversity and Toward a Shared Future for All" is the Chinese outlook.[13]

But this modest and accommodating self-presentation is countered by a much more confrontational stance, primarily for Chinese consumption. Following China's initially successful response to COVID-19, and suppression and integration of Hong Kong, Xi has asserted that "the East is rising and the West is declining." And, behind closed doors, he warned party officials: "The United States is the biggest threat to our country's development and security."[14]

At the October 2022 20th Party Congress, Xi doubled down on the threats he saw the United States posing to China's "national rejuvenation." He listed "infiltration, sabotage, subversion, and separatist activities" and "external attempts to blackmail, contain, blockade, and exert maximum pressure on China."[15]

The major fault lines appear to be the role of the public sector in economic transactions and human rights. Western demands that China respect widely recognized human rights and accord them to the Uighurs and recognize the political rights of Hong Kong and Taiwan confront Chinese demands for unrestricted sovereignty. Internal critics, such as the defector (and former Chinese Communist Party ideologist) Cai Xia, dispute the CCP's political clout, claiming: "The CCP has the ambition of a hungry dragon but inside it is a paper tiger."[16] Western experts also identify potential political weaknesses in a lack of enthusiasm among the young for CCP doctrine. Still, China's aggressive moves toward Hong Kong and in the South China Sea are widely popular in mainland China. National glory and economic prosperity continue to sustain an ambitious agenda in which Xi appears determined to maintain China's rise and claim full equality with the United States, at the minimum, and regional hegemony over East Asia and global leadership, at the maximum.[17]

Putin's Russian Resurgence

Like Xi, Putin has said he wants to improve Moscow's ties with Washington, but the United States wants to "hold back" Russia's development. "We need to find ways of looking for a settlement in our relations, which are at an extremely low level now," Putin told the Saint Petersburg International Economic Forum. "But . . . they want to hold back our development, they talk about it publicly."[18] While portrayed as defensive, Putin has also acted aggressively in targeting US elections with cyber destabilization, providing cover for criminal ransomware attacks in the West, invading Ukraine, and engaging in cyber espionage and sabotage against Russia's near neighbors. Some of his rhetoric is also designed to provoke rather than accommodate, as when he equated the insurrection at the US Capitol with political demonstrations in Russia against the attempted assassination of Aleksei A. Navalny. Overall, like Xi, Putin seeks to enhance Russian greatness through diplomatic equality and diplomatic coups as with the successful military interventions in Syria in support of President Bashar al-Assad and in the dispute between Armenia and Azerbaijan, both remarkably successful in comparison to US interventions in Syria and Afghanistan. Indeed, the invasion of Ukraine is Putin's first major overreach and potentially one with devastating consequences unless he can persuade the Russian public that he has achieved a military "victory" and that the new solidarity of NATO (together with the addition of Finland and Sweden) is inconsequential.

Thus, each of the three powers is on a strikingly different and potentially confrontational trajectory. Yet none claim to be seeking a cold war. Biden made this particularly clear at his summit with Putin in 2021: "This is not a 'Kumbaya' moment... but it's clearly not in anybody's interest—your country or mine—for us to be in a situation where we're in a new cold war."[19]

Similarly, during a 2020 visit to Paris, Chinese foreign minister Wang Yi, while complaining that the United States has been "coercing other countries to take sides" and stoking conflict, claimed, "We never wanted to engage in a new Cold War with anyone."[20] President Biden's 2021 UN General Assembly speech again promised, "We are not seeking a new Cold War or a world divided into rigid blocs."[21] But he then went on to declare that championing the "universal rights of all people" is in "our DNA as a nation" and highlighted China's oppression in Xinjiang (inhabited by the Uighurs) and Russia's ruthless rule of Chechnya as instances of abuse. China responded a couple of days later with a "List of facts about U.S. interference in Hong Kong affairs and support of anti-China forces in Hong Kong," calling the list a "criminal record" of "gross interference in Hong Kong affairs" by the United States, which it labeled an "evil backstage manipulator."[22]

Clearly, while neither wants a cold war, both see the other as threatening its ability to make a world safe for democracy or autocracy.

Cooperation in Cold War

It is worth recalling that "cold war" does not preclude cooperation. It does challenge and limit it, often far below the optimum. Even with the extreme tensions between the United States and the Soviet Union, a rivalry that was both geopolitical and ideological, cooperation was achieved.

The development and use of atomic weapons by the United States on the Japanese cities of Hiroshima and Nagasaki in 1945 and the Soviet Union's subsequent development of nuclear capabilities escalated the tension between the two powers. The resulting arms race between the United States and the Soviet Union led to a seemingly imminent threat of nuclear destruction. In the early years of the Cold War, there were various attempts to control nuclear capabilities, such as the Baruch Plan (a plan to establish a supranational governing body with a monopoly over atomic energy and the right to perform intrusive inspections). Not surprisingly, that ambitious plan for global regulation failed. Later, the Limited Test Ban Treaty (a 1963 treaty that banned nuclear testing in the atmosphere, the oceans, and space) marked a positive step toward limited cooperation.[23] However, the first truly successful international efforts at controlling nuclear capabilities were the Strategic Arms Limitation Talks (SALT) of 1969–1972 and the subsequent Strategic Arms Limitation Treaties (SALT I and II). While the United States never ratified SALT II because of the Soviet Union's invasion of Afghanistan,[24] SALT I proved to be a successful means of arms control.

Rather than attempting to reduce nuclear capabilities, which at the time seemed implausible, SALT I focused on slowing the rate of growth of nuclear weapons stockpiles, with the ultimate goal of halting this growth. Signed in 1972 by the United States and the Soviet Union, SALT I consisted of two agreements: the Anti-Ballistic Missile (ABM) Treaty and the "Interim Agreement." In the ABM Treaty, both sides agreed not to build national defenses against nuclear attack, with an exception of two ABM sites allotted to each side.[25] The "Interim Agreement" had many omissions, but it nonetheless limited intercontinental ballistic missiles

(ICBMs) and submarine-launched ballistic missiles to their existing levels for five years, pending negotiations of a follow-up treaty.[26]

Viewed by many as a representation of the strategy of mutual assured destruction, the ABM Treaty translated the realities of the political environment into law. The United States had an ABM system that was minimally effective, expensive, and that the US Senate would not fund. The Soviet Union had an even more limited ABM system, one that was likely to lose the technological race to the United States.[27] Thus, the parties to the ABM Treaty had preexisting incentives to behave in a manner that was consistent with the treaty, and were predisposed to agree to it.

This illustrates that even an existential conflict did not preclude limited, focused cooperation.[28] US-Soviet arms control shows that cooperation could overcome rivalry and ideological antipathy by focusing negotiation on the mutual desire for stabilization and deterrence, constraining the rate of increase of nuclear stockpiles rather than reducing nuclear capacity, and highlighting their dependence on each other (in order to avoid the consequences of noncooperation in an ever-increasing arms race that left both deeply insecure). Other areas of cooperation emerged in limited UN peacekeeping in conflicts that neither superpower wished to escalate (as in the Middle East, India-Pakistan, and, for a while, in the Congo).

Today the emerging features of a new cold war are much less extreme, giving some optimism to cooperation. But the stakes are also higher, with vastly greater interdependence at stake.

CHAPTER NINE

Four Bridges
to a Cold Peace

To head off a full-blown cold war, we need to identify reasonable terms of accommodation among the three powers over key issues that divide them, and then make sure the United States is geared up to manage a prudent grand strategy of cold peace. Let us start with what needs to be done to make the world safer for American democracy and then turn to what needs to be done to make American democracy safe for the world.

A Shared Fate: Climate

The first bridge is the necessity of and opportunity for making progress on climate change amelioration through cooperation with China. Even though the separate effects of unaddressed climate change might seem small,[1] the combined effects—through malnutrition, disasters such as floods and droughts, and sea rise and civil conflicts—on lives lost amount to 250,000 lives per year from 2030 to 2050. All this led *The Lancet* to conclude that "Climate change is the biggest global health threat of the 21st century."[2]

Today, China emits 10 billion tons of CO_2 to the United States' 5 and India's 2.5, illustrating how important cooperation with India and China is for addressing climate change. But the problem is far from being mostly China's. The United States emits 16 tons per capita and China only 7. Moreover, historically, the United States and Europe have emitted more than half of the globe's stock of CO_2; China less than 14 percent.[3]

Translated into economic costs, new research shows that, if current trends continue, the total cost of global warming will be as high as 3.6 percent of GDP. Four global warming effects alone—hurricane damage, real estate losses, energy costs, and water costs—will come with a price tag of 1.8 percent of US GDP, or almost $1.9 trillion annually (in today's dollars) by 2100.[4] The long-run cost is, of course, a function of how severe the rise in temperature becomes. At 2°C above preindustrial levels of warming, the United States would suffer annual losses equivalent to about 0.5 percent of GDP in the years 2080–2099. But if the global temperature increase rises by 4°C, annual losses would be around 2.0 percent of GDP. Rising mortality as well as changes in labor supply, energy demand, and agricultural production are all especially important factors in driving the increasing effects.[5]

Climate envoy John Kerry is attempting negotiations to find a cooperative approach to meet and develop the Paris climate standards, which the Biden administration reaffirmed, following Trump's renunciation. In an April 2021 meeting, China and the United States pledged to cooperate "to strengthen implementation of the Paris Agreement."[6] They promised eleven targeted measures to reduce climate change ("decarbonize industry," invest in "energy efficient buildings," and so forth) and promote multilateral cooperation under the Paris Agreement. The mutual dependence was clear: If China's 1.4 billion people continue to rely on coal and fossil fuels, climate-designed curbs elsewhere will not work. If the United States and the Europeans do not take major steps to curb their own effects and invest in a cleaner global economy, the burdens their past industrialization have placed on the globe will not be sustainable.

Nonetheless, it soon became clear that while the United States seeks major reforms, including reducing China's reliance on coal plants and fossil fuels, the Chinese look to a broader accommodation. Chinese foreign minister Wang Yi called on the United States to stop treating China as "a threat and an adversary." Climate change, in China's view, "cannot be separated" from the broader geopolitical environment. He added: "The U.S. side hopes climate change cooperation can be an oasis in China-U.S. relations. . . . But if the oasis is surrounded by desert, sooner or later the oasis will also become desert."[7]

Cooperation is essential if the climate is to become sustainable. But in themselves measures of climate cooperation will not be enough to head off a cold war. Indeed, if Minister Wang is to be believed, progress on reducing cold war tensions is a prerequisite for successful cooperation in climate change.

Statesmen, thus, will also need to address drivers of conflict. Crimea, Taiwan, and cyber conflict are three of today's axes of confrontation. None can be resolved in a manner that fully satisfies US interests or principles or those of Russia or China for that matter. Each requires a significant compromise, a second best whose justification is that it is better than a full-blown cold war conflict. Fortunately, there are potential compromises that would allow each to be managed in ways that reduce tension and could contribute to a managed cold peace.

Crimea and Ukraine

The second bridge to a cold peace is a negotiated solution to the Russian invasion of Ukraine. The invasion of Crimea by "little green men" (Russian soldiers in disguise) in 2014 set off a deep crisis not only for Ukraine but also for US and European relations with Putin's Russia. The conflict epitomized the mix of clashing interests and principles at the heart of rising cold war tensions. The intervention was illegal, a clear violation of the territorial integrity of Ukraine as Russia took over Crimea, annexed it, and then sent forces into eastern Ukraine, violating UN Charter Article 2(4) on the use of force against "territorial integrity."

The imposition on norms was particularly acute because Ukraine had surrendered its Soviet nuclear weapons as part of an internationally recognized arrangement for its sovereignty. Its national security was seemingly guaranteed by international recognition and appreciation for its voluntary renunciation.

On the other side of the ledger, self-determination is a competing principle of global legitimacy, and Crimea's ethnically Russian population was said to want to unite with Russia. Self-determination in practice has been limited to "external," "saltwater" determinations (ex-colonies, overseas from their metropoles) and not "internal" rebellions against central governments.[8] When the International Court of Justice was given an opportunity to rule on the legality of the independence of Kosovo, it sidestepped the opportunity in favor of a purely procedural ruling. Nonetheless, the political precedents of Kosovo and East Timor did seem relevant. The Russians in Ukraine and in the Baltics were "beached diasporas" (co-ethnics left in post-colonial states)[9] by the retreat of the Soviet and Russian empire, just as Germans in Eastern Europe and the white settlers in southern Africa had been left behind by the retreats of their empires. But the Russians in Ukraine had Putin prepared to back their cause and claims.

Vladimir Putin's own oft-repeated justification for seizing Crimea and intervening in the Donbas region of eastern Ukraine centered on the "direct threat" Ukraine's desire to someday join NATO might pose to Russia.[10] Others were skeptical of NATO tanks ever crossing the Ukrainian-Russian border and noted the coup might satisfy a deep popular Russian desire to reunify and "return" its fellow Russians abandoned by the Soviet Union while earning Putin and his allies a global military coup with domestic political resonance. Putin blithely explained: "Crimea has always been an integral part of Russia in the hearts and minds of people."[11]

The Minsk II Protocol (2015) set out principles for an accommodation between Russia, Ukraine, and the Donbas's restive minorities.[12] Unfortunately, many of the propositions are contradictory, such as recognizing Ukrainian sovereignty and Donbas's separate status, and even more have been neglected, such that few appear to think they constitute a stable basis for peace.

The 2022 invasion of Ukraine by Russia has made an accommodation that could lead to a cold peace immensely more difficult. Everything now depends on the outcome of the war. The two least likely scenarios are: first, a Russian victory that "denazifies" Ukraine and imposes a Russian puppet regime. The successful defense of Kyiv seems to have ruled that out. Second, a Ukrainian armed liberation of eastern Ukraine and Crimea appears equally improbable against the vastly larger and better-equipped Russian army and the support Russia might receive from Russia-leaning populations in the Donbas and Crimea.

Current (October 2022) Russian military aims are to conquer both the eastern border region, linking the Donbas to Crimea through Mariupol, and the Black Sea southern border, linking the Russian-conquered eastern provinces to the breakaway Russia-oriented Transnistria region of Moldova.[13] The eastern conquests would give Russia a vital land bridge that would secure Crimea, provide access to freshwater for Crimea, and absorb rich regions of industrial capacity and oil and gas reserves in the east. The southern conquests would cut off Ukraine from the Black Sea while providing a corridor to protect Transnistria. It is impossible to say whether Russia will succeed in both these campaigns. In August 2022, Ukraine mounted a counteroffensive to liberate Kherson in the south and territory around Kkarkiv in the northeast.

The most likely scenario in either case is a stalemate. Russia will keep some conquered territory in the east, and Ukraine will survive, refuse to recognize the conquest, and inflict substantial and continuing damage on Russian forces occupying eastern Ukraine. If that scenario comes to be, not peace but an armistice—an agreement to stop fighting—might be the most likely outcome. In that case, the results in Ukraine would come to resemble those of the sad Cold War armistices dividing East and West Germany and dividing (and still dividing) North and South Korea.

Can one still visualize compromises that establish a cold peace that permits elements of cooperation between Russia and the West to emerge? Ukraine has a powerful incentive to compromise as a way to gain the return of some of its lost territory. Russia has suffered both on the bat-tlefield and from NATO-led economic sanctions. The Russian economy is experiencing 15 percent inflation and many shortages in stores and facto-ries and overall may shrink almost 10 percent in 2022.[14] But this primarily hurts the Russian people, not Putin or his oligarchic cronies. Indeed, Rus-sian state oil revenues in 2022 *increased* by 38 percent over 2021 (thanks to higher prices due to sanctions and sales to China and India).[15] Only, as persuasively argued by Fareed Zakaria, a more effective program of oil and gas sanctions will likely move him. Europe and Germany vitally depend on Russian oil and gas, and world gas prices over $100 a barrel are straining the coalition; so to cut off the spigot, the United States and its allies need to persuade Saudi Arabia to replace Russian oil and gas with an increased flow from its wells. That will require difficult political com-promises that include stronger backing for Saudi Arabia against Iran and sidestepping Mohammed bin Salman's alleged execution of Saudi Ara-bian journalist Jamal Khashoggi.[16]

With the most likely alternative to a compromise being a continuing full-scale war and the additional costs of a rising democracy-autocracy cold war that would undermine needed cooperation in many other areas, some kind of compromise that, however imperfect, improves legitimacy and stability is clearly worthwhile. Any and all compromise measures should have Ukraine in the lead. Ukraine does not and should not dictate NATO policy, but negotiations with Russia should not be conducted over Ukraine's head and should be informed by the "nothing about Ukraine, without Ukraine" principle. Following a general cease-fire, a negotiated peace might look something like the following in which all sides surren-der interests for the sake of an ameliorating package:

1. The largest legitimacy gain for Russia and largest cost for Ukraine would be the cession of Crimea, provided the wishes of the Crimeans would be legitimately ascertained. The UN Security Council rightly condemned the takeover by a vote of 13 to 1 (Russia vetoing) with China abstaining. The General Assembly condemned the 2014 Russian-organized referendum in Crimea by 100 votes, with 11 opposing and

58 abstentions. UN assistant secretary-general for human rights Ivan Simonovic described the very flawed Russian-conducted referendum in the following words: "Media manipulation significantly contributed to a climate of fear and insecurity in the period preceding the referendum, and the presence of paramilitary and so-called self-defence groups, as well as soldiers in uniform but without insignia, was not conducive to an environment in which voters could freely exercise their right to hold opinions and the right to freedom of expression."[17] Yet, as recently as 2021, polls indicate the vast majority of the inhabitants (some 80 percent) favored unification with Russia. Fifty-eight percent of Crimea is Russian, 24 percent Ukrainian, 12 percent Tartar, and 8 percent others. Reunifying Crimea by force, even if Ukraine were capable of doing so, would today be wrong, violating self-determination and causing unimaginable casualties.

The first step toward a solution thus would be an internationally supervised referendum on unification to be conducted by the Organization for Security and Cooperation in Europe (OSCE) and the United Nations. Crimeans would be given the choice of Russia or Ukraine, with Ukraine being prepared to accept the likely results.[18] Russia would pledge to respect OSCE monitoring of minority rights to property and education.

2. The second part of the package would address complementary issues in the Donbas, where Russians are in a distinct minority but have been sustained by Russian armed intervention. The Donbas is composed of Donetsk and Luhansk, which are 38 percent and 39 percent Russian in ethnicity, respectively. The Donbas would be returned to Ukraine, the titular sovereign under the Minsk II Protocol.[19] Under this new understanding, Russia would withdraw all its military forces and with them all heavy weapons in the hands of its paramilitary allies. Ukrainian forces would return to the international border between Russia and Ukraine. Ukraine would pledge to implement minority rights to property and education and local self-government (as is currently being proposed for all of Ukraine). The OSCE would have guaranteed access in order to monitor compliance on the ground for a following ten years.

3. The European Union and NATO would be pledged to support both territorial arrangements. In addition, to create bulwarks to support the peace, Ukraine and Russia would both withdraw heavy weapons (tanks and artillery) fifty miles from their common borders. Ukraine would reopen the North Crimea Canal that provides water to Crimea. (Without water from the Dnieper River, Crimea's arable land shrank, from 130,000 hectares in 2013—already a fraction of Soviet-era levels— to 14,000 in 2017.)[20] Russia will agree to de-weaponize gas flows to Ukraine (Ukraine has relied on Russia for about 37 percent of its imports) by maintaining a steady flow and compensate Ukraine for any reductions.[21] Russia would also agree not to repeat the 2015 cyber-attack on the Ukrainian power grid, which came very near to causing a catastrophic crisis for Ukrainian public utilities.[22] The United States and the Europeans would lift economic sanctions on Russia specifi-cally tied to the Russian invasions of Ukraine. Ukraine, Russia, and NATO would need to establish a claims commission to assess damage to civilians and civilian structures in Ukraine and arrange for com-pensation from Russian sources. All three of these last arrangements would be nested in a wider Russian protocol on gas flows and more general détente, as described next.

4. The fourth part of the package would be incorporating the Ukraine peace into a wider framework for détente between Russia, NATO and the European Union. The wider framework would build on the initia-tive already launched by the Biden administration in 2021 to extend the New START nuclear arms negotiations by five years in order to develop the terms for a wider agreement.[23] At this point, it would be unwise to restore the Nord Stream 2 pipeline designed to bring natural gas from Russia to Germany, unless backup sources of supply for Ger-many and Europe can be guaranteed so that neither is again subject to Russian economic coercion.[24]

5. Putin is also said to want to "neutralize" Ukraine through an agree-ment to be made between Russia and NATO not to extend further their alliances into Eastern Europe and to recognize the "permanent neutrality" of those states.[25] We must keep in mind that alliances are

a matter of sovereign choice. Ukraine can choose to be neutral; NATO can refuse to admit Ukraine. If, however, Russia insists on Ukrainian neutrality, it is attempting to impose a "protectorate," and that should be rejected. But NATO should also consider that Ukraine lacked in the past the democratic stability to make it a good candidate for membership, and, given Ukraine's geographic proximity to Russia, it is a strategic liability rather than an asset for alliance security. It might thus make sense for NATO to declare that it will not offer membership to Ukraine as long as Russia credibly promises not to destabilize the country and lives up to those promises in practice.

Should these wider steps toward détente succeed and be accompanied by steps to restore respect for international political independence and minimum comity outlined in the discussion of cybersecurity later, the door would be open to a genuine restoration of normal and predictable relations, including the lifting of sanctions. This, after all, is what Russia, the Europeans, and the United States claim to want.

Taiwan and China

The third bridge to cold peace is a détente with China. US relations with China reflect both similarities and differences in a comparison with the relations that have developed between Russia and NATO. The similarities rest on the problems that corporatist, nationalist autocracies pose for liberal, capitalist democracies. The differences reflect China's scale, with China's GDP almost ten times the size of Russia's, and China's historic focus on development, having a number of nuclear warheads almost twenty times less than Russia's (or the United States'). In the succinct phrasing of the RAND Corporation, China is a peer, not a rogue; Russia is a rogue, not a peer.[26] Russia disrupts liberal international order; China flourishes in but threatens to replace it.

But as discussed earlier, the dangers of cold war–style rivalry with China are, nonetheless, real. There are tense confrontations over China's "nine-dash line" claim to have sovereign control over the South China Sea by virtue of various artificial islands (a claim rejected by the Law of the Sea Tribunal). With Japan, China disputes the ownership of the Diaoyu/ Senkaku Islands; with India, the border with Tibet; and with the United States, it conflicts over cyber espionage and technology theft (discussed later). But perhaps the most dangerous tinder in the tense relationship will be Taiwan, a strikingly difficult combination of legitimacy and geo-strategic issues.

Taiwan is the legal and geopolitical opposite of Crimea. Crimea remains legally Ukrainian territory, now ruled by Russia with the apparent self-determining support of a majority of Crimeans. Taiwan is "acknowledged" to be part of the "One China," but ruled by the self-determining population of Taiwan. In contradistinction to US policy on Ukraine and Crimea, the United States legally "recognizes" "One China" and "acknowledges" that China claims Taiwan, but supports effective Taiwanese self-determination by maintaining unofficial relations.[27]

Han Chinese began to settle in and displace the indigenous popula-tion when Taiwan was a Dutch East India Company trading outpost in the sixteenth and seventeenth centuries. Conquered by the Chinese Qing dynasty in 1683, the Qing in turn ceded the island to Japan in 1895, which then held it until 1945. Defeated in the Chinese civil war and retreating from the mainland in 1949, Chiang Kai-shek's Republic of China forces brought almost 2 million "mainlanders" who would form the core of Kuomintang (KMT) Party rulers of the island. The democracy movement within the KMT first began "localization" in 1987 and then split into KMT (pro-unification with China) and Democratic Progressive Party (DPP; pro-independence) factions that continue to compete in Taiwan today. In 2022, the DPP ruled the island nation.

US policy during the Cold War promulgated the bizarre fiction that KMT Taiwan was the "One China" that ruled all China and held the per-manent China seat on the UN Security Council. In 1971, Taiwan lost its permanent UN seat to China. In 1972, US policy shifted with the "Shang-hai Communiqué" and again in 1979 when President Carter recognized China and only one China, as Taiwan was demoted to unofficial status well short of diplomatic recognition. The US Congress responded with the Taiwan Relations Act, which established an "institute" in place of an embassy and initiated the US understanding that China would not use force to seize Taiwan but could proceed to woo the island into unification. China never forswore armed unification, and, indeed, Xi Jinping has promised unification by the 100th anniversary of the Chinese revolution, in 2049; still, despite armed crises, China has pursued diplomatic isolation of Taiwan, not armed invasion . . . so far.[28]

Taiwan is the epitome of a new cold war legitimacy conflict: the self-determination of the functionally independent Taiwanese people against China's claim to sovereignty resting on a memory of a hundred years of colonial humiliation. But it is not the only conflict. As noted in the previous chapters, China and the United States are at loggerheads over the cultural genocide of the Uighurs, China's extraordinary sovereignty claims on the South China Sea, and material clashes (discussed later) on cyber security and industrial espionage and the wider contest on whether the world should be made safe for democracy or autocracy.

No overall condominium or even settled international order is in the offing, but as with Russia we can imagine the contours of pragmatic compromises that could greatly improve the prospects of necessary cooperation in managing the global commons, climate change, and global pandemics central among them.

If we assume that the United States' primary strategic interests in the western Pacific are protecting key allies, keeping the sea lanes open, and avoiding the invasion of democratic Taiwan, then the United States should be willing to compromise. If we assume that China's key interests are avoiding war, maritime security in its region, the principle of territorial integrity, economic growth, and the national prestige of leading its region, then it too should be willing to compromise. We can also assume that both the United States and China want to avoid even the economic costs (to the global economy) of confrontation, which are estimated by Nikkei Asia at $2.6 trillion if sanctions equivalent in scope to those imposed on Russia were imposed on China in the wake of an invasion of Taiwan.

Robert D. Blackwill and Philip Zelikow have argued a sensible set of conditions for a US strategy on Taiwan, shaped by three planks: (1) "affirm that we are not trying to change Taiwan's status; (2) work with our allies, especially Japan, to prepare new plans that could challenge Chinese military moves against Taiwan and help Taiwan defend itself, yet put the burden of widening a war on China; and (3) visibly plan, beforehand, for the disruption and mobilization that could follow a wider war, but without assuming that such a war would or should escalate to the Chinese, Japanese, or American homelands."[29]

One set of compromises that would effectuate that strategy might look like this:

1. The "constructive ambiguity" on Taiwan's territorial status as part of China, but self-governing, would be acknowledged jointly and publicly by China and the United States and combined with an explicit guarantee that China would not use force to unify Taiwan as long as Taiwan refrained from declaring independence.

2. Maritime and aerial security would be defined by special, agreed-upon zones barring military transit. As a way to reduce the chances of inadvertent military clashes, the United States and China and Taiwan would bar naval vessels and military aircraft from the Taiwan Strait, which separates Taiwan from mainland China, while recognizing the right of commercial vessels and civilian airliners to treat the waterway as an international passage.[30]

3. As an alternative, should this confidence-building, arms control arrangement fail, the United States would assist Taiwan in acquiring defensive weapons (anti-ship missiles, sea mines, shoulder-fired Stinger missiles) and help it build up its civil defense.[31] This offers a much more credible deterrent than building up US naval forces in the region sufficient to deter the Chinese fleet (with the Chinese fleet's significant advantages of proximity). Defending the outlying Taiwanese islands is nearly impossible. Instead, a 2021 war-game analysis proposed that "[g]iven the inherent difficulty of defending small, distant offshore islands like Dongsha, Taiwan and the United States should strive to turn them into what the players called 'poison frogs.' This

approach would make Chinese attempts to seize these islands so militarily, economically, and politically painful from the outset that the costs of coercion or aggression would be greater than the benefits."[32] The clear corollary is that Taiwan itself should have self-defense capabilities sufficient to make the entire island a "poison frog."

Unfortunately, in response to Speaker Nancy Pelosi's visit to Taiwan in 2022, China revealed its effective response to the "poison frog" strategy by demonstrating that it could blockade the island. Taiwan and the United States need to consider how they would respond short of escalating to an all-out war. Stockpiling supplies (to give the time diplomacy and sanctions will require) or other measures clearly are required.[33]

4. The United States would inform China of the movement of its naval vessels in the South China Sea, while China would cease the construction of artificial islands that it has used to claim sovereign control and guarantee free passage for all vessels and noninfringement on the territorial seas and economic zones of all the littoral powers.

5. A wider set of security guarantees might also involve integrating China into the New START nuclear arms negotiations. Up until recently, China has very prudently stayed within the "minimum deterrent" levels of Britain, France, India, Pakistan, and Israel, and not sought to compete with Russia and the United States. Recent construction in submarines and new missile silos, however, suggests a change. If so, better that would be done in a multilateral framework with the United States and Russia so that monitoring would be shared and any changes could be agreed upon through formal negotiation.

There is of course no assurance that the compromise offer would be accepted. The US alternative if those and other arrangements in cybersecurity collapsed would be waging a carefully modulated containment response designed to bolster US actual and potential allies and perhaps "triangulate," exploiting divides between Russia and China. The original Quad (Japan, Australia, India, and the United States) could well be supplemented as it recently has been by New Zealand, South Korea, Vietnam, and the fuller cooperation of Europe.[34] Difficulties are likely to arise in keeping India within this fold, given Indian prime minister Narendra Modi's erratic policy and the long tradition of Indian neutrality that only the recent tension with China has begun to overcome. Triangulating between China and Russia will run up against their recent success in coordinating policy and the deepening sense of mutual threat from the allied democracies being mobilized by Biden.[35]

Success in moderating tensions with Russia and China also hinges on a geoeconomic détente in cyber that regulates cyber espionage, curbs intellectual property theft, and stops sabotage (both political and industrial).

Cyber Peace?

The fourth bridge to accommodation is to reach new rules for cyber.[36] Any discussion of cyber conflict needs to start with an understanding that every major-power state capable of engaging in cyber espionage seems to have done it; and the major players—the United States, Israel, China, and Russia—all seem to have engaged in cyber sabotage at one point or another.[37] They have included US, Russian, and Chinese cyberattacks as espionage; private-sector hacks and ransomware (as with Colonial Pipeline and JBS); and public-sector hacks (on infrastructure—Stuxnet on Iran by the United States and Israel; Russia on Ukraine, and Russia on politics in the US 2016 election). Adding new complications, both Iran and North Korea have demonstrated a capacity for cyberattacks.[38] As noted in Chapter Two, the CSIS has documented more than twenty-five major cyberattacks in the past fifteen years.[39]

Efforts have been made to reduce the harms associated with cyber hacking. The Tallinn Manuals 1 and 2, beginning with publication in 2013, examined the international law governing cyber warfare, considering cyber operations both as state instruments in national policy and as methods of armed conflict. Negotiated among a group of academic experts, and nonbinding, the basic premise of the norms in the Manuals is that the existing laws of war cover cyber and are applicable. Thus the manuals focus on armed attacks that warrant state responses of self-defense and offer legal protection to "noncombatants" in the private sector. The manuals are a valuable academic restatement of the law, but they leave many of the newer forms of conflict short of "war" open. The Tallinn Manual 3.0 is currently under preparation.[40]

An important complement to Tallinn was 2018's Paris Call for Trust and Security in Cyberspace, issued by French president Emmanuel Macron in partnership with Microsoft and civil society organizations. More than 1,100 government, corporate, civil society, and public authority supporters have backed this call to action, resulting in its becoming the largest multi-stakeholder cybersecurity initiative in the world. The goal of the call is to engage diverse stakeholders in discussions of shared values regarding safety, draw key distinctions that protect the "private" sector from cyber conflict, and hold each other accountable to make cyberspace a free, secure, and open place. However, the United States, Russia, and China—the three nations with the most cyber operations active—were not among the signatories. The organizers plan to involve stakeholders in emerging countries, promoting a multi-stakeholder approach in UN cyber negotiations, and creating a cyberspace stability index, among other steps.[41]

Again, despite the conflicts of interest and aspirations, compromises can be envisioned that moderate the competition for advantage and limit the harms being inflicted between countries.

Superpower agreements to curb attacks can have positive effects. In 2015, US president Barack Obama and Chinese president Xi Jinping formally agreed not to knowingly conduct or support cyber operations against each other's countries. Washington and Beijing would also provide timely responses to requests for cybersecurity assistance and cooperate with each other to prevent and halt cybercrime. The agreement raised doubts among many onlookers who saw it as an opportunity for China to avoid sanctions imposed by Washington. However, as documented a year later, Chinese hacking attacks on US corporations and individuals decreased dramatically following the agreement. Unfortunately, in subsequent years both Chinese and Russian hacks have increased.[42]

President Biden and President Putin reached a similar arrangement in mid-June of 2021 in Geneva. Biden declared that the United States will act against Russia if it continues with its patterns of behavior that harm the United States. Here, the harms cited are the recent JBS and Colonial Pipeline hacks conducted by Russian operatives. Biden gave Putin a list of twenty potential targets of US infrastructure that were off limits and urged the Russian president to curb ransomware hacking sites in his country.[43] Biden also drew attention to human rights violations occurring in Russia and urged progress in nuclear arms control strategic-stability talks.[44] Soon thereafter, Blackmatter (a revival of DarkSide, responsible for the Colonial Pipeline ransomware attack) said that it was moderating its targets and would no longer go after critical infrastructure.[45] Other agreements could substantially assist a cyber détente, including:

- The summits could be supplemented with a tripartite agreement among the United States, Russia, and China to adopt two key standards.[46] The first would agree to cooperate in preventing and sanctioning private ransomware attacks. Reflecting the difficulty of controlling cyber technologies, an established expert in the field, Joseph Nye, has suggested an agreement to avoid state-led sabotage against critical infrastructure targets (hospitals, banks, power plants, pipelines, and so forth).[47] Similar arrangements were codified in the United Nations to prohibit terrorist attacks on airlines, nuclear plants, and other critical targets, even though no shared definition of "terrorism" could be agreed upon. These limited-target arms control strategies were adopted because the United States and its allies wanted to prohibit all non-state attacks, and the anti-colonial movement wanted to except anti-colonial struggles such as South Africa's democratic resistance led by the African National Congress (ANC).

- Similar prohibitions should be established for attacks on political systems and existing territorial status quos. Repeats of the 2016 attacks on the United States would produce a significant escalation in cold war tensions. Attempts to encourage the separation of Hong Kong, Tibet, or Xinjiang from China would be equally disruptive. Countries

will want to continue public diplomacy and advocacy. Covert propaganda campaigns, like the one that targeted the US Women's March
in 2017, are the destabilizing problem.[48] An accord to make public the
sources of state-directed advocacy campaigns and funding is the minimum guarantee of improved détente.

There is, of course, no guarantee that these accords would work to
reduce tension and restore a better prospect of stability to great power
rivalries. It is also very unlikely that any one of the three powers would
credibly forswear pure espionage activity—it can be an essential guarantee
of compliance by the other powers. However, it can also be seen as an additional arms control measure.[49] Moreover, the United States and its democratic allies cannot, and should not, forswear human rights diplomacy
that publicly criticizes abuses wherever they occur. But, if the big three do
want to achieve a détente, measures that prohibit sabotage and political
destabilization could be essential parts of what makes it last. Together
they would make a world safer for democracy (and for autocracy too).

A Caucus of Democracies

When the number one power (the United States) is faced with a coalition between the number two military power (Russia) and the number
two economic power (China), balance-of-power logic suggests that one
should try to split them, winning one or the other to its side. During the
Cold War, encouraging Yugoslav dissent from the Warsaw Pact and, even
more, Kissingerian triangulation with China against the USSR were diplomatic coups.

This an attractive strategy today, especially given China's greater stake
in a globalized economy. But the problem is that the symmetrical balancing strategy is for the number twos to stick together to offset the number
one. Concretely, why would China prefer to abandon Russia, which use-
fully disrupts the West? The prospect of a Ukrainian victory in the current war against Russia (and thus a NATO victory, too) that leaves Russia
bankrupt and in domestic turmoil is a China alone against a reinvigo-

rated democratic coalition that is determined to curb its regional take-over of East Asia and block its globally scaled industrial espionage . . . and stand up for human rights and democracy in ways that discredit China.

The better assumption is that Russia and China will stick together. The right response for the United States is to strengthen the democratic coalition of states prepared to balance against the autocratic coalition of Russia and China and their allies.

Achieving a democratic caucus will call for reinforcing the liberal order supporting human rights. It calls for reasserting international rule-of-law principles, reaffirming existing alliances (while constructing new ones measuring up to new challenges, especially in the Pacific), and developing better balanced trade regimes across the Atlantic and the Pacific that are open to all who are willing to abide by their rules.[50]

As effective caucuses do, the democracies should strive to convene regularly to coordinate common action and thus signal common resolve. The door should be open as wide as possible to welcome any autocracy willing to cooperate, issue by issue, and any autocracy contemplating a transition to democratic rule.

It is time to form and rely on a caucus of democracies but not a "League of Democracies," such as was proposed by Senator John McCain. The latter was envisioned as a substitute legal order to authorize the use of force to address humanitarian emergencies when the United Nations is stalemated. The league's substitute legal order raises unnecessary walls in world politics. Forming a league, rather than a caucus, will exacerbate cold war tensions while missing the real opportunities for genuine compromise along the lines of the measures recommended earlier. It prematurely abandons the universal, multilateral restraints now embodied in UN Charter law against unilateral uses of nondefensive force and loses the multilateral standards that can sometimes encourage compromises through invoking established multilateral norms.[51]

For those who doubt the potential for multilateral compromise within the UN context, it is worth recalling the impressive negotiations that led to the 2021 renewal of cross-border access for humanitarian assistance in Syria (UN Security Council Resolution 2585 of July 2021). Russia and

China were demanding exclusive access through the Syrian government as a way to reinforce Assad's claims to exclusive sovereign dominance. The West, led by the United States and the Europeans, sought to protect the direct cross-border access (authorized in UN Security Council Resolution 2332 of December 2016) that permitted the Syrian opposition to survive. In the end, the Security Council agreed unanimously to extend the cross-border access at one crossing point (not three) for six months (conditioned on the Syrian government permitting assistance to cross internal lines) . . . or for twelve months. The text is unclear. Indeed, the ambiguities seem to have been vital in permitting a non-vetoed outcome.[52] Although far from ideal, the result kept the Security Council together and provided a better prospect of assistance reaching the armed opposition. And that may keep open the doors for further negotiation for a political settlement in Syria. The war in Ukraine has put even this cooperation under strain, yet it continues.

But even with a Russian and Chinese response to rational stabilization, the pillars of stability will require a United States that is less vulnerable to international tension and more prepared to conduct a steadying foreign policy that avoids the erratic behavior of the Trump administration's flirtation with the autocrats and provocation toward democratic allies.

The United States itself must be made safer for a stable world.

US Reform

Ironically, the best and most productive focus of a liberal defense of national security and human rights may be inside the democratic West. Sometimes, the best defense is a good offense. But today, in response to the threats from a new cold war, the best defense is a good defense.

The first measures of defense are identifying threats to democratic stability, ensuring the integrity of electoral systems, and combatting "fake news" campaigns designed to destabilize them.[53]

Successful democracy rests on the realization of good governance through majority rule. It relies, as Jan-Werner Müller has argued well, on "political equality" and "facts" (accurate information).[54] All citizens need to count as one, and none for more or less. Elections need to be open to all relevant citizens on equal terms. Citizens need access to reliable information through a free press and public statements from accountable authorities.

Democracy, Freedom House memorably declared in its 2021 report, is "under siege."[55] Forty-five more countries declined in democracy than improved in 2020, a trend that started in 2006. One problem related to this is "truth decay." Facts, data, and analysis seem to play an ever reducing role in political and civil discourse. Technology such as Facebook and personalized news feeds offer continual access to unfiltered information of varying quality and credibility, information that often blurs the lines between fact-based evidence and argument and pure opinion.[56]

The United States has begun to address the problem of foreign interference in US elections and campaigns. "Fortunately," David Petraeus and Sheldon Whitehouse argue, "the United States has begun to take steps to harden its rule-of-law defenses and push back against foreign adversaries." They cite the Global Magnitsky Act of 2016 as a new tool for targeting corruption, but they add that the United States will go after kleptocrats, who secretly transfer funds or hide assets behind shell corporations that finance foreign interference in American democracy.[57]

Domestic threats to democratic elections also need to be addressed with significant reforms, such as those embodied in HR 1 (the "For the People Act, 2021") and HR 4 (the "John Lewis Voting Rights Advancement Act, 2021"). Both have passed the House but (in 2022) await Senate passage.

- HR 1 expands voter registration (for example, automatic and same-day registration) and voting access (for example, vote-by-mail and early voting), protects voter rolls, and mandates states to establish independent redistricting commissions to carry out congressional redistricting. In addition, the bill enhances election security and addresses campaign finance, prohibiting campaign spending by foreign nationals and calling for disclosure of campaign-related fundraising and spending. And, lastly, it strengthens safeguards for governmental ethics by prohibiting Members of the US House of Representatives from serving on the board of a for-profit entity, establishing additional conflict-of-interest and ethics provisions for federal employees and the White House, and requiring the president, the vice president, and certain candidates for those offices to disclose ten years of tax returns.[58]

- HR 4 would modernize and restore "preclearance" for voting laws that unevenly burden voters of color. It would also limit gerrymandering that allows politicians to handpick their voters and entrench their power.[59]

A second threat to democracy—even when elections are free and fair—is the condition of the electorate. To promote democratic good governance, it is important that decisions have wide support and that they reflect the long-run interests of large numbers of citizens. Promoting socioeconomic equality can build that wide middle ground and is thus also vital for democratic legitimacy and stability.[60] Practically, having a large middle class, and no extremes of deprivation or domination, means having many voters around the proverbial median voter (or median party) who typically shapes democratic governance when elections are working fairly. The normative socio-demographic bell-shaped curve illustrates this well. In addition, in large, diverse democratic republics, cross-cutting coalitions contribute, as James Madison famously argued in Federalist No. 10, to stability by requiring factions to moderate their demands to accommodate allies.

Unfortunately, the United States is eroding the root sources of democratic stability and legitimacy. The United States has experienced growing economic inequality, declining social mobility, and increasing racial religious and political divides, all playing themselves out in regional and party divisions.[61] Demographic trends exacerbate these dangers when a minority of the nation's voters (rural, white, elderly) inhabiting less populous states will have a blocking vote in the Senate. Moreover, today, with single-issue voting blocs, political coalitions seem to contribute to instability and polarization. Fundamentalists and anti-abortion voters link with rural voters, white supremacists, and the anti-taxation wealthy to create Trumpism; and minorities, the young, educated professionals, and urban voters line up with Democrats. Factions accommodate the single maximalist demands of each other. In the Republican Party, the (otherwise) socially liberal rich support anti-abortion policies and racial discrimination, as the rural poor accept the tax privileges of the wealthy. In the Democratic Party, minorities support Green New Deal policies, and urban professionals wind up supporting "woke" education. The result is a polarized polity that empowers each of the factional interests through logrolling (quid pro quo deals) and elections whose results appear existential.

A related and also alarming trend is the emergence of factions committed to white supremacy, many fearing "replacement" by minorities. A distinct faction has formed (before Trump), defined by that hostility to minorities—including Blacks, Jews, Muslims, gays, and Latinos—and a lack of commitment to democratic legitimacy. This group found Trump as their spokesman and, whatever their previous political party (most were identified as Republicans or Independents), shifted to vote for and support his divisive agenda.[62]

Lastly, socioeconomic divides have widened in ways that undermine democracy. Some reflect major shifts in the makeup of the electorate. The college educated formerly were mostly Republican; now they are mostly Democratic. GDP per Democratic congressional seat in 2008 was $39,741; per Republican congressional seat, $33,254. In 2018, for Democrats $48,502; for Republicans $32,596. The improving seats were or became Democratic; the declining seats, Republican—reflecting noticeably differing fates. Similarly, median household income for 2008 Republican seats was $55,000 and for Democratic seats $54,000. And in 2018, $53,000 for Republican seats and $61,000 for Democratic seats. Again, a significant reversal.[63]

One characteristic assessment and denunciation of the current equality thus runs as follows: "Over the past four decades, most Americans have seen wages stagnate against the cost of living. The Trump-era tax laws of 2017 legislated breaks that disproportionately benefited the rich. And we, like the medieval peasantry, are surrounded by the spectacle of high net worth individuals and their expensive adventurism. The fortunes of American billionaires grew by 70 percent in the pandemic—and as we learned this summer, some regularly pay nothing or next to nothing in taxes."[64]

This played out in the 2016 election. "Trump's supporters," Richard Reeves of the Brookings Institution has noted, "are not especially poor or suffering from free-trade policies, according to a comprehensive study by Gallup. But they are more likely to live in areas with low rates of upward mobility and shorter-than-average life expectancy. In TrumpLand, compared with the rest of America, prospects are limited and life is short."[65] Indeed, Republicans tend not to be themselves poor (they do not predominate in the bottom US quintile, and they do dominate the top quintile). But the most significant driver appears to be a neighborhood effect: They live in areas that appear to be missing out on the American dream of upward mobility.

The deeper root is the increasing inequality in the American economy as a whole that both disadvantages Trumpian districts and skews money away from the middle class. In a powerfully evocative graph, David Leonhardt has shown the diverging conditions of the poor and middle class, on the one hand, and the very richest fraction of the top 1 percent, on the other. From 1946 to 1980, the poor and middle class received the largest income growth (income, post tax and transfers), and then growth in income declined all the way to the top 1 percent, which received the least increase. From 1980 to 2014, the poor received the lowest shares, and then income grew in slowing increasing rates to the top 5 percent and then top 1 percent—a small fraction of which received by far the largest share.[66] Current trends suggest that this pattern will only get more extreme. The millennial rich and upper middle class (overwhelmingly white) will inherit the assets of their parents to become the wealthiest cohort America has ever known. Working-class millennials, meanwhile, are poised to enjoy less economic security than their parents, as their wages fail to keep pace with the rising costs of housing and health care.[67]

What is at stake are the deepest sources of American political and social resilience.

Eric Liu, the author and activist, memorably drew the comparisons with Russia and China in his sermons in *Become America*, where he wrote: "American history is a record of small groups of people who keep remaking this country over and over, and who reveal to us all that the perpetual remaking is the greatest statement of fidelity to our creed and our national purpose, which is not to be like Russia, white and stagnant and oligarchic, or like China, monoethnic and authoritarian and centralized, but to be more like America, hybrid and dynamic and democratic and free to be remade."[68]

Reforms are readily within reach. Deepening democracy in the 1960s by ending Jim Crow discrimination required civil disobedience, marches, and sit-ins with laws broken and lives put on the line. Deepening democracy today just demands political activism, turning out to vote, and defending the law. The key is making sure the benefits of globalization are shared, not monopolized by the dominant elites. An ill-founded faith in perfectly operating markets blinded the United States to the potentially adverse effects of technological automation, trade, and unregulated immigration on the less skilled and those in industries directly competing with imports. It is difficult to imagine any strategy to sustain globalization and grow national and global GDP without policies that also invest in education, repair an eroded infrastructure, boost demand for industrial skills idled by international competition, and, where needed, offer direct compensation through negative income taxes.

Recent legislation has moved in the right direction to revive the economy and sustain those who are destitute, promote opportunity, and grow the American middle class while building resilience in the face of global competition and climate change.

- The $1 trillion bipartisan infrastructure bill (The Infrastructure and Investment Act, 2021) was an important step to repair and upgrade America's physical infrastructure and the largest infusion of federal investment into infrastructure projects in more than a decade. Funding would focus on the nation's power grid and projects to better manage climate risks. Hundreds of billions of dollars would go to repairing and replacing aging public works projects. With $450 billion of already authorized and $550 billion in new federal spending, the bill would provide "$65 billion to expand high-speed Internet access; $110 billion for roads, bridges and other projects; $25 billion for airports; and the most funding for Amtrak since the passenger rail service was founded in 1971."[69]

- The CHIPS and Science Act (2022), focused on strengthening the domestic foundations of the US semiconductor industry and improving its capacity to compete with China, will secure supply chains at home.

- The Biden administration's decision in 2022 to cancel up to $10,000 of federal student debt for most borrowers (and up to $20,000 for a subset of debtors) was another step to relieve the middle class. (It is limited to those who make less than $125,000 per year, or married couples or heads of households earning less than $250,000.)

- And fourth, The Inflation Reduction Act (2022) is designed to invest in climate sustainability and improve the affordability and accessibility of health care by extending premium subsidies in the Affordable Care Act's (ACA) marketplaces and lowering prescription drug prices and out-of-pocket costs for Medicare beneficiaries.

Even together, they do not add up to the ambitious 2021 $3.5 trillion version of the bill that included universal pre-K, housing, Pell grants for low-income students, immigration reform, paid family leave, many of Biden's climate priorities, and investments in public housing, job training, and an expansion of the Affordable Care Act.[70] Especially controversial for the Republicans was the expected funding that relied on raising taxes on big corporations and wealthy Americans, something Republicans saw as a rejection of their 2017 tax cuts. The bill also added changes to immigration policy, including a pathway to citizenship for undocumented immigrants and green cards for "Dreamers"—children brought to the United States illegally—and for farmworkers.[71]

Nonetheless, modest as these steps were, they are downpayments on the foundations of long-term security. They reflect the lesson of the grim politics of the past years in both Europe and the United States that international security will not be achieved without first rebuilding the economic foundations of liberal democracy at home.

Conclusion

Statespersons around the world rightly worry that we are entering an especially difficult decade. Ideologies, political systems, and power are each clashing and the potential results are deeply uncertain. The prospect of a "decade of living dangerously"[72] shakes political Beijing and Washington, and we could add more of the same for Moscow.

The United States and its democratic liberal allies seem to be headed toward another "long twilight struggle" with China, Russia, and their autocratic allies. As shown in the previous chapters and as "fought" through cyber warfare, sabotage for profit, industrial espionage, and political subversion and destabilization, this struggle could have immense negative consequences in excess spending on arms and on missed opportunities to combat the common challenges of climate change, pandemics, and promoting a shared interest in global prosperity.

This contest is deeply rooted in the power transition now under way between China and the United States and in the domestic systems of liberal, capitalist democracies and nationalist, corporatist autocracies. Both systems see short-run benefits in confrontation against ideological adversaries. Both seek to make the world around them safe for democracy or autocracy in order to create a milieu in which they can bask in international legitimacy and avoid concerted pressure and constrained opportunities for trade and security.

Yet, as this chapter has argued, a "cold war" that challenges basic security interests by putting political independence and territorial integrity at risk is not inevitable. A "cold peace" can be envisioned. We can identify reasonable compromises over current questions in contention such as Crimea and Ukraine, Taiwan, and cyber conflict that can open the door for the cooperation elsewhere. Each side can credibly pledge that political destabilization and territorial interference are out of bounds.

Moreover, because there is no guarantee that diplomacy will achieve those compromises or that the guardrails of coexistence will hold, the United States and its allies can bolster a democratic caucus that leverages multilateral assistance. The days when such a caucus would have produced more strife than the caucus was worth are over. The strife already exists. The caucus can assemble the much-needed cooperation among the democracies to balance the coordination now occurring between Russia and China.

The most important bolster to long-run security must be found at home, for it is here that democracies are most at threat. Domestic right-wing terrorism has inflicted much more damage since 9/11 than international terrorism. The Trump putsch of January 6 may have had roots in Putin's 2016 disruption of US electoral politics, but its deepest and widest roots are thoroughly American. They link to historic racism now reignited by the increasingly multiracial character of the United States and to the increasing inequality in the US economy that has made many in the middle class feel economically disenfranchised from the hope for shared prosperity. This was further fueled under President Trump by a disdain for historic allies and a propensity to threaten and engage in military force as a form of propaganda.

Here, too, there are readily available measures that will protect the conduct of our elections from subversion, both foreign and domestic, and there are reforms in material and human infrastructure that can rebuild a dynamic middle class that has been the foundation of US democratic resilience for almost a century.

Making a world safe for America requires making an America safer from and safer for the world.

Afterword and
Acknowledgments

Thinking for this book began many years ago when I first began wondering what sort of international order the world would have after Gorbachev dismantled the Soviet empire. In 1992, Sandy Berger, having seen some of my work on democratic peace and being a distinguished advisor to and friend of President-elect Bill Clinton, encouraged me to send him and the Clinton Transition Team some thoughts. I sent two memos. One proposed a grand strategy of democratic enlargement to expand the zone of liberal democratic peace through peaceful means.[1] This elicited a short note of appreciation. The other proposed a European Treaty Organization to replace NATO and better reflect a world in which a democratizing Russia would no longer be a threat and in which Russia deserved and would benefit from equal status as a founding member of a collective security organization (no longer, as NATO was, a collective defense organization focused on an external enemy). The second memo produced silence. (I print the earlier op-ed version, written in 1990 but never published, in the endnote.)[2] Richard Ullman, a friend and mentor at Princeton University (where I was then teaching), explained the differing receptions by noting that victors don't innovate, they repeat.

Although I have been thinking about these questions for many years, the research and writing on the threat of a new cold war began in 2017 when I was asked by Mats Karlsson to talk at UI, an influential think tank in Stockholm, which he directed. The comments and suggestions I received then and in later versions delivered at the Seoul Forum for International Affairs (arranged by Shin-wha Lee), in Mexico City at the School of Global Studies, Anáhuac University (invited by Jessica de Alba-Ulloa), in Lillehammer at the Inland Norway University (invited by Lars Christie) and to colleagues in Paris were all immensely helpful in shaping my ideas. The last presentation noted was also a tribute to former prime minister Michel Rocard, someone whose statesmanship, philosophy, and association I had enjoyed with our colleagues at the Collegium International.

I published versions of those talks as "A New Cold War?," UI Paper no. 2 (June 2018), https://www.ui.se/butiken/uis-publikationer/ui-paper/2018/a-new-cold-war/; "New World Disorder," *Dissent* (Winter 2017): 123–128; and in "Un Nouveau Monde Desordonne," translation by Jean-Pierre Fournier, *Pour Michel Rocard* (Paris: Flammarion, 2018), 171–186.

I have benefited from expert research assistance by brilliant students at Columbia University in political science, the School of International and Public Affairs, and the Law School. Nathan Feldman, Theo Milonopoulos, Rachel Hulvey, Emma Borgnas, Katharine Yusko, Greg Smith, Cameron Ford Wallace, Ryan Safiry, and Hannah Houpt all labored in various ways to improve this manuscript.

My colleague Nadia Urbinati was a generous guide into the literature on Fascism and populism that she knows so well. I thank old friend and former editor Roby Harington of W. W. Norton for encouraging me to write this book and his colleagues Michael Wright and Vincent Yu of W. W. Norton for advising me on improvements throughout the writing process.

I thank the Endeavor Foundation and the Carnegie Corporation whose grants have supported my various research projects over many years. Olena Jennings, as she has many times before, assisted me with the management of the text and grants.

The last stages of editing have taken place in the lovely and comfortable confines of the WZB (the Berlin Social Science Center) whose hospitality has been outstanding and whose Global Governance group, led by Michael Zürn, has been a source of stimulating ideas. As usual, I have tried out some of these ideas on my dear wife, Amy Gutmann. She has inspired so much of my happiness and best thinking. Of course, none of the views in this book necessarily reflect her views or those of the United States Government which she now represents so impressively for the Biden Administration in Germany.

Michael Doyle
Berlin, Germany, and Philadelphia, Pennsylvania
October 2022

Notes

Introduction

1. "Gorbachev at the United Nations," C-SPAN video, 1:35:15, December 7, 1988, https://www.c-span.org/video/?5292-1/gorbachev-united-nations.

2. Chris Buckley, "The Rise and Fall of the Goddess of Democracy," Sinosphere (blog), June 1, 2014, https://sinosphere.blogs.nytimes.com/2014/06/01/the-rise-and-fall-of-the-goddess-of-democracy/.

3. John le Carré, "In the Place of Nations," *The Nation*, April 9, 2001, 13.

4. David Cornwell, "Speech Given at the Olof Prize Ceremony in Stockholm, Sweden" (January 2020), published as "John le Carré on Brexit: 'It's Breaking My Heart,'" *The Guardian*, February 1, 2020, https://www.theguardian.com/books/2020/feb/01/john-le-carre-breaking-heart-brexit.

5. Joe Biden, "Remarks by President Biden in Press Conference" (speech, Washington, DC, March 25, 2021), White House, https://www.whitehouse.gov/briefing-room/speeches-remarks/2021/03/25/remarks-by-president-biden-in-press-conference/.

6. Democracies, like autocracies, *have* imposed forcible regime changes, often as a measure to try to help a conquest hold, as was done by the US and its allies after the military defeats of Nazi Germany and Imperial Japan in 1945. But such impositions rarely succeed. Afghanistan is just the latest demonstration of this. For discussion, see among many sources my *The Question of Intervention* (New Haven, CT: Yale University Press, 2015).

7. And $350 billion in foreign aid. See Graham Allison and Gregory Treverton, eds., "National Security Portfolio Review," in *Rethinking America's Security* (New York: Norton, 1992), 40; and for Cold War wars, Paul Thomas Chamberlin, *The Cold War's Killing Fields: Rethinking the Long Peace* (New York: HarperCollins, 2019) and for casualties, Andrew Mack, "Global Trends in Armed Conflicts," *Global Political Violence* (International Peace Institute, 2007), http://www.jstor.org/stable/resrep09553.6.

PART ONE : A NEW COLD WAR?

1. Gordon Chang, "China, Losing Pakistan, Calls America and India 'Enemies,'" *Newsweek*, August 24, 2021, https://www.newsweek.com/china-losing-pakistan -calls-america-india-enemies-opinion-1622297.

Chapter One: Defining Cold War

1. "Kissinger Says U.S. and China in 'Foothills of a Cold War,'" Bloomberg News, November 21, 2019, https://www.bloomberg.com/news/articles/2019-11-21/ kissinger-says-u-s-and-china-in-foothills-of-a-cold-war.

2. "Syria Crisis: UN Chief Says Cold War Is Back," BBC News, April 13, 2018, https:// www.bbc.com/news/world-middle-east-43759873. Other prominent scholars and commentators using similar language of the "new cold war" include Robert Legvold, *Return to Cold War* (Cambridge, UK: Polity, 2016); Dmitri Treinin, "Welcome to Cold War II," *Foreign Policy,* March 4, 2014, https://foreignpolicy.com/ articles/2014/03/04/welcome_to_cold_war_ii; Kevin Rudd and Justina Crabtree, "There's an 'Undeclared New Cold War' Between the US and China—and It's in Tech, Australia Ex-Leader Says," CNBC, April 30, 2018, https://www.cnbc.com/2018/04/30/ us-and-china-in-a-cold-war-over-tech-australia-rudd-says.html.

3. Uri Friedman, "The World According to HR McMaster," *The Atlantic,* January 8, 2018, https://www.theatlantic.com/international/archive/2018/01/hr-mcmaster -trump-north-korea/549341/. McMaster also confusingly compares the world of today to pre-1914 Europe, an era notorious for "sleepwalking" complacency.

4. Lawrence Freedman, "Putin's New Cold War," *New Statesman,* March 13, 2018, https:// www.newstatesman.com/politics/uk/2018/03/putin-s-new-cold-war. For a related article on the Trump administration, see Peter Beinart, "Trump Is Preparing for a New Cold War," *The Atlantic,* February 27, 2018, https://www.theatlantic.com/international/ archive/2018/02/trump-is-preparing-for-a-new-cold-war/554384/.

5. Michael Klare, "The New Cold War Is Here—and Now 3 Major Powers Are Involved," *The Nation,* March 8, 2018, https://www.thenation.com/article/the-new -cold-war-is-here-and-now-three-major-powers-are-involved/.

6. Legvold, *Return to Cold War,* 6.

7. Alexander Cooley and Daniel Nexon, "How Hegemony Ends: The Unraveling of American Power," *Foreign Affairs,* July/August 2020, https://www.foreignaffairs.com/articles/

united-states/2020-06-09/how-hegemony-ends. Cooley and Nexon provide an insightful comparison between the unipolar 1990s and the period of tension that followed. My interpretation places the more significant inflection point at 2012 rather than in the 1990s, for the reasons noted below.

8. Kenneth Weinstein, "A New Cold War Between the US and China," *Aspen Review*, March 15, 2019, https://www.aspen.review/article/2019/new-cold-war-us-china/.

9. Noah Feldman, *Cool War: The United States, China and the Future of Global Competition* (New York: Random House, 2015); Michael McFaul, *From Cold War to Hot Peace* (Boston: Houghton Mifflin, 2018).

10. John Haltiwanger, "Blinken Refuses to Call Biden's Superpower Competition with China a 'New Cold War,'" *Business Insider*, May 4, 2021, https://www.businessinsider.com/blinken-refuses-call-biden-us-china-competition-new-cold-war-2021-5.

11. Antony Blinken, "The Administration's Approach to the People's Republic of China" (speech, The George Washington University, Washington, DC, May 26, 2022).

12. McFaul, *From Cold War to Hot Peace*. This led to one scholar developing the concept of "hot peace" where two or more states each accept each other's political independence and territorial integrity but nonetheless clash in minor conflicts, often in the "peripheral" world in colonial campaigns.

13. Walter Lippman, *The Cold War: A Study in U.S. Foreign Policy* (New York: Harper, 1947), 29–31. Curiously, nostalgic as he was for the prewar European balance of power, Lippman's critique of containment was close to the views that Kennan himself would later advocate.

14. Paul Chamberlin, *The Cold War's Killing Fields: Rethinking the Long Peace* (New York: HarperCollins, 2019). But note the Cold War involved extensive conflict, including proxy wars, in the peripheries.

15. Derek McKay and H. M. Scott, *The Rise of Great Powers: 1648-1815* (London: Longman, 1983), 126. McKay and Scott in their widely read text describe the contentious relations between France and Britain, on the one hand, and Austria and Spain, on the other, in the 1720s as a "Cold War in Europe, 1724-1728."

16. See, for example, Stephen Walt, *Revolution and War* (Ithaca, NY: Cornell University Press, 1996).

17. I offered an interpretation of this liberal peace in a set of paired essays in 1983 in *Philosophy and Public Affairs*. For a valuable debate on the issue, see Michael E. Brown, Sean Lynn-Jones, and Steven E. Miller, eds., *Debating the Democratic Peace* (Cambridge, MA: MIT Press, 1996).

18. Samuel Charap and Timothy J. Colton, "Cold Peace," in *Everyone Loses: The Ukraine Crisis and the Ruinous Contest for Post-Soviet Eurasia* (London: Routledge, 2017), copy at http://www.tinyurl.com/y3hj93z4. "Cold peace" is used differently by Charap and Colton to describe the lose-lose outcome of the 2014 conflict over Ukraine.

19. Charap and Colton, "Cold Peace."

20. White House, *National Security Strategy of the United States of America* (Washington, DC, 2017), https://trumpwhitehouse.archives.gov/wp-content/uploads/2017/12/

NSS-Final-12-18-2017-0905.pdf. There is no evidence that President Trump read the document he signed, with implications as discussed below. On the other hand, it closely reflects the known views of his then national security advisor, the eminent military intellectual, Gen. H. R. McMaster.

21. White House, *National Security Strategy*, 1–2.

22. Kenneth Waltz, *Theory of International Politics* (Long Grove, IL: Waveland Press, 1979).

23. Henry John Temple, "Treaty of Adrianople—Charges Against Viscount Palmerston" (speech, London, March 1, 1848), Hansard, https://api.parliament.uk/historic-hansard/commons/1848/mar/01/treaty-of-adrianople-charges-against. One of the attractive features of Palmerston's speeches was that they were so inconsistent: quotable for every purpose, including this one. Am I right to say that inconsistency is attractive? For a more complex and contextualized discussion of Palmerston's foreign policy, see Jasper Ridley's sympathetic and magisterial biography *Lord Palmerston* (London: Constable, 1970) and my *Question of Intervention* (New Haven, CT: Yale University Press, 2015) for Palmerston's strategy for intervention in Portugal in 1846.

24. Jeffrey Goldberg, "A Senior White House Official Defines the Trump Doctrine: 'We're America, Bitch,'" *The Atlantic*, June 11, 2018, https://www.theatlantic.com/politics/archive/2018/06/a-senior-white-house-official-defines-the-trump-doctrine-were-america-bitch/562511/.

25. Dexter Filkins, "John Bolton on the Warpath," *New Yorker*, April 29, 2019, https://www.newyorker.com/magazine/2019/05/06/john-bolton-on-the-warpath. It should be noted that this is a caricature of Hobbes's much more subtle and reasoned doctrine, as I argue in *Ways of War and Peace* (New York: Norton, 1997).

26. Richard Haass and Charles Kupchan, "The New Concert of Powers: How to Prevent Catastrophe and Promote Stability in a Multipolar World," *Foreign Affairs*, March 23, 2021, https://www.foreignaffairs.com/articles/world/2021-03-23/new-concert-powers.

27. Ludwig Dehio, *The Precarious Balance* (New York: Vintage, 1965).

28. Henry A. Kissinger, "The Congress of Vienna: A Reappraisal," *World Politics* 8, no. 2 (January 1956): 279, https://www.jstor.org/stable/2008974.

29. Harold Nicolson, *The Congress of Vienna—A Study in Allied Unity: 1812–1822* (New York: Grove, 2001), 260.

30. Charles Lipson, "Is the Future of Collective Security Like the Past?," in *Collective Security Beyond the Cold War*, ed. George W. Downs (Ann Arbor: University of Michigan Press, 1994), 121–122.

31. Lipson, "Future of Collective Security," 120.

32. Henry A. Kissinger, *A World Restored* (Boston: Houghton Mifflin, 1957; repr. Gainesville, FL: Peter Smith, 1973), 328–329. Citations refer to the Peter Smith edition.

33. Joe Biden, "My Trip to Europe Is About America Rallying the World's Democracies," *Washington Post*, June 5, 2021, https://www.washingtonpost.com/opinions/2021/06/05/joe-biden-europe-trip-agenda/.

34. Charles VI went to the trouble of securing "The Pragmatic Sanction of 1713" in order to legitimize his daughter's claim to her Austrian inheritance over the claims of his nieces, who formally preceded her.

35. For general sources, see Patrice Louis-René Higonnet, "The Origins of the Seven Years' War," *Journal of Modern History* 40, no. 1 (March 1968): 57–90, https://doi.org/10 .1086/240165; Walter Dorn, *Competition for Empire, 1740-1763*, vol. 9, ed. William L. Langer (New York: Harper & Brothers, 1940). And Henry Kissinger drew similar distinctions in his landmark interpretation of the Congress of Vienna, where he drew distinctions between legitimate and revolutionary international systems. Robert Tucker made a similar point when he distinguished contests over who ruled from contests over what the rules should be. See Kissinger, *A World Restored*; Robert W. Tucker, *The Inequality of Nations* (New York: Basic Books, 1977).

36. Zbigniew Brzezinski and Samuel P. Huntington, *Political Power: USA/USSR* (New York: Viking Press, 1964). See also the archbishop's notorious speech before Henry V in Shakespeare's *Henry V*. William Shakespeare, *King Henry V*, 3rd ed. (London: Arden Shakespeare, 1995).

37. Fredrik Logevall, *JFK: Coming of Age in the American Century, 1917–1956* (New York: Random House, 2021), 221. And prior to that of course Stalin (to avoid becoming the isolated target) and Hitler formed the Nazi-Soviet Pact in 1939, prodding one British wag to remark, "All the isms are now wasms."

38. Quoted in Nigel Hamilton's excellent history of the war, *Commander in Chief: FDR's Battle with Churchill* (New York: Houghton Mifflin, 2016), 393.

39. "Declaration of the Constitution of the Soviet Union of 1924," *Vestnik TsIK, SNK i STO Soiuza SSR*, no. 2 (1924): art. 24, quoted in Milton H. Andrew, *Twelve Leading Constitutions with Their Historical Backgrounds* (Compton, CA: American University Series, 1931), 327.

40. For important background to the article, see John Gaddis, *George F. Kennan: An American Life* (New York: Penguin, 2011). See especially chap. 12, "Mr. X: 1947."

41. *NSC 68: United States Objectives and Programs for National Security* (Washington, DC: National Security Council, 1950), https://digitalarchive.wilsoncenter.org/ document/116191.pdf.

42. Office of Legislative Counsel, *Memorandum Re: Constitutional and Legal Basis for So-Called Covert Activities of the Central Intelligence Agency* (Washington, DC: Department of Justice, 1962), 7, https://s3.documentcloud.org/documents/5836225/73-1501862.pdf.

Chapter Two: Cold War II?

1. David E. Sanger, *The Perfect Weapon: War, Sabotage, and Fear in the Cyber Age* (New York: Broadway Books, 2019); Joseph S. Nye, "Is Deterrence Possible in Cyberspace?," *International Security* 42, no. 2 (2017): 196–199, https://doi.org/10.1162/ISEC_c_00290.

2. Michael C. Horowitz, "Do Emerging Military Technologies Matter for International Politics?," *Annual Review of Political Science* 23 (2020): 385–400, https://doi.org/10.1146/ annurev-polisci-050718-032725. It is worth remembering that millions of cyberattacks occur every day around the world but, unlike kinetic uses of force, both governments and non-state actors use cyberweapons for various purposes that do not always fit neatly into our traditional understandings of weapons.

3. Center for Strategic and International Studies (CSIS), *Significant Cyber Incidents Since*

2006, https://csis-websiteprod.s3.amazonaws.com/s3fspublic/210604_Significant_ Cyber_Events.pdf.

4. Henry Farrell and Abraham L. Newman, "Weaponized Interdependence: How Global Economic Networks Shape State Coercion," *International Security* 44, no. 1 (2019): 42–79, https://doi.org/10.1162/isec_a_00351. Growing interdependence creates the possibility for great powers to have strategic vantage points over Internet exchange points and technology firms, where most of the world's traffic collides.

5. David E. Sanger, Nicole Perlroth, and Julian E. Barnes, "As Understanding of Russian Hacking Grows, So Does Alarm," *New York Times*, last modified May 28, 2021, https://www.nytimes.com/2021/01/02/us/politics/russian-hacking-government.html.

6. Monique Beals, "New Report Uncovers Massive Chinese Hacking of Trade Secrets," *The Hill*, May 4, 2022. Chinese state spokespersons denied the hack.

7. Michael Schwartz and Nicole Perlroth, "DarkSide, Blamed for Gas Pipeline Attack, Says It Is Shutting Down," *New York Times*, last modified June 8, 2021, https://www.nytimes.com/2021/05/14/business/darkside-pipeline-hack.html; Stephanie Kelly and Jessica Resnick-ault, "One Password Allowed Hackers to Disrupt Colonial Pipeline, CEO Tells Senators," Reuters, June 8, 2021, https://www.reuters.com/business/colonial-pipeline-ceo-tells-senate-cyber-defenses-were-compromised-ahead-hack-2021-06-08/.

8. "JBS: FBI Says Russia-Linked Group Hacked Meat Supplier," BBC News, June 3, 2021, https://www.bbc.com/news/world-us-canada-57338896; Rebecca Robbins, "Meat Processor JBS Paid $11 Million in Ransom to Hackers," *New York Times*, June 9, 2021, https://www.nytimes.com/2021/06/09/business/jbs-cyberattack-ransom.html.

9. See "Our Country Is Being Attacked," *New York Times*, June 11, 2021, https://www.nytimes.com/2021/06/11/podcasts/ransomware-hacking.html; Julian E. Barnes, "Russia Influences Hackers but Stops Short of Directing Them, Report Says," *New York Times*, September 9, 2021, https://www.nytimes.com/2021/09/09/us/politics/russia-ransomware-hackers.html.

10. Kim Zetter, "How Digital Detectives Deciphered Stuxnet, the Most Menacing Malware in History," *Wired*, July 11, 2011, https://www.wired.com/2011/07/how-digital-detectives-deciphered-stuxnet/.

11. Andy Greenberg, "How an Entire Nation Became Russia's Test Lab for Cyberwar," *Wired*, June 20, 2017, https://www.wired.com/story/russian-hackers-attack-ukraine/; Kim Zetter, "Inside the Cunning, Unprecedented Hack of Ukraine's Power Grid," *Wired*, March 3, 2016, https://www.wired.com/2016/03/inside-cunning-unprecedented-hack-ukraines-power-grid/; Paul Shinkman, "Russia Ramps Up Cyberattacks in Ukraine Amid Fears of War," *US News & World Report*, April 20, 2021, https://www.usnews.com/news/world-report/articles/2021-04-20/us-helping-ukraine-foil-russian-cyberattacks-as-hacking-spikes-sources.

12. Abigail Abrams, "Here's What We Know So Far About Russia's 2016 Meddling," *Time*, April 18, 2019, https://time.com/5565991/russia-influence-2016-election/; Nicole Perlroth, Michael Wines, and Matthew Rosenberg, "Russian Election Hacking Efforts,

Wider than Previously Known, Draw Little Scrutiny," *New York Times*, September 1, 2017, https://www.nytimes.com/2017/09/01/us/politics/russia-election-hacking.html; "Twelve Russians Charged with US 2016 Election Hack," BBC News, July 13, 2018, https://www.bbc.com/news/world-us-canada-44825345; Alex Ward, "Russia Hacked Voting Systems in 39 States Before the 2016 Presidential Election," *Vox*, June 13, 2017, https://www.vox.com/world/2017/6/13/15791744/russia-election-39-states-hack-putin -trump-sessions.

13. "Global Threats and National Security," C-SPAN video, 2:40:39, February 13, 2018, https://www.c-span.org/video/?440888-1/fbi-director-rob-porter-background-check -completed-july.

14. Luke Harding, Julian Borger, and Dan Sabbagh, "Kremlin Papers Appear to Show Putin's Plot to Put Trump in White House," *The Guardian*, July 15, 2021, https:// www.theguardian.com/world/2021/jul/15/kremlin-papers-appear-to-show-putins -plot-to-put-trump-in-white-house.

15. Kathleen Hall Jamieson, "How Russia Cyber Attacks Helped Trump to the US Presidency," *The Guardian*, October 22, 2018, https://www.theguardian.com/ commentisfree/2018/oct/22/russia-cyber-theft-trump-us-election-president-clinton.

16. Bill Whitaker, "When Russian Hackers Targeted the US Election Infrastruc-ture," *CBS News*, April 8, 2018, https://www.cbsnews.com/news/when-russian -hackers-targeted-the-u-s-election-infrastructure/.

17. Michael Wines, "Russian Breached Florida County Computers Before 2016 Elec-tion, Mueller Report Says," *New York Times*, April 18, 2019, https://www.nytimes .com/2019/04/18/us/florida-russia-2016-election-hacking.html.

18. Rachel Smith, "Sounding the Alarm About a New Russian Cyber Threat," NPR, April 24, 2018; see "Alert (TA 18-106a): Russian State-Sponsored Cyber Actors Targeting Net-work Infrastructure Device," Cybersecurity & Infrastructure Security Agency, 2018, https://www.cisa.gov/uscert/ncas/alerts/TA18-106A.

19. Mark Landler and Stephen Castle, "'No One' Protected British Democracy from Russia, U.K. Report Concludes," *New York Times*, July 21, 2020, https://www.nytimes .com/2020/07/21/world/europe/uk-russia-report.html?referringSource=articleShare.

20. Jean-Baptiste Jeangene Vilmer, A. Escorcia, M. Guillaume, and J. Herrera, *Information Manipulation: A Challenge for Our Democracies* (Paris: Policy Planning Staff [CAPS] of the Ministry for Europe and Foreign Affairs and the Institute for Strategic Research [IRSEM] of the Ministry for the Armed Forces, 2018).

21. Andrew Desiderio, "Senate Intel Chair Privately Warned That GOP's Biden Probe Could Help Russia," *Politico*, February 27, 2020, https://www.politico.com/news/2020/02/27/ richard-burr-joe-biden-probe-russia-118025.

22. Zolan Kanno-Youngs, "Cyberwarfare Is Top Threat Facing US, Nielsen Says," *New York Times*, March 19, 2019, https://www.nytimes.com/2019/03/18/todayspaper/ quotation-of-the-day-cyberwarfare-is-top-threat-facing-us-nielsen-says.html. The administration then proposed an $86 billon budget for cyberweapons for the upcom-ing year, a 6 percent rise, in a budget cutting domestic programs. The single most

thorough report on the wider scope of Russian cyber operations throughout Europe is Vilmer et al., *Information Manipulation*.

23. CSIS, *Significant Cyber Incidents Since 2006*.

24. Michael Schwartz, "Top Secret Russian Unit Seeks to Destabilize Europe, Security Officials Say," *New York Times*, October 8, 2019, https://www.nytimes.com/2019/10/08/world/europe/unit-29155-russia-gru.html.

25. David Sanger and Nicole Pertroth, "Russia Appears to Carry Out Hack Through System Used by U.S. Aid Agency," *New York Times*, May 28, 2021, https://www.nytimes.com/2021/05/28/us/politics/russia-hack-usaid.html.

26. Jocelyn Grzeszczak, "Biden Says Russia and China Are Trying to Undermine U.S. Elections," *Newsweek*, July 18, 2020, https://www.newsweek.com/biden-says-russia-/china-are-engaging-undermine-us-elections-1518872.

27. "Statement by the North Atlantic Council in Solidarity with Those Affected by Recent Malicious Cyber Activities Including the Microsoft Exchange Server Compromise" (Brussels: North Atlantic Treaty Organization, 2021), https://www.nato.int/cps/en/natohq/news_185863.htm.

28. Zolan Kanno-Youngs and David Sanger, "US Accuses China of Hacking Microsoft," *New York Times*, July 19, 2021, https://www.nytimes.com/2021/07/19/us/politics/microsoft-hacking-china-biden.html.

29. Nicole Perlroth and David Sanger, "China Breached Dozens of Pipeline Companies in Past Decade, US Says," *New York Times*, July 20, 2021, https://www.nytimes.com/2021/07/20/us/politics/china-hacking-pipelines.html.

30. "Worldwide Threats Briefing: 5 Takeaways, from Russia to China," *Wired*, February 2, 2018, https://www.wired.com/story/worldwide-threats-briefing-russia-election-china/. The January 2020 preliminary trade agreement with China includes provisions in which China pledges to curb these practices in the future.

31. *Survey of Chinese Espionage in the United States Since 2000*, Center for Strategic & International Studies, 2022, https://www.csis.org/programs/technology-policy-program/survey-chinese-linked-espionage-united-states-2000.

32. Matt Apuzzo and Benjamin Novak, "Russian Banks Welcome in Hungary Stirs Spy Fears," *New York Times*, March 19, 2019, https://www.nytimes.com/2019/03/18/world/europe/hungary-russian-bank-spy-orban-putin.html.

33. Bob Davis, "US Chip Makers Fear Trap in a Trade Deal with China," *Wall Street Journal*, March 19, 2019, https://www.wsj.com/articles/u-s-chip-industry-cool-on-chinese-purchase-offer-11552936389.

34. Amy Qin, "China's New Rules Could Hit U.S. Firms and Send a Message to Biden," *New York Times*, January 9, 2021, https://www.nytimes.com/2021/01/09/business/china-rules-trump-biden-sanctions.html.

35. U.S. House Permanent Select Committee on Intelligence, *The China Deep Dive: A Report on the Intelligence Community's Capabilities and Competencies with Respect to the People's Republic of China*, September 2020, 5.

36. UN Security Council Report, *Syria: Humanitarian Briefing via VTC*, What's In Blue

(blog), June 27, 2020, https://www.securitycouncilreport.org/whatsinblue/2020/06/ syria-humanitarian-meeting-via-vtc.php. The UN Board of Inquiry found that it was "highly probable" that four attacks on medical facilities were "carried out by the Government of Syria and/or its allies [signifying Russia]." Speaking to the Security Council on June 16, 2019, Russian Permanent Representative Vassily Nebenzia spoke at length about the report's findings, concluding that Russia's "analysis of the summary of the [BOI] report leads to one more conclusion: the deconflicting mechanism has more than just gaps—to put it mildly—but it is used for misinformation" and the board itself had been created on the basis of "false data." See also Charlie Savage, Eric Schmitt, and Michael Schwirtz, "Russia Secretly Offered Afghan Militants Bounties to Kill U.S. Troops, Intelligence Says," *New York Times*, June 26, 2020, https://www.nytimes .com/2020/06/26/us/politics/russia-afghanistan-bounties.html.

37.   Clifford D. May and H. R. McMaster, "Future Wars: A Conversation with H. R. McMaster," March 4, 2019, in *Foreign Podicy*, produced by Foundation for the Defense of Democracies, podcast, MP3 audio, 00:06:38—00:07:00, https://www.fdd.org/ analysis/2019/03/04/future-wars-featuring-h-r-mcmaster/.

38.   Kevin Rudd, "Beware the Guns of August—in Asia: How to Keep U.S.-Chinese Tensions from Sparking a War," *Foreign Affairs*, August 3, 2020, https://www.foreignaffairs.com/ articles/united-states/2020-08-03/beware-guns-august-asia.

39.   Senators Michael Bennet et al. to Executive Officials Michael Pompeo et al. (letter), June 8, 2018, https://www.rubio.senate.gov/public/_cache/files/e191e7b0-e562 -450d-b4d8-2b958c489130/60A010F8B76E93F482F6678EF444085B.chinese -influence-operations-without-footnotes-1-.pdf. "Public assessments from our intelligence community, independent researchers and representatives of allied governments illustrate the tools China systematically employs in its influence activities. Organizations and individuals linked to the Chinese Communist Party (CCP) use financial ties to political elites, propaganda filtered through local media outlets and academic institutions, highly managed cultural events, and even coercion of nationals of Chinese ancestry to manipulate democratic political environments to serve China's interests. The CCP's long-term objectives with these operations are to undermine liberal democracies, erode the strength of US alliances, weaken the ability of democracies to work against China, supplant U.S. leadership in the world and shape the future of the international order." The letter is co-signed by US senators Michael Bennet (D-Colo.), Sherrod Brown (D-Ohio), Catherine Cortez Masto (D-Nev.), Ted Cruz (R-Texas), Cory Gardner (R-Colo.), Angus King (I-Maine), Ed Markey (D-Mass.), Jeff Merkley (D-Ore.), Gary Peters (D-Mich.), Marco Rubio (R-Fla.), and Elizabeth Warren (D-Mass.).

40.   Kinling Lo, "China Calls on Russia to Hold the Line Against 'US Perverse Acts,'" *South China Morning Post*, June 5, 2021, https://www.scmp.com/news/china/diplomacy/ article/3136187/china-calls-russia-hold-line-again-us-perverse-acts.

41.   Tony Munroe, Andrew Osborn, and Humeyra Pamuk, "China, Russia Partner Up Against West at Olympics Summit," Reuters, February 4, 2022, https://www.reuters.com/world/

europe/russia-china-tell-nato-stop-expansion-moscow-backs-beijing-taiwan-2022-02
-04/.

42. Marc Bennetts, "Putin and Xi Plot a New World Order to Challenge America's Might," *Sunday Times*, September 13, 2022.

43. "Summit for Democracy Summary of Proceedings," White House Briefing Room, press release, December 23, 2021, https://www.whitehouse.gov/briefing-room/ statements-releases/2021/12/23/summit-for-democracy-summary-of-proceedings/.

44. Lingling Wei and Bob Davis, "China's Message to America: We're an Equal Now," *Wall Street Journal*, April 13, 2021, https://www.wsj.com/articles/america-china-policy -biden-xi-11617896117.

45. Eric Schmitt, "Russia's Military Mission Creep Advances to a New Front: Africa," *New York Times*, March 31, 2019, https://www.nytimes.com/2019/03/31/world/africa/ russia-military-africa.html.

46. "Kremlin Aide to Chair Organizing Committee for 2019 Russia-Africa Summit," *Tass*, February 25, 2019, https://tass.com/world/1046329.

47. Dionne Searcey, "Gems, Warlords and Mercenaries: Russia's Playbook in Central African Republic," *New York Times*, September 30, 2019, https://www.nytimes.com/2019/09/30/ world/russia-diamonds-africa-prigozhin.html.

48. Damien Cave, "Why a Chinese Security Deal in the Pacific Could Ripple Through the World," *New York Times*, April 22, 2022, https://www.nytimes.com/2022/04/20/world/ australia/china-solomon-islands-security-pact.html.

49. Kalinga Seneviratne, "COVID-19: Bio-Warfare Conspiracy Theories Need Investigation," *InDepth News*, March 26, 2020, https://www.indepthnews.net/index.php/sustainability/ health-well-being/3411-covid-19-bio-warfare-conspiracy-theories-need-investigation.

50. Javier Hernandez, "China Peddles Falsehoods to Obscure Origin of Covid Pandemic," *New York Times*, December 6, 2020, https://www.nytimes.com/2020/12/06/world/asia/ china-covid-origin-falsehoods.html.

51. Joseph Biden, *Interim National Security Strategic Guidance: March 2021* (Washington, DC: White House, 2021), https://www.whitehouse.gov/wp-content/uploads/2021/03/ NSC-1v2.pdf.

52. Andrew Desiderio, "Senate Advances a Rare Bipartisan Deal on Countering China," *Politico*, May 17, 2021, https://web.archive.org/web/20210610141333/https:/www .politico.com/news/2021/05/17/senate-bipartisan-deal-countering-china-489152.

53. John Haltiwanger, "China Blasts US Bill Aimed at Challenging Its Growing Global Influ-ence as 'full of Cold War Mentality,'" *Business Insider*, June 9, 2021, https:/www.business insider.com/china-blasts-us-global-competition-bill-full-cold-war-mentality-2021-6.

54. Amanda Macias and Kayla Tausche, "U.S. Needs to Work with Europe to Slow China's Innovation Rate, Raimondo Says," CNBC, September 28, 2021, https://www.cnbc.com/2021/09/28/us-needs-to-work-with-europe-to-slow -chinas-innovation-rate-raimondo-says.html.

55. But military assistance to the direct parties was massive and significant: In November 1968, the Soviet Union and North Vietnam signed military and economic agreements

in which the USSR agreed to supply deliveries of food, petroleum, transportation equipment, iron and steel, other metals, fertilizers, arms, munitions, and other commodities. Chinese aid to North Vietnam between 1950 and 1970 was estimated at $20 billion. Of course, the United States provided even larger quantities of aid to South Korea and South Vietnam while fighting directly on their side. Moreover, the USSR fought to support its clients in Afghanistan while the United States provided large quantities of weapons—most famously Stingers—to the Afghan resistance.

56. Joe Biden, State of the Union Address (speech, Washington, DC, March 1, 2022), White House, https://www.whitehouse.gov/state-of-the-union-2022/.

57. Resolution adopted by the European Parliament on March 12, 2019, with 402 votes in favor of it, 163 against, and 89 abstentions. See "European Parliament Resolution of 12 March 2019 on the State of EU-Russia Political Relations," Voltaire Network, March 12, 2019, https://www.voltairenet.org/article205701.html.

58. Matt Clinch, "Afghanistan Pullout Sparks EU Calls for More Military Might," CNBC, September 4, 2021, https://www.cnbc.com/2021/09/04/commissioner-gentiloni -on-eu-army-after-afghanistan-conclusion.html.

59. Paul Charon and Jean-Baptiste Jeangène Vilmer, *Les Opérations d'influence chinoises. Un moment machiavélien* (Paris: Ministère des Armées, 2021).

60. Silvia Amaro, "'Russianization' of China? French Military Think Tank Says Beijing Borrowing from Moscow Playbook," CNBC, September 29, 2021, https://www.cnbc .com/2021/09/29/french-military-think-tank-warns-of-beijing-russia-like-global -influence-.html.

61. Anatoly Kurmanaev, "Russia Stands with Maduro (While Hedging Bets)," *New York Times*, March 8, 2019, https://www.nytimes.com/2019/03/08/world/americas/ russia-venezuela-maduro-putin.html.

62. Katie Rogers, "US Revokes More Visas from Allies of Maduro," *New York Times*, March 8, 2019, https://www.nytimes.com/2019/03/07/world/americas/us-venezuela-visas.html.

63. David Smith and Sabrina Siddiqui, "New Details of Russia Election Hacking Raise Questions About Obama's Response," *The Guardian*, June 23, 2017, https://www .theguardian.com/us-news/2017/jun/23/obama-cia-warning-russia-election-hack -report.

64. Zach Dorfman, Kim Zetter, Jenna McLaughlin, and Sean D. Naylor, "Exclusive: Secret Trump Order Gives CIA More Powers to Launch Cyberattacks," *Yahoo! News*, July 15, 2020, https://news.yahoo.com/secret-trum-order-gives-cia-more -powers-to-launch-cyberattacks-090015219.html.

65. Lucian Kim, "Trump Vs. Biden: How Russia Sees the U.S. Election," NPR, October 14, 2020, https://www.npr.org/2020/10/14/923380941/trump-vs-biden-how-russia -sees-the-u-s-election.

66. Paulina Dedaj, "China Slams NBC for Airing 'Incomplete' Map During Olympic Coverage," *Fox News,* July 24, 2021, https://www.foxnews.com/sports/china-nbc -incomplete-map-olympic-coverage.

67. Kari Soo Lindberg, "China Lists 102 Examples of U.S. 'Interference' in Hong

Kong," Bloomberg, September 24, 2021, https://www.bloomberg.com/news/articles/2021-09-24/china-lists-102-examples-of-u-s-interference-in-hong-kong.

68. Joseph Biden, "Remarks Before the 76th Session of the United Nations General Assembly," (speech, New York, NY, September 21, 2021), https://www.whitehouse.gov/briefing-room/speeches-remarks/2021/09/21/remarks-by-president-biden-before-the-76th-session-of-the-united-nations-general-assembly/.

69. It should be mentioned that US support was especially confused and ineffective, attacking Assad's main rival (ISIS) while supporting Assad's opposition.

70. Andrew Roth, "Putin Threatens US Arms Race with New Missiles Declaration," *The Guardian*, March 1, 2018, https://www.theguardian.com/world/2018/mar/01/vladimir-putin-threatens-arms-race-with-new-missiles-announcement. And Keir Giles describes cyber and info war in *The Next Phase of Russian Information Warfare* (Riga, Latvia: NATO Strategic Communications Centre of Excellence, 2016), https://stratcomcoe.org/publications/the-next-phase-of-russian-information-warfare/176. And Brad Lendon, "China Boosts Military Spending 8% Amidst Ambitious Modernization Drive," CNN, March 5, 2018, https://www.cnn.com/2018/03/04/asia/chinese-military-budget-intl/index.html.

71. Julian Barnes and David Sanger, "Russia Deploys Hypersonic Weapon, Potentially Renewing Arms Race," *New York Times*, December 27, 2019, https://www.nytimes.com/2019/12/27/us/politics/russia-hypersonic-weapon.html.

72. For an enlightening discussion of how EU experts see the "return of great power rivalry," see European Political Strategy Centre, *Geopolitical Outlook for Europe: Confrontation vs Cooperation* (Brussels: European Commission, 2018), https://op.europa.eu/en/publication-detail/-/publication/97534e02-10dc-11ea-8c1f-01aa75ed71a1/language-en.

73. Gerry Shih, "China Is Trying to Mend Fences in Europe. It's Not Going Well," *Washington Post*, September 2, 2020, https://www.washingtonpost.com/world/asia_pacific/china-europe-relations-us/2020/09/02/63d963e0-ece1-11ea-bd08-1b10132b458f_story.html.

74. Biden, "Remarks Before the 76th Session of the United Nations General Assembly."

75. The most thoughtful argument I have read along these lines is Thomas Christensen, "There Will Not Be a New Cold War: The Limits of US Chinese Competition," *Foreign Affairs*, March 24, 2021, https://www.foreignaffairs.com/articles/united-states/2021-03-24/there-will-not-be-new-cold-war.

76. James Dobbins, Howard J. Shatz, and Ali Wyne, *Russia Is a Rogue, Not a Peer; China Is a Peer, Not a Rogue: Different Challenges, Different Responses* (Santa Monica, CA: RAND Corporation, 2019), https://www.rand.org/pubs/perspectives/PE310.html.

77. Dobbins, Shatz, and Wyne, *Russia Is a Rogue*.

78. For a good survey of what "authoritarian international law" looks like in comparison to liberal international law, see Tom Ginsburg, "Authoritarian International Law?," *American Journal of International Law* 114, no. 2 (2020): 221–260, https://doi.org/10.1017/ajil.2020.3.

79. This point is argued persuasively by Thomas Christensen, *No New Cold War: Why the US Strategic Competition Will Not Be Like the US-Soviet Cold War* (Seoul: Asan Institute for Policy Studies, 2020).

80. Robert Legvold, *Return to Cold War* (Cambridge, UK: Polity, 2016), 43–46.

81. Hannah Beach, Abdi Atif Dahir, and Oscar Lopez, "With Us or with Them? In a New Cold War, How About Neither," *New York Times*, April 24, 2022, https://www.nytimes.com/2022/04/24/world/asia/cold-war-ukraine.html.

82. This section benefited from the suggestions of Nathan Feldman.

83. This section draws on an unpublished research memorandum by Michael Doyle, Alicia Evangelides, and Christopher Kaoutzanis prepared for the Multilateralism Project of the International Peace Institute (2016), on file with the authors. For another thoughtful, much more extensive account along these lines, see Richard Haass, *A World in Disarray: American Foreign Policy and the Crisis of the Old Order* (New York: Penguin, 2017).

84. Horizontal inequalities are financial inequalities divided along demographic lines—race, religion, ethnicity, or region. For information about the political, social, and economic consequences of extreme inequalities, see Michael W. Doyle and Joseph E. Stiglitz, "Eliminating Extreme Inequality: A Sustainable Development Goal, 2015-2030," *Ethics and International Affairs* 28, no. 1 (March 2014): 5–13.

85. Khalid Koser and Frank Laczko, *World Migration Report 2010* (Geneva: International Organization for Migration, 2010), 3, https://publications.iom.int/system/files/pdf/wmr_2010_english.pdf.

86. United Nations High Commissioner for Refugees, "Situations: Syria," https://data.unhcr.org/en/situations/syria.

87. Michèle Griffin, "The UN's Role in a Changing Global Landscape," in *The Oxford Handbook on the United Nations*, ed. Thomas Weiss and Sam Daws (Oxford: Oxford University Press, 2018), 2:827–828.

88. *Resilient People, Resilient Planet: A Future Worth Choosing; The Report of the United Nations Secretary-General's High-Level Panel on Global Sustainability* (New York: United Nations, 2012), 11, http://www.acp.int/sites/acpsec.waw.be/files/GSP_Report_web_final.pdf.

89. John Mueller, *Overblown: How Politicians and the Terrorism Industry Inflate National Security Threats, and Why We Believe Them* (New York: Free Press, 2006); and John Mueller, *Chasing Ghosts: The Policing of Terrorism* (New York: Oxford University Press, 2016).

90. Edith Lederer, "Russia Spars with EU and US at Meeting on EU-UN Cooperation," Associated Press, June 11, 2021, https://apnews.com/article/joe-biden-russia-united-nations-middle-east-health-ea6635f5fbb0e33287519be62fb21213.

91. Ellen Nakashima, "The US Is Urging a No Vote on Russian-Led UN Resolution Calling for Global Cybercrime Treaty," *Washington Post*, November 15, 2019, https://www.washingtonpost.com/national-security/the-us-is-urging-a-no-vote-on-a-russian-led-un-resolution-calling-for-a-global-cybercrime-treaty/2019/11/16/b4895e76-075e-11ea-818c-fcc65139e8c2_story.html.

92. Security Council Report, *DPRK (North Korea): Yesterday's Vote on a Sanctions*

Resolution, What's In Blue, May 26, 2022, https://www.securitycouncilreport.org/whatsinblue/2022/05/dprk-north-korea-yesterdays-vote-on-a-sanctions-resolution.php.

93. Julian E. Barnes and Michael Venutolo-Mantovani, "Race for Coronavirus Vaccine Pits Spy Against Spy,' *New York Times*, September 5, 2020, https://www.nytimes.com/2020/09/05/us/politics/coronavirus-vaccine-espionage.html.

94. "Gorbachev at the United Nations," C-SPAN video, 1:35:15, December 7, 1988, https://www.c-span.org/video/?5292-1/gorbachev-united-nations.

95. Kristine Lee and Alexander Sullivan, *People's Republic of the United Nations: China's Emerging Revisionism in International Organizations* (Washington, DC: Center for a New American Security, 2019), 4.

96. David Lawler, "The 53 Countries Supporting China's Crackdown on Hong Kong," Axios, July 3, 2020, https://www.axios.com/2020/07/02/countries-supporting-china-hong-kong-law.

97. UN General Assembly Resolution 75/277 (May 18, 2021).

98. See Hernandez, "China Peddles Falsehoods."

99. See Richard Gowan, "Three Troubling Trends at the UN Security Council," International Crisis Group, November 6, 2019, https://www.crisisgroup.org/global/three-troubling-trends-un-security-council; Richard Gowan, "UN Peacekeeping in a Fragmenting International Order," International Crisis Group, December 9, 2020, https://www.crisisgroup.org/global/un-peacekeeping-fragmenting-international-order.

100. Michelle Ye Hee Lee, "China Draws North Korea Closer than Ever as Biden Visits Region," *Washington Post*, May 18, 2022.

101. Jolie Myers and Ari Shapiro, "U.N. Chief: Security Council Gridlock Blocks Effective Coronavirus Response," NPR, June 9, 2020, https://www.npr.org/sections/coronavirus-live-updates/2020/06/09/873060941/u-n-chief-security-council-gridlock-blocks-effective-coronavirus-response.

102. Nicholas Burns and Douglas Lute, *NATO at Seventy: An Alliance in Crisis* (Boston: Belfer Center for Science and International Affairs, 2019).

PART TWO: THE SOURCES OF CONFLICT

1. The war in Korea was the most striking exception. US and Chinese soldiers (and Soviet pilots) directly engaged each other. The absence of direct military conflict between the two blocs was what led the eminent military historian John Gaddis to memorably call the era "The Long Peace" in "The Long Peace: Elements of Stability in the Postwar International System," *International Security* 10, no. 4 (1986): 99–142, https://doi.org/10.2307/2538951.

2. Andrew Roth, "Putin Threatens US Arms Race with New Missiles Declaration," *The Guardian*, March 1, 2018, https://www.theguardian.com/world/2018/mar/01/vladimir-putin-threatens-arms-race-with-new-missiles-announcement. Keir Giles describes cyber and info war in *The Next Phase of Russian Information*

Warfare, prepared by NATO Strategic Communications Centre of Excellence, May 2016, https://www.stratcomcoe.org/next-phase-russian-information-warfare-keir -giles. And Brad Lendon, "China Boosts Military Spending 8% Amidst Ambitious Modernization Drive," CNN, March 5, 2018, https://www.cnn.com/2018/03/04/asia/ chinese-military-budget-intl/index.html.

3. For an enlightening discussion of how EU experts see the "return of great power rivalry," see European Commission, European Political Strategy Centre, *Geopolitical Outlook for Europe: Confrontation vs Cooperation,* June 8, 2018, https://data.europa.eu/ doi/10.2872/153229.

4. Amy Zegart, "American Spies Are Fighting the Last War, Again," *The Atlantic,* September 6, 2021.

5. I discuss Hobbesian structural realism and Kantian liberalism as philosophies of world politics in *Ways of War and Peace* (New York: Norton, 1997), chap. 3 and 8.

6. Mancur Olson, *The Logic of Collective Action* (Cambridge, MA: Harvard University Press, 1965); Alphons van der Kragt, John Orbell, and Robyn Dawes, "The Minimal Contributing Set as a Solution to Public Goods Problems," *APSR* 77 (1983): 112–122; and Kenneth Oye, "Explaining Cooperation Under Anarchy," *World Politics* 38, no. 1 (October 1985): 1–24, for the role of issues and numbers in cooperation. For some current implications, see Richard Haass, "The Unraveling," *Foreign Affairs,* November 13, 2014.

7. On hegemony's capacity to overcome the tendency to free ride, see Mancur Olson and Richard Zeckhauser, "An Economic Theory of Alliances," *Review of Economics and Statistics* 48, no. 3 (August 1966): 266–279; and Robert Keohane, *After Hegemony* (Princeton, NJ: Princeton University Press, 1984). For bipolarity and international monetary order, see Fred Hirsch and Michael Doyle, *Alternatives to Monetary Disorder* (New York: McGraw Hill/Council on Foreign Relations, 1977).

8. Robert Axelrod, *The Evolution of Cooperation* (New York; Basic Books, 1984), chap. 6.

9. Elinor Ostrom, *Governing the Commons: The Evolution of Institutions for Collective Action* (Cambridge, UK: Cambridge University Press, 1990).

10. Robert Ellickson, *Order Without Law: How Neighbors Settle Disputes* (Cambridge, MA: Harvard University Press, 1991), chap. 16.

11. For a thoughtful study of how legitimacy in its various forms enhances or, in its absence, impedes cooperation in international organizations, see Michael Zürn, *A Theory of Global Governance* (Oxford: Oxford University Press, 2018), especially chap. 3, "Legitimation Problems."

Chapter Three: Superpower Systems, Hegemonic Transitions, and Multidimensional Polarity

1. On hegemony's capacity to overcome the tendency to free ride, see Mancur Olson and Richard Zeckhauser, "An Economic Theory of Alliances," *Review of Economics and Statistics* 48, no. 3 (August 1966): 266–279; and Robert Keohane, *After Hegemony* (Princeton,

NJ: Princeton University Press, 1984). For bipolarity and international monetary order, see Fred Hirsch and Michael Doyle, *Alternatives to Monetary Disorder* (New York: McGraw Hill/Council on Foreign Relations, 1977).

2. Francis Fukuyama, "The End of History," *National Interest* 16 (Summer 1989): 3–18.

3. Measuring power is notoriously difficult, and on some accounts alliances can substitute for "poles" (but only if they are credible). For the classic and best account of an attempt to form a general power-based theory, see Kenneth Waltz, *The Theory of International Politics* (New York: McGraw Hill, 1979).

4. William C. Wohlforth, "The Stability of a Unipolar World," *International Security* 24, no. 1 (Summer 1999): 5–41.

5. G. John Ikenberry, *After Victory* (Princeton, NJ: Princeton University Press, 2001).

6. Jeanna Smialek, "These Will Be the World's 20 Largest Economies in 2030," Bloomberg, April 10 2015, http://www.bloomberg.com/news/articles/2015-04-10/the-world-s-20-largest-economies-in-2030.

7. "International Macroeconomic Data Set," US Department of Agriculture, last modified February 14, 2022, http://www.ers.usda.gov/data-products/international-macroeconomic-data-set.aspx.

8. The 1969 GDP of the USSR (in 2010 US dollars) was calculated by adding the 1969 GDP values of the fifteen countries that formed the USSR: Armenia, Azerbaijan, Belarus, Estonia, Georgia, Kazakhstan, Kyrgyzstan, Latvia, Lithuania, Moldova, Russia, Tajikistan, Turkmenistan, Ukraine, and Uzbekistan. ("Union of Soviet Socialist Republics." 2015. In *Encyclopedia Britannica*, http://www.britannica.com/EBchecked/topic/614785/Union-of-Soviet-Socialist-Republics.)

9. According to the US Department of Agriculture ("International Macroeconomic Data Set"), Russia had the eleventh largest GDP in 2014, in a ranking of real GDP by country (in 2010 US dollars).

10. According to the US Department of Agriculture ("International Macroeconomic Data Set"), Russia will have the tenth largest GDP in 2030, in a ranking of real GDP by country (in 2010 US dollars).

11. "Catching the Eagle: Chinese and American GDP Forecasts," *The Economist*, August 22, 2014, http://www.economist.com/blogs/graphicdetail/2014/08/chinese-and-american-gdp-forecasts.

12. Organization for Economic Co-operation and Development (OECD), "GDP Long Term Forecast" (Paris: OECD, 2016), cited in Michael O'Hanlon, *The Senkaku Paradox: Risking Great Power War over Small Stakes* (Washington, DC: Brookings, 2019), 55. O'Hanlon's fine book assumes that the overall state of rivalry remains at pre-2016 levels and warns of the dangers of allowing conflicts over small stakes (for example, the Senkaku Islands) to escalate. He also prescribes hybrid strategies for the United States to better manage the rivalry. I return to the valuable strategic lessons he offers in the last two chapters of *Cold Peace*, but in the meantime, I raise the sources of increasing tension, tending toward a cold war, that are deepening the rivalry among the powers.

13. Clearly, the likelihood of the United Kingdom remaining closely aligned with the European Union is questionable, and the European Union uniting into a coherent superpower is very low, at least as seen from the vantage point of 2022.

14. Some of the above estimates use exchange rate measures; others use purchasing power measures of GDP in which China has already passed the United States (though such measures may not well reflect the ability to fund advanced weapons systems and other measures of modern national power). These figures also downplay India's position, because its per capita GDP and industrialization are low.

15. Minxin Pei on why China will not surpass the United States, *The Economist*, https://www.economist.com/by-invitation/2021/08/30/minxin-pei-on-why-china -will-not-surpass-the-united-states?utm_campaign=a_21americanpower&utm_ mediu.

16. Joseph Nye, *Soft Power: The Means to Success in World Politics* (New York: Public Affairs Press, 2004).

17. Stanley Hoffmann, "The Sound and the Fury: The Social Scientists vs War and History," in *Janus and Minerva* (Boulder, CO: Westview, 1987), 439–457.

18. Table of Global Nuclear Weapons Stockpiles, 1945–2002, Natural Resources Defense Council, https://nuke.fas.org/norris/nuc_01049601a_160.pdf.

19. Benjamin Mainardi, "Yes, China Has the World's Largest Navy. That Matters Less than You Might Think," *The Diplomat*, April 7, 2021, https://thediplomat.com/2021/04/ yes-china-has-the-worlds-largest-navy-that-matters-less-than-you-might-think/.

20. O'Hanlon, *Senkaku Paradox*, 56–57.

21. Stanley Hoffmann has articulated the multiple chessboards view of world politics in many publications, including *World Disorders: Troubled Peace in the Post-Cold War Era* (Lanham, MD: Rowman & Littlefield, 1998).

22. The concepts are from Edward Gulick, *Europe's Classical Balance of Power* (New York: Norton, 1967). For evidence, see Michael Doyle, *Ways of War and Peace* (New York: Norton, 1997), chap. 5 passim and pp. 191–193 for the evidence during the classical eighteenth-century European balance of power.

23. I discuss the operation of the classical, eighteenth-century balance of power in "Balancing Power Classically," chap. 5 of *Ways of War and Peace*.

24. Thomas J. Christensen and Jack Snyder, "Chain Gangs and Passed Bucks: Predicting Alliance Patterns in Multipolarity," *International Organization* 44, no. 2 (Spring 1990): 137–168. And Robert Jervis, "Cooperation Under the Security Dilemma," *World Politics* 30, no. 2 (1978): 167–214.

25. Kenneth N. Waltz, "The Stability of a Bipolar World," *Daedalus* 93, no. 3 (Summer 1964): 881–909.

26. Carl von Clausewitz, *On War* (Princeton, NJ: Princeton University Press, 1989), chap. 1.

27. The terms *big-endian* and *little-endian* were applied to international politics by Danny Cohen in 1980 in *Internet Engineering Note 137*, a memorandum entitled "On Holy Wars and a Plea for Peace," subsequently published in print form in *IEEE Computer* 14, no. 10 (1981): 48–57.

28. I explored these affinities in the context of distinguishing the systemic sources of informal and formal empires in *Empires* (Ithaca, NY: Cornell University Press, 1986), chap. 20.

29. Thucydides's own argument was more nuanced and the "international" order of ancient Greece was more complicated than a simple bipolar balance of power; see Richard Lebow and Barry Strauss, eds., *Hegemonic Rivalry* (Boulder, CO: Westview, 1991).

30. Graham Allison, *Destined for War: Can America and China Escape the Thucydides Trap* (New York: Houghton Mifflin, 2017). And for a theoretical exploration of international hegemony, see Robert Gilpin, *War and Change in World Politics* (New York: Cambridge University Press, 1981).

31. Steven Lee Myers, "Biden Has Angered China, and Beijing Is Pushing Back," *New York Times*, July 20, 2021.

32. Timothy R. Heath, Derek Grossman, and Asha Clark, *China's Quest for Global Primacy: An Analysis of Chinese International and Defense Strategies to Outcompete the United States* (Santa Monica, CA: RAND Corporation, 2021), https://www.rand.org/pubs/research_reports/RRA447-1.html. Also available in print form.

33. Richard Bitzinger, "China's Double-Digit Defense Growth and What It Means for a Peaceful Rise," *Foreign Affairs*, April 6, 2015, 1, https://www.foreignaffairs.com/articles/china/2015-03-19/chinas-double-digit-defense-growth.

34. Bitzinger, "China's Double-Digit Defense Growth," 2.

35. Chun Han Wong, "China to Expand Naval Operations Amid Growing Tensions with US," *Wall Street Journal*, May 26, 2015, https://www.wsj.com/articles/china-shifts-maritime-military-focus-to-open-seas-1432648980.

36. Hal Brands, "The Danger of China's Decline," *Foreign Policy*, April 14, 2022. But also see Oriana Mastro and Derek Scissors, "China Hasn't Reached the Peak of its Power," *Foreign Affairs*, August 2022, which contests Brand's assessment of Chinese decline.

37. The classic argument along these lines is Olson and Zeckhauser, "An Economic Theory of Alliances."

38. Europe's production of natural gas has fallen from 300 billion cubic meters in 2010 to 200 billion cubic meters in 2021. Russia has increased its exports to 200 billion cubic meters from under 140 billion cubic meters a decade ago. James Marson and Joe Wallace, "Russia Steps In to Fill Demand as Europe Pumps Less Gas," *Wall Street Journal*, September 25, 2021.

39. Bojan Pancevski, "Merkel Era Ends with Cooler US Alliance," *Wall Street Journal*, September 25, 2021.

40. Ricci Shyrock, "For a Former Rebel the Decision to Take Moscow's Side in Its War with Ukraine Was Never in Doubt," *New York Times*, August 22, 2022.

Chapter Four: Corporatist, Nationalist Autocracies

1. Francis Fukuyama, *The End of History and the Last Man* (New York: Free Press, 1992).

2. Clearly, CNAs bear a relationship to twentieth-century Fascism, memorably defined by

Mussolini as "organized, concentrated, authoritarian democracy on a national basis"; but, as Ernst Nolte persuasively argues, twentieth-century Fascism has to be understood in the light of Socialism, which it saw as its key rival and from which it borrowed many strategies, while (as Nolte didn't fully appreciate) discarding Socialism's rationalism and cosmopolitanism. Nolte states that "without Marxism there is no fascism." See Ernst Nolte, *Three Faces of Fascism: Action Francaise, Italian Fascism, National Socialism,* trans. Leila Vennewitz (New York: Holt, Rinehart and Winston, 1966), 7, 21. I take up these points in Chapters 6 and 7, where I discuss liberal approaches to Mussolini's Italy and post-Taisho Japan.

3. Philippe C. Schmitter, "Still the Century of Corporatism?" *Review of Politics* 36, no. 1 (1974): 93–94, http://www.jstor.org/stable/1406080.

4. Schmitter, "Still the Century of Corporatism?," 103–104, 105–106. For varieties of democratic corporatism, see Peter Katzenstein, *Corporatism and Change: Austria, Switzerland, and the Politics of Industry* (Ithaca, NY: Cornell University Press, 1987).

5. Karl Polanyi, *The Great Transformation: The Political and Economic Origins of Our Time* (1944; repr. New York: Beacon Press, 1980).

6. Theoretically, any trade, even arm's-length, should equalize factor prices, but tariff, transportation, and other barriers muted trade's effects. Movements of factors—labor, capital, or technology—multiply the effects of trade in commodities. The key theoretical contributions were made by Heckscher, Ohlin, Rybczynski, Stolper, and Samuelson. For a nontechnical survey, see Chapter 3 in John Williamson, *The Open Economy and the World Economy: A Textbook in International Economics* (New York: Basic Books, 1983). For a contemporary study of the collapse of market globalization, see Harold James, *The End of Globalization: Lessons from the Great Depression* (Cambridge, MA: Harvard University Press, 2001).

7. Gulnara Aitova, "From the Soviet Model of Labour Relations to Social Partnership: The Limits of Transformation," *World Review of Political Economy* 6, no. 2 (Summer 2015): 252, https://www.jstor.org/stable/10.13169/worlrevipoliecon.6.2.0252.

8. Simon Clarke, "Trade Unions, Industrial Relations and the State in Russia," *Transfer: European Review of Labour and Research* 3, no. 2 (August 1997): 377–389, https://doi.org/10.1177%2F102425899700300208.

9. Timothy Frye, *Property Rights and Property Wrongs: How Power, Institutions and Norms Shape Economic Conflict in Russia* (Cambridge, UK: Cambridge University Press, 2017), 202–204.

10. Thomas Grove, "Putin Retains Popularity Despite Wave of Protests," *Wall Street Journal,* April 21, 2012.

11. Alexander Abramov, Alexander Radygin, and Maria Chernova, "State-Owned Enterprises in the Russian Market: Ownership Structure and Their Role in the Economy," *Russian Journal of Economics* 3, no. 1 (March 2017): 1–23, https://doi.org/10.1016/j.ruje.2017.02.001. Also see "The Party Winds Down," *The Economist,* May 6, 2016, https://www.economist.com/international/2016/05/07/the-party-winds-down.

12. "2017 Investment Climate Statements," US State Department, Bureau of Economic and Business Affairs, 2017, https://www.state.gov/reports/2017-investment-climate-statements/.

13. Anton Troianovski and Ivan Nechepurenko, "Russian Tycoon Criticized Putin's War. Retribution Was Swift," *New York Times*, May 1, 2022, https://www.nytimes.com/2022/05/01/world/europe/oligarch-putin-oleg-tinkov.html.

14. Elizabeth C. Economy, *The Third Revolution: Xi Jinping and the New Chinese State* (New York: Oxford University Press, 2018), 95.

15. *Global Times*, March 2, 2021.

16. Donald C. Clarke, "Corporate Governance in China: An Overview," *China Economic Review* 14 (September 2003): 495, doi:10.1016/j.chieco.2003.09.019.

17. Emily Feng, "Xi Jinping Reminds China's State Companies of Who's the Boss," *New York Times*, October 13, 2016, https://www.nytimes.com/2016/10/14/world/asia/china-soe-state-owned-enterprises.html. Also see World Bank Group, *Corporate Governance of State-Owned Enterprises* (Washington, DC: World Bank Group, 2014), https://openknowledge.worldbank.org/bitstream/handle/10986/20390/9781464802225.pdf; and Economy, *Third Revolution*, 106.

18. Economy, *Third Revolution*, 110.

19. Ellen Nakashima, Gerry Shin, and John Hudson, "Leaked Documents Reveal Huawei's Secret Operations to Build North Korea's Wireless Network," *Washington Post*, July 22, 2019, https://www.washingtonpost.com/world/national-security/leaked-documents-reveal-huaweis-secret-operations-to-build-north-koreas-wireless-network/2019/07/22/583430fe-8d12-11e9-adf3-f70f78c156e8_story.html?noredirect=on.

20. Raymond Zhong, "Jailed Huawei Workers Raised a Forbidden Subject: Iran," *New York Times*, April 25, 2020, https://www.nytimes.com/2020/04/25/technology/china-huawei-iran-arrests.html?smid=url-share. The article reports that China arrested five former employees who had discussed the tech giant's Iranian sales in a chat group, raising questions about its government ties.

21. Minxin Pei, "Crony Communism in China," *New York Times*, October 17, 2014, https://www.nytimes.com/2014/10/18/opinion/crony-communism-in-china.html. As Pei argues, President Xi's efforts to stem corruption are in tension with his equal imperative to restrict the independence of civil society and the courts, which could play a vital role in identifying and containing corrupt officials.

22. Scott Livingston, *The Chinese Communist Party Targets the Private Sector* (Washington, DC: Center for Strategic and International Studies, 2020), https://www.csis.org/analysis/chinese-communist-party-targets-private-sector.

23. Jing Yang and Lingling Wei, "China's President Xi Jinping Personally Scuttled Jack Ma's Ant IPO," *Wall Street Journal*, November 12, 2020, https://www.wsj.com/articles/china-president-xi-jinping-halted-jack-ma-ant-ipo-11605203556.

24. Jing Yang, "Jack Ma's Ant Group Bows to Beijing with Company Overhaul," *Wall Street Journal*, April 12, 2021, https://www.wsj.com/articles/ant-group-to-become-a-financial-holding-company-overseen-by-central-bank-11618223482.

25. Lingling Wei, "Xi Jinping Aims to Rein in Chinese Capitalism, Hew to Mao's Socialist Vision," *Wall Street Journal*, September 20, 2021, https://www.wsj.com/

articles/xi-jinping-aims-to-rein-in-chinese-capitalism-hew-to-maos-socialist
-vision-11632150725.

26. Stephan Haggard and Barry Naughton, "The United States, China and the Asia-Pacific:
The Shifting Economic Agenda," Working Paper, East Asia Institute, April 17 2019,
http://www.eai.or.kr/m/eng/research_view.asp?intSeq=10002&code=1&keyword_
option=&keyword=&menu=study.

27. For quote, see Vikram Khanna, "Still America First in Trade," https://rightwayspro
.blogspot.com/2021/03/still-amrica-first-in-trade.html. For further comment,
see Chris Buckley, "'The East Is Rising': Xi Maps Out China's Post-Covid Ascent,"
New York Times, March 3, 2021, https://www.nytimes.com/2021/03/03/world/asia/
xi-china-congress.html.

28. Li Yuan, "What China Expects from Businesses: Total Surrender," *New York
Times*, July 19, 2021, https://www.nytimes.com/2021/07/19/technology/
what-china-expects-from-businesses-total-surrender.html.

29. See Keith Bradsher and Ana Swanson, "U.S.-China Trade Talks Stumble on Beijing's Spending at Home," *New York Times*, May 12, 2019, https://www.nytimes
.com/2019/05/12/business/china-trump-trade-subsidies.html.

30. Alexandra Stevenson, "Business Embraces Hong Kong's Security Law. The Money
Helps," *New York Times*, June 30, 2020, https://www.nytimes.com/2020/06/30/business/
china-hong-kong-security-law-business.html?referringSource=articleShare.

31. Yi-Zheng Lian, "Trump Is Wrong About TikTok. China's Plans Are Much More Sin-
ister," *New York Times*, September 17, 2020, https://www.nytimes.com/2020/09/17/
opinion/tiktok-china-strategy.html.

32. Nicole Perlroth, "How China Transformed into a Prime Cyber Threat to the U.S.,"
New York Times, July 19, 2021, https://www.nytimes.com/2021/07/19/technology/
china-hacking-us.html.

33. James R. Hollyer, B. Peter Rosendorff, and James Raymond Vreeland, *Information,
Democracy, and Autocracy: Economic Transparency and Political (In)Stability* (Cambridge,
UK: Cambridge University Press, 2018).

34. Adler-Karlsson, Gunnar, *Western Economic Warfare 1947–1967* (Stockholm: Almqvist &
Wiksell, 1968).

35. Jaime Lowe, "With 'Stealth Politics,' Billionaires Make Sure Their Money Talks,"
New York Times, April 6, 2022, https://www.nytimes.com/2022/04/06/magazine/
billionaire-politics.html?referringSource=articleShare.

36. For example, according to the Federal Reserve Bank of St. Louis in 2014, SOEs made
up 10.2 percent of the US GDP: World Bank, "Credit to Government and State-Owned
Enterprises to GDP for United States [DDEI08USA156NWDB]," retrieved from
FRED, Federal Reserve Bank of St. Louis, May 28, 2022, https://fred.stlouisfed.org/
series/DDEI08USA156NWDB. Furthermore, "according to a 2009 OECD survey, 25
OECD countries had a total of some 2,050 SOEs valued at US$1.2 trillion. These SOEs
accounted for 15 percent of gross domestic product (GDP), as measured by the valua-
tion of SOE sectors relative to GDP, and, in countries still undergoing the transition to

a more market-based economy, for 20–30 percent of GDP (OECD 2011)." (World Bank Group, *Corporate Governance of State-Owned Enterprises*, 4.)

37. Kate Kelly, "At Saudi Investment Conference, Trump Allies Remain Front and Center," *New York Times*, October 31, 2021, https://www.nytimes.com/2021/10/31/us/politics/saudi-investment-conference-trump-allies.html. And for a corresponding phenomenon of US receptiveness to flight capital, see Casey Michel, *American Kleptocracy: How the US Created the World's Greatest Money Laundering Scheme in History* (New York: St. Martins, 2021).

38. Andreas Wimmer, "Why Nationalism Works: And Why It Isn't Going Away," *Foreign Affairs*, March/April 2019, https://www.foreignaffairs.com/articles/world/2019-02-12/why-nationalism-works; and see Jack Snyder, "The Broken Bargain: How Nationalism Came Back," *Foreign Affairs*, March/April 2019, https://www.foreignaffairs.com/articles/world/2019-02-12/broken-bargain.

39. The "Black Nationalism" espoused by a few of the African American dissenting groups of the 1960s was both similar and different; similar in race-based identity; different in that it espoused separation by a minority, not domination by a majority.

40. Brexit Opinion Poll, Statista, https://www.statista.com/statistics/987347/brexit-opinion-poll/.

41. Federico Finchelstein, *From Fascism to Populism in History* (Berkeley: University of California Press, 2017), 103–104.

42. Nadia Urbinati, *Me the People* (Cambridge, MA: Harvard University Press, 2019), 57.

43. Stephen Kotkin, "Russia's Perpetual Geopolitics: Putin Returns to the Historical Pattern," *Foreign Affairs*, May/June 2016, https://www.foreignaffairs.com/articles/ukraine/2016-04-18/russias-perpetual-geopolitics.

44. Many sources, but see Katie Sander, "Did Vladimir Putin Call the Breakup of the USSR 'the Greatest Geopolitical Tragedy of the 20th Century?,'" *Politifact*, March 6, 2014, https://www.politifact.com/factchecks/2014/mar/06/john-bolton/did-vladimir-putin-call-breakup-ussr-greatest-geop/.

45. John Haaga, "High Death Rate Among Russian Men Predates Soviet Union's Demise," Population Reference Bureau, April 1, 2000, https://www.prb.org/resources/high-death-rate-among-russian-men-predates-soviet-unions-demise/.

46. Hannah Arendt, *Origins of Totalitarianism* (New York: Shocken, 1951), preface.

47. Timothy Snyder, *The Road to Unfreedom: Russia, Europe, America* (New York: Tim Duggan Books, 2018), 194–195.

48. Grove, "Putin Retains Popularity Despite Wave of Protests."

49. Isaiah Berlin, "The Bent Twig," *Foreign Affairs*, October 1972, https://www.foreignaffairs.com/articles/1972-10-01/bent-twig; and for a discussion of the wider applicability, see Fareed Zakaria, "Who Understands Our Times, Bernie or The Donald?" *Washington Post*, April 11, 2019, https://fareedzakaria.com/columns/2019/4/11/who-understands-our-times-bernie-or-the-donald.

50. Timothy Snyder, "The War in Ukraine Has Unleashed a New Word," *New York Times*, April 22, 2022, https://www.nytimes.com/2022/04/22/magazine/ruscism-ukraine-russia-war.html.

51. Snyder, *Road to Unfreedom*, 8–83.

52. Timothy Snyder, "God Is a Russian," *New York Review of Books*, April 5, 2018, https://www.nybooks.com/articles/2018/04/05/god-is-a-russian/. But we should not assume a neat essentialist correspondence with all good and bad things going together. The Enlightenment philosophers who inspired modern liberalism expressed many nationalist and even racist sentiments. Enlightenment rationality, individualism, universalism (as in Kant and Voltaire) contributed to democratic sentiments but did not guarantee universal tolerance or equality. And romantic communalism (Herder) did not preclude toleration or the rule of law. See Kwame Anthony Appiah, "Dialectics of Enlightenment," *New York Review of Books,* May 9, 2019, https://www.nybooks.com/articles/2019/05/09/irrationality-dialectics-enlightenment/.

53. Anna Nemtsova, "Putin's Crackdown on Dissent Is Working," *The Atlantic,* March 22, 2019, https://www.theatlantic.com/international/archive/2019/03/putins-new-law-makes-it-illegal-disrespect-russia/585502/.

54. Lionel Barber, Henry Foy, and Alex Barker, "Vladimir Putin Says Liberalism Has 'Become Obsolete,'" *Financial Times*, June 27, 2019, https://www.ft.com/content/670039ec-98f3-11e9-9573-ee5cbb98ed36.

55. Gordon G. Chang, "Xi Changed My Mind About Trump," *Wall Street Journal*, July 24, 2019, https://www.wsj.com/articles/xi-changed-my-mind-about-trump-11564008053. Notably, Chang is the author of a book titled *The Coming Collapse of China*.

56. See Jessica Chen Weiss, "A World Safe for Autocracy? China's Rise and the Future of Global Politics," *Foreign Affairs*, July/August 2019, https://www.foreignaffairs.com/articles/china/2019-06-11/world-safe-autocracy. For a wide-ranging discussion of the Chinese world view that is relevant in these respects, see Alastair Iain Johnston, "China in a World of Orders: Rethinking Compliance and Challenge in Beijing's International Relations," *International Security* 44, no. 2 (Fall 2019): 9–60, https://doi.org/10.1162/isec_a_00360.

57. Chris Buckley, "China Warns Officials Against 'Dangerous' Western Values," *New York Times*, May 13, 2013, https://www.nytimes.com/2013/05/14/world/asia/chinese-leaders-warn-of-dangerous-western-values.html.

58. Sebastian Veg, "The Rise of China's Statist Intellectuals: Law, Sovereignty, and 'Repoliticization,'" *China Journal* 82 (July 2019): 23–45, https://doi.org/10.1086/702687.

59. Jiang Shigong, "The Internal Logic of Super-Sized Political Entities: 'Empire' and World Order," trans. David Ownby, https://www.readingthechinadream.com/jiang-shigong-empire-and-world-order.html.

60. John Lewis Gaddis, *Now We Know* (Oxford: Oxford University Press, 1997), especially chap. 7.

61. Barrington Moore, Jr., *Social Origins of Dictatorship and Democracy: Lord and Peasant in the Making of the Modern World* (Boston: Beacon Press, 1966).

62. Juan Linz, "An Authoritarian Regime: The Case of Spain," in *Cleavages, Ideologies and Party Systems: Contributions to Comparative Political Sociology*, Transactions of the Westermarck Society, vol. 10, ed. Erik Allardt and Yrjö Littunen (Helsinki: Distributed by the Academic Bookstore, 1964), 291–341.

63. Richard Fontaine and Kara Frederick, "The Autocrat's Toolkit," *Wall Street Journal*, March 15, 2019, https://www.wsj.com/articles/the-autocrats-new-tool-kit-1155266 2637.

64. Hope Reese, "It's Time to Become Aware of How Machines 'Watch, Judge, and Nudge Us,' Says Zeynep Tufekci," *Tech Republic*, September 29, 2015, https://www.techre public.com/article/its-time-to-become-aware-of-how-machines-watch-judge -and-nudge-us-says-zeynep-tufekci/.

65. Anders Aslünd estimates that Putin has moved more $100 Billion out of Russia since 2006; Anders Aslund, "Vladimir Putin Is Russia's Biggest Oligarch," *Washington Post*, June 5, 2019, https://www.washingtonpost.com/opinions/2019/06/05/ vladimir-putin-is-russias-biggest-oligarch/.

66. Karen Dawisha, *Putin's Kleptocracy: Who Owns Russia* (New York: Simon and Schuster, 2014); and Michael McFaul, *From Cold War to Hot Peace: An American Ambassador in Putin's Russia* (New York: Houghton Mifflin Harcourt, 2018). On the significance of the 2011–2012 Moscow demonstrations and Putin's reassertion of presidential power, see McFaul, *From Cold War to Hot Peace,* 240–250.

67. Matthew Schmidt, "The One Thing That Could Deter Putin," CNN, February 21, 2022, https://www.cnn.com/2022/02/20/opinions/ukraine-forces-russia-matthew-schmidt/ index.html.

68. Dawisha, *Putin's Kleptocracy,* 4.

69. Alex Abramovich, "Dons of the Gulag," *New York Review of Books,* May 9, 2019, https:// www.nybooks.com/articles/2019/05/09/russia-mafia-dons-gulag/.

70. Alexander Vershbow, "ESDP and NATO: Better Cooperation in View of the New Security Challenges" (speech, Interparliamentary Conference on CFSP/CSDP, Riga, Latvia, March 5, 2015), NATO, https://www.nato.int/cps/en/natohq/opinions_117919.htm.

71. Andrew Higgins, "As Putin Era Begins to Wane, Russia Unleashes a Sweeping Crackdown," *New York Times,* October 24, 2019, https://www.nytimes.com/2019/10/24/world/ europe/russia-protests-putin.html.

72. Daria Litinova, "Russia Labels Media Outlet, 2 Rights Groups 'Foreign Agents,'" AP News, September 29, 2021, https://apnews.com/article/business-europe-russi -media-moscow-9e78875b5298e0c78a588badd15dac9a.

73. T. Frye, *Property Rights and Property Wrongs: How Power, Institutions, and Norms Shape Economic Conflict in Russia* (Cambridge, UK: Cambridge University Press. 2017), 83, discussing Georgiy Suynyaev, "Is Propaganda Effective? Evidence on Framing Responsibility by State-Owned Media in Russia" (Research paper, September 2020).

74. Anton Troianovski and Adam Satoriano, "Google and Apple, Under Pressure from Russia, Remove Voting App," *New York Times,* September 17, 2021, https://www.nytimes .com/2021/09/17/world/europe/russia-navalny-app-election.html.

75. Lawrence Freedman, "The Crisis of Liberalism and the Western Alliance," *Survival* 63, no. 6 (2021): 37–44.

76. Immanuel Kant, *Perpetual Peace: A Philosophical Sketch*, ed. H. S. Reiss (Cambridge, UK: Cambridge University Press, 1991), 100.

77. Jessica L. P. Weeks, *Dictators at War and Peace* (Ithaca, NY: Cornell University Press, 2014).

78. Andrew J. Nathan, "China's Changing of the Guard: Authoritarian Resilience," *Journal of Democracy* 14, no. 1 (January 2003): 6–17.

79. The "third revolution" is Elizabeth Economy's apt label from *The Third Revolution: Xi Jinping and the New Chinese State* (Oxford: Oxford University Press, 2018), 10. For the roots of recent changes, see Minxin Pei, *China's Crony Capitalism: The Dynamics of Regime Decay* (Cambridge, MA: Harvard University Press, 2016).

80. Steven Lee Myers and Paul Mozur, "China Is Waging a Disinformation War Against Hong Kong Protesters," *New York Times*, August 13, 2019, https://www.nytimes .com/2019/08/13/world/asia/hong-kong-protests-china.html?partner=IFTTT. For a careful analysis of the wider capacities of the Chinese state's media control strategy, see Gary King, Jennifer Pan, and Margaret E. Roberts, "How the Chinese Government Fabricates Social Media Posts for Strategic Distraction, Not Engaged Argument," *American Political Science Review* 111, no. 3 (July 2017): 484–501, doi:10.1017/S0003055417000144.

81. Chun Han Wong, "From Falun Gong to Xinjiang: China's Repression Maestro," *Wall Street Journal*, April 9, 2019, A1, A10.

82. Elizabeth C. Economy, *Third Revolution*, 79–80. Current numbers with deficit scores run about 13 million according to Nicole Kobie, "The Complicated Truth About China's Social Credit System," *Wired*, June 7, 2019, https://www.wired.co.uk/article/ china-social-credit-system-explained.

83. Russia, like the United States, has experienced internationally organized terror attacks. Most recent was the ISIS-inspired attack in the St. Petersburg subway, presented by ISIS as revenge for Russian intervention in Syria.

84. See Michael McFaul's discussion of the Moscow demonstrations and their effect on the second Putin presidency in *From Cold War to Hot Peace.*

85. Jane Perlez, "China Reacts to Trade Tariffs and Hong Kong Protests by Blaming U.S.," *New York Times*, August 2, 2019, https://www.nytimes.com/2019/08/02/world/asia/ china-trump.html.

86. Xi Jinping, "Full Text of President Xi's Speech at Opening of Belt and Road Forum" (speech, Beijing, China, May 14, 2017), Ministry of Foreign Affairs of the People's Republic of China, https://www.fmprc.gov.cn/mfa_eng/wjdt_665385/zyjh_665391/201705/ t20170527_678618.html#:~:text=Ladies%20and%20Gentlemen%2C-Dear%20 Friends%2C,namely%2C%20the%20maritime%20Silk%20Road.

87. For a good survey of the literature on "autocratic" foreign policy, see Katsiaryna Yakouchyk, "Beyond Autocracy Promotion: A Review," *Political Studies Review* 17, no. 2 (May 2019): 147–160, https://doi.org/10.1177/1478929918774976. The Fascist autocracies of Mussolini and Hitler actively engaged in autocracy promotion; both Russia and China focus more on autocracy protection through anti-liberalization.

88. See for discussion Kerry Brown, *China's World: The Foreign Policy of the World's Newest Superpower* (London: I. B. Tauris, 2017); Gerald Chan, *Understanding China's New Diplomacy: Silk Roads and Bullet Trains* (Cheltenham, UK: Edward Elgar, 2018); Antonio Fiori and Matteo Dian, eds., *The Chinese Challenge to the Western Order* (Trento, Italy: Fondazione

Bruno Kessler, 2014); and an excellent student paper by Simon Ma, "Harmony or Hegemony" (Political Science Department, Columbia University, 2019).

89. For a valuable survey, see Jonathan E. Hillman, *The Emperor's New Road: China and the Project of the Century* (New Haven, CT: Yale University Press, 2020).

90. Ana Swanson, "A New Red Scare Is Reshaping Washington," *New York Times*, July 20, 2019, https://www.nytimes.com/2019/07/20/us/politics/china-red-scare-washington.html.

91. Josh Rogin, *Chaos Under Heaven: Trump, Xi, and the Battle for the 21st Century* (Boston: Houghton Mifflin Harcourt, 2021), xvi.

92. Mahalia Dobson, "Lobster or Legitimacy? A Key U.S. Ally Embraces the West—and Pays the Price with China," *NBC News*, June 20, 2021, https://www.yahoo.com/entertainment/lobster-legitimacy-key-u-ally-083312781.html.

93. Jennifer Hillman and David Sacks, *Independent Task Force Report No. 79, China's Belt and Road Implications for the United State*s (New York: Council on Foreign Relations, 2021), https://www.cfr.org/report/chinas-belt-and-road-implications-for-the-united-states/findings.

94. David Stanway, "China's Belt and Road Plans Losing Momentum as Opposition, Debt Mount—Study," Reuters, September 29, 2021, https://www.reuters.com/world/china/chinas-belt-road-plans-losing-momentum-opposition-debt-mount-study-2021-09-29/.

95. David E. Sanger, *The Perfect Weapon: War, Sabotage, and Fear in the Cyber Age* (New York: Broadway Books, 2018); and Richard J. Harknett and Joseph S. Nye, Jr., "Is Deterrence Possible in Cyberspace?" *International Security* 42, no. 2 (November 2017): 196–199, https://doi.org/10.1162/ISEC_c_00290. For a thorough exploration of the stabilizing and destabilizing implications of cyber conflict in various strategic scenarios, see Jason Healey and Robert Jervis, "The Escalation Inversion and Other Oddities of Situational Cyber Stability," *Texas National Security Review* 3, no. 4 (Fall 2020): 30–53, http://dx.doi.org/10.26153/tsw/10962.

96. Elsa Kania, Samm Sacks, Graham Webster, and Paul Triolo, "China's Strategic Thinking on Building Power in Cyberspace," *New America*, September 25, 2017, https://www.newamerica.org/cybersecurity-initiative/blog/chinas-strategic-thinking-building-power-cyberspace/; and see Johnston, "China in a World of Orders," 53–56, for comments on the information order and cybersecurity.

97. Duncan B. Hollis, "China and the US Strategic Construction of Cybernorms: The Process Is the Product." Aegis Paper Series No. 1704, Hoover Institution Paper Series on National Security, Technology, and Law (Stanford: Hoover Institution, 2017), 1–2, https://www.hoover.org/research/china-and-us-strategic-construction-cybernorms-process-product.

98. Sarah E. Kreps, Miles McCain, and Miles Brundage, "All the News That's Fit to Fabricate: AI-Generated Text as a Tool of Media Misinformation," *Journal of Experimental Political Science* 9, no. 1 (Spring 2022): 104–117, https://doi.org/10.1017/XPS.2020.37; and Jack Goldsmith and Stuart Russell, "Strengths Become Vulnerabilities: How a Digital World Disadvantages the United States in Its

International Relations," *Lawfare*, June 6, 2018, 1–24, https://www.lawfareblog.com/ strengths-become-vulnerabilities-how-digital-world-disadvantages-united-states-its -international-0.

99. Henry Farrell and Abraham L. Newman, "Weaponized Interdependence: How Global Economic Networks Shape State Coercion," *International Security* 44, no. 1 (July 2019): 42–79, https://doi.org/10.1162/isec_a_00351.

100. Sulmaan Wasif Khan, "Wolf Warriors Killed China's Grand Strategy: And We'll All Come to Miss It," *Foreign Policy*, May 28, 2021, https://foreignpolicy.com/2021/05/28/ china-grand-strategy-wolf-warrior-nationalism/.

101. Norman Kempster, "Just Kidding, Russian Says After Cold War Blast Stuns Europeans," *Los Angeles Times*, December 15, 1992, https://www.latimes.com/archives/ la-xpm-1992-12-15-mn-2214-story.html.

102. Chris Blattman, "The Strategic Logic of Russia's War on Ukraine," *Wall Street Journal*, April 25, 2022, https://www.wsj.com/articles/the-strategic-logic-of-russia-war -on-ukraine-putin-leverage-western-europe-invasion-peace-negotiations-sanctions -weaken-russia-11650917047.

103. Andrei Makhovsky and Polina Devitt, "Battling Protests, Lukashenko Says Putin Agreed to Help Security of Belarus," Reuters, August 15, 2020, https://www.usnews.com/ news/world/articles/2020-08-15/baltic-leaders-urge-belarus-to-hold-free-and -fair-elections?context=amp.

104. UN Press Release, SC/93255, March 19, 2018.

105. David Petraeus and Sheldon Whitehouse, "Putin and Other Authoritarians' Corruption Is a Weapon—and a Weakness," *Washington Post*, March 8, 2019, https://www.washingtonpost.com/opinions/2019/03/08/putin-other -authoritarians-corruption-is-weapon-weakness/.

106. Tom Miles, "China: U.S. Resembles "Don Quixote" in Seeing Other Powers as Threats," Reuters, May 22, 2019, https://www.reuters.com/article/us-usa-china-nuclear/ china-u-s-resembles-don-quixote-in-seeing-other-powers-as-threats-idUSKCN 1SS1E5.

107. Jeremy Page, "China Promises Further Military Cooperation with Russia," *Wall Street Journal*, July 24, 2019, https://www.wsj.com/articles/china -promises-further-military-cooperation-with-russia-11563973937.

108. China's defense white paper, July 2019, emphasizes partnership with Russia but also focuses on domestic sources of insecurity, such as Xinjiang, Tibet, and Taiwan. See State Council Information Office of the People's Republic of China, "China's National Defense in the New Era" (Beijing: Foreign Languages Press, 2019), http://www .chinadaily.com.cn/specials/whitepaperonnationaldefenseinnewera.pdf.

Chapter Five: Liberal, Capitalist Democracies

1. Isaiah Berlin, "Two Concepts of Liberty," in *Four Essays On Liberty* (Oxford: Oxford University Press, 1969), 8.

2. This section draws on my "Liberalism and World Politics," *American Political Science Review* 80, no. 4 (December 1986): 1151–1169; http://www.jstor.org/stable/1960861.

3. Stephen Skowronek, "The Reassociation of Ideas and Purposes: Racism, Liberalism, and the American Political Tradition," *American Political Science Review* 100, no. 3 (August 2006): 385, http://www.jstor.org/stable/27644362.

4. Stephen Taylor Holmes, "Aristippus in and Out of Athens," *American Political Science Review* 73, no. 1 (March 1979): 115, https://doi.org/10.2307/1954734.

5. Francis Fukuyama, "The End of History," *National Interest* 16 (Summer 1989): 3–18.

6. Fred Hirsch, *Social Limits to Growth* (Cambridge, MA: Harvard University Press, 1976).

7. John Rawls, *The Law of Peoples* (Cambridge, MA: Harvard University Press, 1999), 50.

8. Robert A. Dahl, "Can International Organizations Be Democratic? A Skeptic's View," in *Democracy's Edges*, ed. Ian Shapiro and Casiano Hacker-Cordón (Cambridge, UK: Cambridge University Press, 1999), 19–36.

9. Michael Tomz and Jessica Weeks, "Public Opinion and the Democratic Peace," *American Political Science Review* 107, no. 4 (November 2013): 862, http://www.jstor.org/stable/43654037.

10. Freedom House, *Freedom in the World: 2019* (Washington, DC: Freedom House, 2019), 3, https://freedomhouse.org/sites/default/files/Feb2019_FH_FITW_2019_Report_ForWeb-compressed.pdf.

11. Sheri Berman, *Democracy and Dictatorship in Europe: From the Ancien Régime to the Present Day* (Oxford: Oxford University Press, 2019).

12. For a landmark analysis of the Bretton Woods order, see G. John Ikenberry, *After Victory: Institutions, Strategic Restraint, and the Rebuilding of Order After Major Wars* (Princeton, NJ: Princeton University Press, 2000).

13. See Graham Allison, *Destined for War: Can America and China Escape Thucydides's Trap?* (Boston: Houghton Mifflin Harcourt, 2017); and see the cautions of Jonathan Kirshner, "Handle Him with Care: The Importance of Getting Thucydides Right," *Security Studies* 28, no. 1 (January 2019): 1–24, https://doi.org/10.1080/09636412.2018.1508634.

14. Recent examples include the US State Department's annual human rights report, which stated that China was "in a league of its own" when it comes to human rights violations, with roundup of Muslims not matched "since the 1930s" and millions of Uighurs detained in reeducation camps, which Beijing compares to "boarding schools." But the same report fails to blame Mohammed bin Salman for murders of Saudi dissidents. See David E. Sanger, "State Dept. Accuses China of Rights Abuses Not Seen 'Since the 1930s,'" *New York Times*, March 13, 2019, https://www.nytimes.com/2019/03/13/us/politics/state-department-human-rights-abuses.html.

15. I first discussed these features of liberalism in "Kant, Liberal Legacies, and Foreign Affairs: Part I," *Philosophy and Public Affairs* 12, no. 3 (June 1983): 205–235, https://www.jstor.org/stable/2265298; and in "Kant, Liberal Legacies, and Foreign Affairs: Part II," *Philosophy and Public Affairs* 12, no. 4 (October 1983): 323–353, https://www.jstor.org/stable/2265377. Stefano Recchia and I survey the wider field of empirical democratic peace studies in "Liberalism in International Relations," *International Encyclopedia of*

Political Science, ed. Bertrand Badie, Dirk Berg-Schlosser, and Leonardo Morlino (Los Angeles: Sage, 2011), 5:1434–1439.

16. The paragraphs below draw on arguments initially made in Doyle, "Liberal Legacies and Foreign Affairs: Part II."

17. Steve Chan, "Mirror, Mirror on the Wall . . . Are the Freer Countries More Pacific?," *Journal of Conflict Resolution* 28, no. 4 (December 1984): 636, http://www.jstor.org/stable/173984.

18. Walter Clemens, "The Superpowers and the Third World: Aborted Ideals and Wasted Assets," in *Sage International Yearbooks in Foreign Policy Studies*, vol. VII: *Foreign Policy: USA/USSR*, ed. C. W. Kegley and P. J. McGowan (Beverly Hills: Sage, 1982), 117–118.

19. Barry Posen and Stephen W. van Evera, "Overarming and Underwhelming," *Foreign Policy*, no. 40 (Autumn 1980): 105, https://www.jstor.org/stable/1148343.

20. "Herbert Hoover to President Wilson (29 March 1919)," in *Major Problems in American Foreign Policy*, vol. 1, ed. Thomas Paterson (Boston: Houghton Mifflin Harcourt, 1978), 95. The actual US intervention in the Soviet Union was limited to supporting anti-Bolshevik Czechoslovak soldiers in Siberia and to protecting military supplies in Murmansk from German seizure.

21. US Senate, *Hearings Before the Committee on Foreign Relations on the Nomination of John Foster Dulles, Secretary of State Designate*, 83rd Congress, 1st session, January 15, 1953 (Washington, DC: GPO, 1953), 5–6.

22. Michael Doyle, *Empires* (Ithaca, NY: Cornell University Press, 1986); and for an example, see Alexis De Tocqueville, *Democracy in America*, trans. Henry Reeve (1835; repr. New York: Knopf, 1945), 351.

23. See Paterson, ed., *Major Problems in American Foreign Policy*, vol. 1, 328.

24. Jeane J. Kirkpatrick, "Dictatorships and Double Standards," *Commentary* 68 (November 1979): 1–32, https://www.commentary.org/articles/jeane-kirkpatrick/dictatorships-double-standards/.

25. Richard Barnet, *Intervention and Revolution: The United States in the Third World* (New York: Meridian, 1968), chap. 10.

26. Arthur Schlesinger, *A Thousand Days: John F. Kennedy in the White House* (Boston: Houghton Mifflin Harcourt, 1965), 769; also quoted in Barnet, *Intervention and Revolution*, 158.

27. L.R. Simon and J.C. Stephens, *El Salvador Land Reform 1980–1981* (Boston: Oxfam America, *1981*), 38.

28. I offer an interpretation, updating, and critical appreciation of Mill's "Nonintervention" in *The Question of Intervention: John Stuart Mill and the Responsibility to Protect* (New Haven, CT: Yale University Press, 2015).

29. This sections draws on and updates Michael W. Doyle, "The Liberal Peace, Democratic Accountability, and the Challenge of Globalization," in *Globalization Theory: Approaches and Controversies*, ed. David Held and Anthony Grew (Cambridge, UK: Polity, 2007), 190–206.

30. See John Ruggie's "International Regimes, Transactions and Change: Embedded Liberalism in the Postwar Economic Order," *International Organization* 36, no. 2 (Spring 1982): 379–415, https://www.jstor.org/stable/2706527.

31. Peter Drucker calls this "transnational strategy": Peter F. Drucker, "The Global Economy and the Nation-State," *Foreign Affairs*, September/October 1997, https://www .foreignaffairs.com/articles/1997-09-01/global-economy-and-nation-state. Marina von Neumann Whitman, *New World, New Rules: The Changing Role of the American Corporation* (Cambridge, MA: Harvard Business School Press, 1999) explores how American companies that were once stable, lumbering, globe-striding giants with paternalistic ties to their home communities have become lean, mean, and footloose.

32. I draw on and update parts of Michael Doyle, "A More Perfect Union? The Liberal Peace and the Challenge of Globalization," *Review of International Studies* 26 (December 2000): 81–94, https://www.jstor.org/stable/20097713.

33. Arvind Panagariya, "International Trade," *Foreign Policy*, no. 139 (November/December 2003): 22, https://doi.org/10.2307/3183727. Also see the UN annual *Millennium Goals Report* at https://doi.org/10.18356/98544aa9-en.

34. Robert Gilpin, *The Challenge of Global Capitalism* (Princeton, NJ: Princeton University Press, 2000), 307. For global GDP comparisons, see Tahir Beg, "Globalization, Development and Debt-Management," *The Balance* (Spring 2000), table 2, http:// balanceddevelopment.org/articles/globalization.html; and Nancy Birdsall, "Why Inequality Matters: Some Economic Issues," *Ethics and International Affairs* 15, no. 2 (September 2001): 3–28, doi:10.1111/j.1747-7093.2001.tb00356.x.

35. "OECD Now Accounts for Slightly Less than 50% of World GDP, Large Emerging Economies for About 30%," OECD, April 30, 2014, https://www.oecd.org/sdd/prices-ppp/oec dnowaccountsforslightlylessthan50ofworldgdplargeemergingeconomiesforabout30 .htm.

36. United Nations Conference on Trade and Development, *2004 Development and Globalization: Facts and Figures* (Geneva: UNCTAD, 2004), 18.

37. Christoph Lakner and Branko Milanovic, *Global Income Distribution: From the Fall of the Berlin Wall to the Great Recession* (Washington, DC: World Bank, 2013), 31, http://hdl .handle.net/10986/16935.

38. Homi Kharas and Brina Seidel, *What's Happening to the World Income Distribution? The Elephant Chart Revisited* (Washington, DC: Brookings, 2018), 2, https://www.brookings .edu/research/whats-happening-to-the-world-income-distribution-the-elephant-chart -revisited/.

39. James B. Davies and James Shorrocks, *The World Distribution of Household Wealth, Discussion Paper 2008/003* (Helsinki: UNU-WIDER, 2006), 7, https://www.wider.unu.edu/ publication/world-distribution-household-wealth.

40. For valuable context for these strains on liberal globalization, see Peter Katzenstein and Jonathan Kirshner, eds., *The Downfall of the American Order?* (Ithaca, NY: Cornell University Press, 2022); and Jonathan Kirshner, *American Power After the Financial Crisis* (Ithaca, NY: Cornell University Press, 2014).

41. This sections draws on and updates Michael W. Doyle, "The Liberal Peace, Democratic Accountability, and the Challenge of Globalization," in *Globalization Theory: Approaches and Controversies*, ed. David Held and Anthony Grew (Cambridge, UK: Polity, 2007), 190–206.

42. US National Security Council, *Defense Planning Guidance, FY 1994–1999* (Washington, DC, 1992), 2, https://www.archives.gov/files/declassification/iscap/pdf/2008-003-docs1-12 .pdf. The regional engagement is revised as [emphasis supplied]: "The third goal is to preclude any hostile power from dominating a region critical to our interests, and also thereby to strengthen the barriers against the reemergence of a global threat to the interests of the U.S. **and our allies**. These regions include Europe, East Asia, the Middle East/Persian Gulf, and Latin America. Consolidated, **nondemocratic** control of the resources of such a critical region could generate a significant threat to our security."

43. Mary Elise Sarotte, "A Broken Promise? What the West Really Told Moscow About NATO Expansion," *Foreign Affairs*, September/October 2014, https://www.foreignaffairs .com/articles/russia-fsu/2014-08-11/broken-promise.

44. See the informative study in the National Security Archive (December 12, 2017), "NATO Expansion: What Gorbachev Heard." Valuable background is in James Goldgeier, *Not Whether, but When* (Washington, DC: Brookings, 2010); and Joshua Shiffrinson, "Deal or No Deal," *International Security* (Spring 2016).

45. For a thorough account grounded in a close reading of the Russian perceptions of the US and NATO expansion, see Andrey A. Sushentzov and William C. Wohlforth, "The Tragedy of US-Russian Relations: NATO Centrality and the Revisionists' Spiral," *International Politics* 57 (March 2020): 427–450, https://doi.org/10.1057/s41311-020-00229-5. They argue that both the United States and Russia had expansionist aims, rather than purely defensive ones, making any stable accommodation exceptionally difficult. Disclosure: I sent a short memo to the Clinton Transition Team in 1992 proposing an "Organization of European States" along these lines.

46. "Exclusive—As War Began, Putin Rejected a Ukraine Peace Deal Recommended by His Aide: Sources," Reuters, September 14, 2022.

47. As a further irony, the United States under Clinton became dependent on Yeltsin's cooperation in reducing loose nuclear weapons and may have encouraged his nondemocratic manipulations that brought Putin to power. See Svetlana Savranskaya and Mary Sarotte, "The Clinton-Yeltsin Relationship in Their Own Words," National Security Archive (October 2, 2018).

48. See Kimberly Marten, "NATO Enlargement: Evaluating Its Consequences in Russia," *International Politics* 57, no. 3 (April 2020): 401–426, https://doi.org/10.1057/ s41311-020-00233-9 for a similar argument; and James Goldgeier and Joshua R. Itzkowitz Shiffrinson, "Evaluating NATO Enlargement: Scholarly Debates, Policy Implications, and Roads Not Taken," *International Politics* 57 (2020): 291–321, https://doi .org/10.1057/s41311-020-00243-7 for a survey of the academic literature.

49. See Independent International Commission on Kosovo, *The Kosovo Report: Conflict, International Response, Lessons Learned* (Oxford: Oxford University Press, 2000); I discuss the case in Chapter 4 of *The Question of Intervention* (New Haven, CT: Yale University Press, 2015).

50. For an argument advancing the defensive motive (against NATO expansion) for Putin's invasion, see Philip Short, "After Six Months of Bloody War and Terrible War, What Exactly Does Putin Want from Ukraine," *The Guardian*, August 22, 2022.

51. Ross Douthat, "Putin Is Losing in Ukraine. But He's Winning in Russia," *New York Times*, April 2, 2022, https://www.nytimes.com/2022/04/02/opinion/putin-ukraine-russia .html.

52. Significantly, it was just this threat of Ukrainian membership in the European Union that led Putin to pull the plug on Ukrainian independence and insist that his client stop negotiating with the European Union in 2013.

53. White House, *National Security Strategy of the United States of America* (Washington, DC, 2017), 3, https://trumpwhitehouse.archives.gov/wp-content/uploads/2017/12/ NSS-Final-12-18-2017-0905.pdf.

54. Ana Swanson, "A New Red Scare Is Reshaping Washington," *New York Times*, July 20, 2019, https://www.nytimes.com/2019/07/20/us/politics/china-red-scare-washington .html.

55. For the thoughts of an eminent US economist with deep knowledge of China, see Gregory C. Chow, "The Impact of Joining the WTO on China's Economic, Legal and Political Institutions," *Pacific Economic Review* 8, no. 2 (June 2003): 105–115, http://dx.doi .org/10.1111/j.1468-0106.2003.00213.x. I once joined Professor Chow and other Princeton economists to brief members of the New Jersey congressional delegation in favor granting China MFN status.

56. John Mearsheimer, *The Tragedy of Great Power Politics* (New York: Norton, 2001), 400.

57. Thomas J. Christensen, "Fostering Stability or Creating a Monster? The Rise of China and U.S. Policy Toward East Asia," *International Security* 31, no. 1 (Summer 2006): 123–126, https://www.jstor.org/stable/4137540. And see for background, David Lampton, *Same Bed, Different Dreams: Managing U.S.-China Relations, 1989–2000* (Berkeley: University of California Press, 2001) and James B. Steinberg, "What Went Wrong? U.S.-China Relations from Tiananmen to Trump," *Texas National Security Review* 3, 1 (Winter 2019/2020), 119–133.

58. For a thoughtful paper exploring policy alternatives, see Miles Kahler, "Reconsidering Engagement with China: Always Different Dreams of World Order?" Working Paper 2022 for the LSE-Princeton Project on Reconsidering the 1990s.

59. Tony Romm and Drew Harwell, "TikTok Raises National Security Concerns in Congress as Schumer, Cotton Ask for a Federal Review," *Washington Post*, October 24, 2019, https://www.washingtonpost.com/technology/2019/10/24/tiktok-raises -national-security-concerns-congress-schumer-cotton-ask-federal-review/.

60. Jamelle Bouie, "Anti-Abortion and Pro-Trump Are Two Sides of the Same Coin," *New York Times*, May 20, 2019, https://www.nytimes.com/2019/05/20/opinion/ anti-abortion-pro-trump.html.

61. See John Ikenberry's eloquent description of this liberal international order tradition in *Liberal Leviathan* (Princeton, NJ: Princeton University Press, 2012).

62. See the insightful discussions in the *Wall Street Journal* by Daniel Michaels and Jason Marson, "NATO and Other Alliances Face Unprecedented Strains," *Wall Street Journal*, January 20, 2020, https://www.wsj.com/articles/nato-and-other-alliances-face-unprecedented -strains-11579542294; and Greg Ip, "What 'America First' Means Under Trump Is

Coming Into Focus," *Wall Street Journal*, January 19, 2020, https://www.wsj.com/articles/what-america-first-means-under-trump-is-coming-into-focus-11579469762. And for an illuminating study of the various ways the Trump administration challenged the standards of international law, see Harold Koh, *The Trump Administration and International Law* (Oxford: Oxford University Press, 2018).

63. Park Si-soo, " 'Stop Provoking Ally': Korea's Conservatives Slam Trump," *Korea Times*, August 14, 2019, http://www.koreatimes.co.kr/www/nation/2019/08/356_273906.html.

64. Mathew Haag, "Robert Jeffress, Pastor Who Said Jews Are Going to Hell, Led Prayer at Jerusalem Embassy," *New York Times*, May 14, 2018, https://www.nytimes.com/2018/05/14/world/middleeast/robert-jeffress-embassy-jerusalem-us.html.

65. Mitch Prothero, "Some Among America's Military Allies Believe Trump Deliberately Attempted a Coup and May Have Had Help from Federal Law-Enforcement Officials," *Business Insider*, January 7, 2021, https://www.businessinsider.com/trump-attempted-coup-federal-law-enforcement-capitol-police-2021-1.

66. Emily Tamkin, "How the American Right Stopped Worrying and Learned to Love Russia," *New York Times*, February 27, 2022, https://www.nytimes.com/2022/02/27/opinion/ukraine-putin-steve-bannon.html.

67. For a disturbing study of the vulnerability of electoral democracies to authoritarian subversion, see Steven Levitsky and Daniel Ziblatt, *How Democracies Die* (New York: Crown, 2018).

68. For a good survey of the issues, see Brendan O'Connor, "Who Exactly Is Trump's 'Base'? Why White, Working-Class Voters Could Be Key to the US Election," *The Conversation*, October 28, 2020, https://theconversation.com/who-exactly-is-trump-base-why-white-working-class-voters-could-be-key-to-the-us-election-147267.

69. John M. Owen, "How Liberalism Produces Democratic Peace," *International Security* 19, no. 2 (Fall 1994), https://www.jstor.org/stable/2539197.

70. Fareed Zakaria, "Xi's China Can't Seem to Stop Scoring Own Goals," *Washington Post*, May 27, 2021, https://www.washingtonpost.com/opinions/2021/05/27/xis-china-cant-seem-stop-scoring-own-goals/.

71. Democracies, as have autocracies, *have* imposed forcible regime changes, often as a measure to try to help a conquest hold, as was done by the United States and its allies after the military defeats of Nazi Germany and Imperial Japan in 1945. But such impositions rarely succeed. Afghanistan is just the latest demonstration of this. For discussion, see among many sources my *The Question of Intervention* (New Haven, CT: Yale University Press, 2015).

Chapter Six: Italian Fascism and American Politics

1. The quotes above all come from Ira Katznelson's magisterial account of the United States during the Great Depression, *Fear Itself: The New Deal and the Origins of Our Time* (New York: Norton, 2014), 58–68. Long was the same diplomat who later became notorious for the exclusion of Jewish refugees seeking asylum in the U.S.

2. A good account of isolationism in this period is in Dexter Perkins, "The Department of

State and American Public Opinion," in *The Diplomats,* ed. Gordon Craig and Felix Gilbert (Princeton, NJ: Princeton University Press, 1981), 282–398; and Charles Kupchan, *Isolationism: A History of America's Efforts to Shield Itself from the World* (Oxford: Oxford University Press, 2020).

3. Henry R. Spencer, "European Dictatorships," *American Political Science Review* 21, no. 3 (1927): 537, https://doi.org/10.2307/1945508.

4. William Kilborne Stewart, "The Mentors of Mussolini," *American Political Science Review* 22, no. 4 (1928): 860–861, https://doi.org/10.2307/1945351.

5. Jonathan Alter, *The Defining Moment: FDR's Hundred Days and the Triumph of Hope* (New York: Simon and Schuster, 2007), 4–5. FDR's draft phrase ran, "As new commander in chief under the oath to which you are still bound I reserve to myself the right to command you in any phase of the situation which now confronts us."

6. The discussion of American scholarly views on the state and the challenges of the 1930s draws on helpful advice from Nathan Feldman and reading a chapter of his forthcoming dissertation on these issues (Political Science Department, Columbia University, forthcoming).

7. Charles E. Merriam, "Planning Agencies in America," *American Political Science Review* 29, no. 2 (1935): 209, https://doi.org/10.2307/1947501.

8. "Bishop Praises Mussolini: 'We Talk About Slums, He Tears Them Down,' says Prelate," *New York Times,* October 2, 1936, https://timesmachine.nytimes.com/timesmachine/1936/10/02/88697309.html?pageNumber=20.

9. Richard Washburn Child, *The Writing on the Wall: Who Shall Govern Us Next?* (New York: J. H. Sears, 1928), 93.

10. Child, *Writing on the Wall,* 269–270.

11. William Yandell Elliott, *The Pragmatic Revolt in Politics* (New York: Macmillan, 1928), 497. Liberals also were among Fascism's earliest critics. In 1928, William Yandell Elliott published *The Pragmatic Revolt in Politics,* which criticized the collectivism and utilitarian "pragmatism" he saw in Fascism and denounced its evils: "Fascism denies the right of the individual as well as the group to a purposive attitude of his own toward the organic state."

12. Walter J. Shepard, "Democracy in Transition," *American Political Science Review* 29, no. 1 (1935): 18–19, https://doi.org/10.2307/1947163.

13. Charles E. Merriam, *The New Democracy and the New Despotism* (New York: McGraw Hill, 1939), 208, 258.

14. Franklin Delano Roosevelt, "Declaration of War on Germany" (speech, Washington, DC, December 11, 1941), Franklin D. Roosevelt Presidential Library and Museum, http://www.fdrlibrary.marist.edu/_resources/images/msf/msfb0006.

15. Franklin Delano Roosevelt, "Address of the President at the University of Virginia" (speech, Richmond, VA, June 10, 1940), Franklin D. Roosevelt Presidential Library and Museum, http://www.fdrlibrary.marist.edu/_resources/images/msf/msf01330.

16. Sohrab Ahmari, Patrick Deneen, and Gladden Pappin, "Hawks Are Standing in the Way of a New Republican Party," *New York Times,* February 5, 2022, https://www.nytimes.com/2022/02/05/opinion/republicans-national-conservatives-hawks.html.

17. This section especially benefited from the research suggestions of Nadia Urbinati and Bruno Settis. For the distinctions between Fascism and modern populism (including LePen, AfD, Trump, and others), see Nadia Urbinati, "Political Theory of Populism," *Annual Review of Political Science* 22, no. 1 (2019): 111–127, https://doi.org/10.1146/annurev-polisci-050317-070753.

18. Katznelson, *Fear Itself,* 63.

19. Benito Mussolini and Giovanni Gentile, *Fascism Doctrine and Institutions* (Rome: Ardita Publishers, 1932), republished as Benito Mussolini, "The Doctrine of Fascism," World Future Fund, https://ia600800.us.archive.org/14/items/TheDoctrineOfFascismByBen itoMussolini/The%20Doctrine%20of%20Fascism%20by%20Benito%20Mussolini.pdf.

20. Mussolini, "Doctrine of Fascism."

21. Antonio Gramsci, *Prison Notebooks*, ed. and trans. Quentin Hoare and Geoffrey Smith (London: Lawrence and Wishart, 1971), 263–271.

22. See Walter L. Adamson, "Gramsci's Interpretation of Fascism," *Journal of the History of Ideas* 41, no. 4 (1980): 615–633, https://doi.org/10.2307/2709277.

23. Robert Paxton, *The Anatomy of Fascism* (New York: Random House, 2004), 218.

24. Benito Mussolini, "Mussolini's Speech-Broadcast, October 2, 1935," History Central, http://www.historycentral.com/HistoricalDocuments/Mussolini%27sSpeech.html.

25. Mussolini, "Doctrine of Fascism," 17.

26. Mussolini, "Doctrine of Fascism," 3.

27. Mussolini, "Doctrine of Fascism," 4.

28. Milo Boyd, "Putin's Chilling Warning to Oligarchs in Bizarre Rant About Oysters and Gender," *The Mirror*, March 16, 2022, https://www.mirror.co.uk/news/world-news/putins-chilling-warning-oligarchs-bizarre-26486740.

29. Mussolini, "Doctrine of Fascism," 8.

30. Umberto Eco, "Ur-Fascism: Freedom and Liberation Are an Unending Task," *New York Review of Books,* June 22, 1995, https://www.nybooks.com/articles/1995/06/22/ur-fascism/.

31. Michael Ledeen, *D'Annunzio: The First Duce* (New Brunswick, ME: Transaction Publishers, 2002), 133–137; Paxton, *Anatomy of Fascism*, 59–60.

32. Mussolini, "Doctrine of Fascism," 10. And see Benito Mussolini, *My Autobiography*, trans. Richard Washburn Child (London: Hutchinson and Co., 1928), chap. 11. "Corporative organization . . . emphasizes Fascist control over unions, including changing Labor Day from May 1 to April 21" (the commemoration of Romulus and Remus's founding of Rome!).

33. Bruce Pauley, *Hitler, Stalin, and Mussolini: Totalitarianism in the Twentieth Century* (Hoboken, NJ: John Wiley and Sons, 2014), 92–93.

34. Louis R. Franck, "Fascism and the Corporate State," *Political Quarterly* 6, no. 3 (1935): 355–368, https://doi.org/10.1111/j.1467-923X.1935.tb01262.x.

35. Franck, "Fascism and the Corporate State," 356–357.

36. Mussolini, "Doctrine of Fascism," 8.

37. Paxton, *Anatomy of Fascism*, 87–91. Paxton notes that the king probably feared that the army would fraternize with and defect to the Fascists.

38. Paxton, *Anatomy of Fascism*, 110.

39. Victoria de Grazia, *The Culture of Consent: Mass Organization of Leisure in Fascist Italy* (Cambridge, UK: Cambridge University Press, 1981).

40. MacGregor Knox, "Fascism: Ideology, Foreign Policy, and War," in *Liberal and Fascist Italy: 1900–1945*, ed. Adrian Lyttelton (Oxford: Oxford University Press, 2002), 110–111.

41. Mussolini, "Mussolini's Speech-Broadcast, October 2, 1935."

42. H. Stuart Hughes, "The Early Diplomacy of Italian Fascism: 1922–1932," in *The Diplomats 1919–1939*, ed. Gordon Craig and Felix Gilbert (Princeton, NJ: Princeton University Press, 1981), 210.

43. Knox, "Fascism," 122.

44. Gian Giacomo Migone, *The United States and Fascist Italy: The Rise of American Finance in Europe*, trans. Molly Tambor (Cambridge, UK: Cambridge University Press, 2015), 287. This section draws on a valuable memorandum researched by Greg Smith.

45. Harold James and Kevin H. O'Rourke, "Italy and the First Age of Globalization, 1861–1940," in *The Oxford Handbook of the Italian Economy Since Unification*, ed. Gianni Toniolo (Oxford: Oxford University Press, 2013), 21.

46. John Patrick Diggins, *Mussolini and Fascism: The View from America* (Princeton, NJ: Princeton University Press, 1972), 32; David Schmitz, *The United States and Fascist Italy, 1922–1940* (Chapel Hill, NC: University of North Carolina Press, 1988).

47. Diggins, *Mussolini and Fascism*, 32.

48. Migone, *The United States and Fascist Italy*, 82.

49. Diggins, *Mussolini and Fascism*, 48.

50. Veronica Binda, "A Short History of International Business in Italy: What We Know and How We Know It," *Journal of Evolutionary Studies in Business* 2, no. 1 (2016): 83, doi. org/10.1344/JESB2016.2.j013.

51. Binda, "Short History of International Business in Italy."

52. Diggins, *Mussolini and Fascism*, 49.

53. James and O'Rourke, "Italy and the First Age of Globalization," 20.

54. Migone, *United States and Fascist Italy*, 318.

55. Migone, *United States and Fascist Italy*, 321. And see Brice Harris, *The United States and the Italo-Ethiopian Crisis* (Stanford: Stanford University Press, 1964).

56. Migone, *United States and Fascist Italy*, 344

57. Migone, *United States and Fascist Italy*, 358.

58. Migone, *United States and Fascist Italy*, 287.

59. James and O'Rourke, "Italy and the First Age of Globalization," 20.

60. Schmitz, *The United States and Fascist Italy*, 98.

61. See the informative discussion in Philip Cannistraro's "Fascism and Italian-Americans in Detroit: 1933–1935," *International Migration Review* 9, no. 1 (Spring 1975): 29–40, https://doi.org/10.2307/3002528.

62. Harris, *United States and the Italo-Ethiopian Crisis*, 21–23.

63. Adam Tooze, "When We Loved Mussolini," *New York Review of Books*, August 18, 2016, https://www.nybooks.com/articles/2016/08/18/when-we-loved-mussolini/, reviewing Migone's *The United States and Fascist Italy: The Rise of American Finance in Europe.*

64. Edward M. Lamont, *The Ambassador from Wall Street: The Story of Thomas W. Lamont. J.P. Morgan's Chief Executive* (Boston: Madison Books, 1994), 221–223.

65. Quoted in Lamont, *Ambassador from Wall Street*, 222.

66. See William Yandell Elliott, "Mussolini: Prophet of the Pragmatic Era in Politics," *Political Science Quarterly* 41, no. 2 (1926): 161–192, https://doi.org/10.2307/2142092. Elliott's critique condemned what he saw as the ethically unaccountable tendencies of pragmatic thought exemplified at its then extreme in Fascism.

67. Other sources of criticism of Mussolini came from the American Federation of Labor (Mussolini suppressed independent unions), from Republicans who compared the New Deal to Mussolini's tyranny, and from anti-Catholic ravers such as Thomas Heflin, US senator from Alabama, who warned about Mussolini's control over Italian immigrants leading to control over the US government (as in 70 Cong. Rec. 3576 [1929]).

68. Diggins, *Mussolini and Fascism*, 292–293.

69. 83 Cong. Rec. 1224 (1938).

70. *Memorandum for the Honorable Norman H Davis: Contribution to the Peace Settlement* (Washington, DC: US Department of State, 1937), 24, housed in Norman H. Davis Papers at the Library of Congress.

71. For excellent surveys, see Warren Cohen, *American Revisionists: The Lessons of Intervention in World War I* (Chicago: University of Chicago Press, 1967), and Brooke Blower, "From Isolationism to Neutrality: A New Framework for Understanding American Political Culture, 1919–1941," *Diplomatic History* 38, no. 2 (2014): 345–376, https://doi.org/10.1093/dh/dht091.

72. Similar skeptical views on the dirigisme of Fascist political economy gained an academic presentation in F. A. Hayek, *The Road to Serfdom*, 2nd ed. (London: Routledge, 2006), 37–38. "Economic liberalism is opposed, however, to competition being supplanted by inferior methods of coordinating individual efforts. And it regards competition as superior not only because it is in most circumstances the most efficient method known, but even more because it is the only method by which our activities can be adjusted to each other without coercive or arbitrary intervention of authority. Indeed, one of the main arguments in favour of competition is that it dispenses with the need for 'conscious social control' and that it gives the individuals a chance to decide whether the prospects of a particular occupation are sufficient to compensate for the disadvantages and risks connected with it."

73. Viscount Halifax, "C.P. 215 – Italy: Economic Situation in Italy," in *CAB 24/279* (London: United Kingdom Cabinet Office, 1938), 118, hosted by National Archives, http://filestore.nationalarchives.gov.uk/pdfs/large/cab-24-279.pdf.

74. Halifax, "C.P. 215 – Italy," 119.

75. Amanda Smith, ed., *Hostage to Fortune: The Letters of Joseph P. Kennedy* (New York: Viking

Press, 2001), 130–132. Also in Fredrik Logevall, *JFK: Coming of Age in the American Century, 1917–1956* (New York: Random House, 2021), 145. In Joseph P. Kennedy, Jr.'s, partial mitigation, Hitler's full crimes were still to come. He volunteered, fought, and died in the war against Nazism.

76. See Katharine Olmstead, *The Newspaper Axis: Six Press Barons who Enabled Hitler* (New Haven, CT: Yale University Press, 2022).

77. Logevall, *JFK*, 198. This did not stop the ambassador and his oldest son, Joe Jr., from complaining about US Jewish interests trying to embroil the United States in war.

78. Associated Press, "Lindbergh's Talk on Arms Embargo," *New York Times*, October 14, 1939, https://timesmachine.nytimes.com/timesmachine/1939/10/14/112718499 .html?pageNumber=10; H. W. Brands, *Traitor to His Class* (New York: Anchor Books, 2009); Logevall, *JFK*, 235. It is not clear whether the Poles were Europeans or something different, Slavic, for Lindbergh.

79. Logevall, *JFK*, 143.

80. Harris, *United States and the Italo-Ethiopian Crisis*, 144. He averred: "The American Government and people had not forgiven Italy for its ruthless campaign against Ethiopia."

81. Charles Lindbergh contributed to the panic with his wild overestimations of German airpower and underestimations of British and French air resources. The literature is extensive. A few high points are Paul Kennedy, "Appeasement," and other chapters in *The Origins of the Second World War Reconsidered*, 2nd ed., ed. Gordon Martel (New York: Routledge, 1999); Herbert Feis, *Seen from E.A.: Three International Episodes* (New York: Knopf, 1947); and Zara Steiner, *Triumph of the Dark: European International History, 1933–1939* (Oxford: Oxford University Press, 2011).

82. Logevall, *JFK*, 194.

Chapter Seven: Japanese Militarism and American Policy

1. This section on Japan has benefited from the research assistance of Theo Milonopoulos.

2. As noted earlier, the United States did restrict Italian immigration in 1922, but Italians were not targeted for limitations on property ownership as were the Japanese.

3. Quoted in Walter LaFeber, *The Clash: U.S.-Japanese Relations Throughout History* (New York: Norton, 1997), 103.

4. 48 Cong. Rec. 10045 (1912). The Japanese government had the company withdraw its investment, mollifying the United States.

5. LaFeber, *The Clash*, 126.

6. LaFeber, *The Clash*, 105-06.

7. Marius B. Jansen, "Yawata, Hanyehping, and the Twenty-one Demands," *Pacific Historical Review* 23, no. 1 (1954): 31–48, https://doi.org/10.2307/3635065.

8. LaFeber, *The Clash*, 116.

9. LaFeber, *The Clash*, 123.

10. LaFeber, *The Clash*, 120.

11. Dexter Perkins, "The Department of State and American Public Opinion," in *The Diplomats*, ed. Gordon Craig and Felix Gilbert (Princeton, NJ: Princeton University Press, 1981), 282–308. Perkins emphasized the deep-seated reluctance of the American public to undertake commitments outside the Americas.

12. For a thorough analysis, see Sadao Asada, "Between the Old Diplomacy and the New, 1918–1922: The Washington System and the Origins of Japanese-American Rapprochement," *Diplomatic History* 30, no. 2 (April 2006), 211–230, https://www.jstor.org/stable/24915091. And for background, W. G. Beasley, *Japanese Imperialism: 1894–1945* (Oxford: Oxford University Press, 1987).

13. LaFeber, *The Clash*, 138.

14. Frederick Dickenson, *World War One and the Triumph of a New Japan, 1919–1930* (Cambridge, UK: Cambridge University Press, 2013). Dickenson contrasts the cooperation of the 1920s to the confrontation of the 1930s.

15. Edward M. Lamont, *The Ambassador from Wall Street. The Story of Thomas W. Lamont, J.P. Morgan's Chief Executive. A Biography* (Lanham MD: Madison Books, 1994).

16. LaFeber, *The Clash*, 131.

17. Letter from The Representative of the American Group (Lamont) to the Representative of the Japanese Group (Kajiwara), in *Papers Relating to the Foreign Relations of the United States, 1920*, ed. Joseph V. Fuller (Washington, DC: US Government Printing Office, 1935), https://history.state.gov/historicaldocuments/frus1920v01/d540.

18. S. C. M. Paine, *The Japanese Empire: Grand Strategy from the Meiji Restoration to the Pacific War* (Cambridge, UK: Cambridge University Press, 2017); Michael Barnhart, *Japan Prepares for Total War: The Search for Economic Security, 1919–1941* (Ithaca, NY: Cornell University Press, 1987).

19. LaFeber, *The Clash*, 140–141, citing Japanese language sources.

20. LaFeber, *The Clash*, 148.

21. Robert Scalapino, *Democracy and the Party Movement in Prewar Japan* (Berkeley: University of California Press, 1975).

22. Marius B. Jansen, *The Making of Modern Japan* (Cambridge, MA: Harvard University Press, 2002).

23. Kato Shuichi, "Taisho Democracy as the Pre-Stage for Japanese Militarism," in *Japan in Crisis*, ed. Bernard Silberman and H. Harootunian (Ann Arbor: University of Michigan Press, 1999); Herbert Bix, *Hirohito and the Making of Modern Japan* (New York: Harper, 2000), 18. Bix discusses the emperor's role in the emerging authoritarian constitution.

24. Louise Young, *Japan's Total Empire: Manchuria and the Culture of Wartime Imperialism* (Berkeley: University of California Press, 1998).

25. The army's institutional role in the war is a major theme of Robert Butow, *Tojo and the Coming of the War* (Princeton, NJ: Princeton University Press, 1961).

26. Shin'ichi Yamamuro, *Manchuria Under Japanese Domination*, trans. Joshua A. Fogel (Philadelphia: University of Pennsylvania Press, 2006); Sadako Ogata, *Defiance in Manchuria: The Making of Japanese Foreign Policy, 1931–1932* (Berkeley: University of California Press, 1964).

27. Young, *Japan's Total Empire.*

28. Margaret S. Culver, "Manchuria: Japan's Supply Base," *Far Eastern Survey* 14, no. 12 (1945): 160–163, https://doi.org/10.2307/3022806.

29. Meirion Harries and Susan Harries, *Soldiers of the Sun: The Rise and Fall of the Imperial Japanese Army* (New York: Random House, 1994).

30. Alexander Gerschenkron, *Economic Backwardness in Historical Perspective* (Cambridge, MA: Harvard University Press, 1962).

31. Richard Samuels, *The Business of the Japanese State: Energy Markets in Comparative and Historical Perspective* (Ithaca, NY: Cornell University Press, 1987), 68.

32. Llewelyn Hughes, *Globalizing Oil: Firms and Oil Market Governance in France, Japan, and the United States* (Cambridge, UK: Cambridge University Press, 2014).

33. Kerry Chase, *Trading Blocs: States, Firms and Regions in the World Economy* (Ann Arbor: University of Michigan Press, 2005), 53. This section draws on arguments in Chase's book.

34. Beasley, *Japanese Imperialism*, 91–100.

35. Francis Jones, *Japan's New Order in East Asia* (London, Oxford University Press, 1954) p. 192; William Lockwood, *The Economic Development of Japan* (Princeton University Press, 1954) p. 50.

36. Toshiyuki Mizoguchi, *The Japanese Informal Empire in China, 1894–1937* (Princeton, NJ: Princeton University Press, 1989).

37. Mariko Hatase, "Devaluation and Exports in Interwar Japan," IMES Discussion Paper, Tokyo, July 2002.

38. Chase, *Trading Blocs*, 59.

39. The decisive effect of the Great Depression in undermining democratic government and exacerbating international strife in Europe is the general theme of Zara Steiner's magisterial *The Lights That Failed: European International History 1919–1933* (Oxford: Oxford University Press, 2007). The indirect effects were experienced across East Asia.

40. Hideaki Miyajima, "Japanese Industrial Policy During the Interwar Period: Strategies for International and Domestic Competition," *Business and Economic History* 21 (1992): 270–279, https://www.jstor.org/stable/23703229.

41. Arthur Tiedeman, *Modern Japan: A Brief History* (Princeton, NJ: Van Nostrand, 1955), 280–281.

42. Hugh Byas, "Regret over Mukden Expressed in Tokyo," *New York Times*, September 20, 1931, https://timesmachine.nytimes.com/timesmachine/1931/09/20/98059603.pdf. The aggressiveness and independence of the Kwantung Army was well recognized in Tokyo and abroad and commented on by foreign correspondent Hugh Byas, who reported from Tokyo: "While this is the Foreign Office attitude [to withdraw and resolve the Mukden crisis diplomatically], the actual question now is whether the Foreign Office or the army is in charge of Japan's policy."

43. G. C. Allen, *Modern Japan and Its Problems* (London: Routledge, 1928), 626–645.

44. Miles Kahler, "External Ambition and Economic Performance," *World Politics* 40, no. 4 (July 1988): 419–451, especially 434, https://doi.org/10.2307/2010313; Jack Snyder,

Myths of Empire (Ithaca, NY: Cornell University Press, 1991), chap. 4. Snyder develops the metaphor of the factional logroll as mechanism for policy formation.

45. See Mira Wilkins, "Japanese Multinationals in the United States, Continuity and Change 1879–1990," *Business History Review* 64, no. 4 (1990): 585, https://doi.org/10.2307/3115500. This section draws on research by Greg Smith.

46. Wilkins, "Japanese Multinationals in the United States," 586.

47. Hisayuki Oshima, "General Trading Companies in the Interwar Period: The Expansion of Asia-Pacific Trade and the Progress of Japanese Trading Companies," *Japanese Research in Business History* 30 (2013): 52, https://doi.org/10.5029/jrbh.30.49.

48. Wilkins, "Japanese Multinationals in the United States," 595.

49. Alejandro Ayuso-Díaz and Antonio Tena-Junguito, "Trade in the Shadow of Power: Japanese Industrial Exports in the Interwar Years," *Economic History Review* 73, no. 3 (2020): 821–825, https://doi.org/10.1111/ehr.12912.

50. Wilkins, "Japanese Multinationals in the United States," 598.

51. Nicolas End, "Japan During the Interwar Period: From Monetary Restraint to Fiscal Abandon," in *Debt and Entanglement Between the Wars*, ed. Era Dabla-Norris (Washington, DC: International Monetary Fund, 2019), available at https://www.imf.org/en/Publications/Books/Issues/2019/11/08/Debt-and-Entanglements-Between-the-Wars-48602.

52. Wilkins, "Japanese Multinationals in the United States," 590.

53. Wilkins, "Japanese Multinationals in the United States," 594.

54. Wilkins, "Japanese Multinationals in the United States," 594.

55. Wilkins, "Japanese Multinationals in the United States," 594.

56. Wilkins, "Japanese Multinationals in the United States," 594.

57. Wilkins, "Japanese Multinationals in the United States," 593.

58. Hirosi Saito, "A Japanese View of the Manchurian Situation," *Annals of the American Academy of Political and Social Science* 165 (1933): 159–161, https://doi.org/10.1177%2F000271623316500122. Saito, a Japanese diplomat soon to represent Japan in Washington, offered a significant counter.

59. Harold Lasswell, "Sino-Japanese Crisis: The Garrison State versus the Civilian State," in *Essays on the Garrison State*, ed. Jay Stanley (New York: Taylor and Francis, 1997), 43–54. Lasswell claimed that total-war militarism was driving all societies toward a garrison state. Nonetheless, because a world of garrison states was not inevitable, it ought to be struggled against. "[T]he friend of democracy views the emergence of the garrison state with repugnance and apprehension. He will do whatever is within his power to defer it. Should the garrison state become unavoidable, however, the friend of democracy will seek to conserve as many values as possible within the general framework of the new society."

60. Harold S. Quigley, "The Far East and the Future," *Virginia Quarterly* 19, no. 1 (1943): 56, https://www.jstor.org/stable/26441808.

61. Oona Hathaway and Scott Shapiro, *The Internationalists* (New York: Simon and Schuster, 2017), 131–182.

62. LaFeber, *The Clash*, 167–168. Strongly pro-Japanese, Assistant Secretary of State William Castle represented what LaFeber calls "the Theodore Roosevelt-Elihu Root strain of U.S. policy that viewed Japan as a force for order" in the region. China, by contrast, was, in Castle's words, "totally unreliable," and he could not conceive of the circumstances under which the United States would go to war either over the Open Door policy or over Japanese annexation of Manchuria. The pro-China camp was embodied by Stanley Hornbeck, head of the State Department's Far Eastern Division, who, according again to LaFeber, "represented the Willard Straight-Paul Reinsch strain that believed cooperation with China offered the great opportunity, and Japan posed the great danger."

63. LaFeber, *The Clash*, 169–170. "Stimson remained torn," LaFeber writes, "between his belief that 'a firm stand' had to be taken against Japan, and, as he confidentially told reporters, that Japan was 'our buffer against the unknown powers' of China and the Soviet Union." Despite Stimson's views that Japan was now "in the hands of virtually mad dogs" with its army "running amok," Hoover and Castle resisted League of Nations efforts to impose an economic embargo on Japan, because that would be perceived as an act of war that could bring the United States into direct confrontation with Japan. "If there is anything left in the stock market," Castle warned, "that little would disappear.... The world is not inclined to take another material kick in the face to maintain the sanctity of treaties which it is not convinced have been violated."

64. William O'Neil, *Interwar U.S. and Japanese National Product and Defense Expenditures* (Alexandria, VA: Center for Naval Analyses, 2003), 7, https://www.cna.org/archive/CNA_Files/pdf/d0007249.a1.pdf. And see for discussion, Henry Rosovsky, *Capital Formation in Japan 1868-1940* (New York: Free Press of Glencoe, 1961).

PART FOUR: COLD PEACE

1. See https://www.newsweek.com/us-nuclear-weapons-spending-compared-china -russia-1715542 for the current data on spending and numbers. Two novels play out the grim possibilities: Elliot Ackerman and Adm. James Stavridis, *2034* (New York: Penguin, 2021), and Peter W. Singer and August Cole, *Ghost Fleet* (New York: Mariner Books, 2016).

2. Parts of this chapter draw on an earlier article in *Dissent* and a tribute to Michel Rocard in *Pour Michel Rocard* (Paris: Flammarion, 2018). They also reflect various helpful suggestions from Rachel Hulvey, Emma Borgnäs, and Nathan Feldman and from meetings at UI (Stockholm) and at the Seoul Forum for International Affairs (arranged by Prof. Shin-wha Lee).

3. Joe Biden, "Remarks by President Biden at the 2021 Virtual Munich Security Conference," (speech, Washington, DC, February 19, 2021), White House, https://www .whitehouse.gov/briefing-room/speeches-remarks/2021/02/19/remarks-by-president biden-at-the-2021-virtual-munich-security-conference/.

4. "Joint Statement of the Russian Federation and the People's Republic of China on

the International Relations Entering a New Era and the Global Sustainable Development," Official Internet Resources of the President of Russia, February 4, 2022, http://en.kremlin.ru/supplement/5770.

5. John Feng, "Xi Jinping Pushes China's Own Vision for 'Global Security,'" *Newsweek*, April 21, 2022, https://www.newsweek.com/china-xi-jinping-global-security-initiative-ukraine-russia-1699553.

Chapter Eight: Future Scenarios

1. Joseph Biden, "Biden's Speech to Congress: Full Transcript," *New York Times*, April 29, 2021, https://www.nytimes.com/2021/04/29/us/politics/joe-biden-speech-transcript.html.

2. Joe Biden, "Joe Biden: My Trip to Europe Is About America Rallying the World's Democracies," *Washington Post*, June 5, 2021, https://www.washingtonpost.com/opinions/2021/06/05/joe-biden-europe-trip-agenda/.

3. Joe Biden, "Remarks by President Biden at an Annual Memorial Day Service" (speech, New Castle, DE, May 30, 2021), White House, https://www.whitehouse.gov/briefing-room/speeches-remarks/2021/05/30/remarks-by-president-biden-at-an-annual-memorial-day-service/.

4. National Intelligence Council, *Global Trends 2040: A Contested World*, NIC 2021-02339, (Washington, DC: US Office of the Director of National Intelligence, 2021), 98, https://www.dni.gov/files/ODNI/documents/assessments/GlobalTrends_2040.pdf. The *Global Trends* report went on to warn that "the risk of interstate conflict is likely to rise because of advances in technology and an expanding range of targets, a greater variety of actors, more difficult dynamics of deterrence, and weakening or gaps in treaties and norms on acceptable use. Major power militaries are likely to seek to avoid high-intensity conflict and particularly full-scale war because of the prohibitive cost in resources and lives, but the risk of such conflicts breaking out through miscalculation or unwillingness to compromise on core issues is likely to increase" (102).

5. White House, *National Security Strategy of the United States of America* (Washington, DC, 2022), https://www.whitehouse.gov/wp-content/uploads/2022/10/Biden-Harris-Administrations-National-Security-Strategy-10.2022.pdf.

6. Alastair Iain Johnson, "The Failures of the 'Failure of Engagement' with China," *Washington Quarterly* 42, no. 2 (June 2019): 99–114.

7. Stephen Krasner, *How to Make Love to a Despot* (New York: Liveright, 2020).

8. John J. Mearsheimer, *The Tragedy of Great Power Politics* (New York: Norton, 2001), 400. Also see Aaron Friedberg, "An Answer to Aggression: How to Push Back Against Beijing," *Foreign Affairs* 99, no. 3 (September/October 2020): 150–164; and Michael D. Swaine and Rachel Odell, "The Overreach of the China Hawks: Aggression Is the Wrong Response to Beijing," *Foreign Affairs*, October 23, 2020, https://www.foreignaffairs.com/articles/china/2020-10-23/overreach-china-hawks.

9. National Intelligence Council, *Global Trends 2040*, 4.

10. See Kurt Campbell and Mira Rapp-Hooper, "China Is Done Biding Its Time: The End of Beijing's Foreign Policy Restraint?," *Foreign Affairs*, July 15, 2020, https://www .foreignaffairs.com/articles/china/2020-07-15/china-done-biding-its-time.

11. This is illustrated by the recent denunciation of Australia and the United States by Foreign Ministry spokesperson Zhao Lijian (Alex W. Palmer, "The Man Behind China's Aggressive New Voice," *New York Times*, July 7, 2021, https://www.nytimes .com/2021/07/07/magazine/china-diplomacy-twitter-zhao-lijian.html).

12. Caitlin McFall, "Trump Demands 100% Tariffs on Chinese Goods, Debt Cancellation, and $10T in Reparations for COVID-19," *Fox News*, June 5, 2021, https://www.foxnews .com/politics/trump-china-pay-10-trillion-in-reparations-for-covid-19.

13. This was also repeated in Xi's speech to the UN General Assembly, 75th session: "Xi Jinping Delivers an Important Speech at the General Debate of the 75th Session of the United Nations (UN) General Assembly," Consulate-General of the People's Republic of China in Mumbai, September 22, 2020, https://www.fmprc.gov.cn/ce/cgmb/eng/zgyw/ t1817766.htm.

14. Chris Buckley, " 'The East Is Rising': Xi Maps Out China's Post-Covid Ascent," *New York Times*, March 3, 2021, https://www.nytimes.com/2021/03/03/world/asia/ xi-china-congress.html.

15. Phelim Kline, "X Jinping Lays Out Vision of Fortress China against Tense Rivalry with the U.S." *Politico*, Oct. 17, 2022.

16. James T. Areddy, "Former Chinese Party Insider Calls U.S. Hopes of Engagement 'Naïve,' " *Wall Street Journal*, June 29, 2021, https://www.wsj.com/articles/ former-chinese-party-insider-calls-u-s-hopes-of-engagement-naive-11624969800.

17. Timothy R. Heath, Derek Grossman, and Asha Clark, *China's Quest for Global Primacy: An Analysis of Chinese International and Defense Strategies to Outcompete the United States* (Santa Monica, CA: RAND Corporation, 2021), https://www.rand.org/pubs/research_reports/ RRA447-1.html. Also available in print form.

18. Kinling Lo, "China Calls on Russia to Hold the Line Against 'US Perverse Acts,' " *South China Morning Post*, June 5, 2021, https://www.scmp.com/news/china/diplomacy/ article/3136187/china-calls-russia-hold-line-again-us-perverse-acts.

19. Niall Stanage, "Five Takeaways from the Biden-Putin Summit," *The Hill*, June 16, 2021, https://thehill.com/homenews/administration/558827-five-takeaways-from-the-biden -putin-summit/.

20. Gerry Shih, "China Is Trying to Mend Fences in Europe. It's Not Going Well," *Washington Post*, September 2, 2020, https://www.washingtonpost.com/world/asia_pacific/ china-europe-relations-us/2020/09/02/63d963e0-ece1-11ea-bd08-1b10132b458f_story .html.

21. Joe Biden, "Remarks by President Biden Before the 76th Session of the United Nations General Assembly" (speech, New York, NY, September 21, 2021), White House, https://www.whitehouse.gov/briefing-room/speeches-remarks/2021/09/21/ remarks-by-president-biden-before-the-76th-session-of-the-united-nations -general-assembly/.

22. Kari Soo Lindberg, "China Lists 102 Examples of U.S. 'Interference' in Hong Kong," *BQ Prime,* September 24, 2021, https://www.bloombergquint.com/politics/china-lists-102-examples-of-u-s-interference-in-hong-kong.

23. "The Limited Test Ban Treaty, 1963," Office of the Historian, US Department of State, https://history.state.gov/milestones/1961-1968/limited-ban, accessed August 8, 2022.

24. "Strategic Arms Limitation Talks," *Encyclopedia Britannica,* last updated February 5, 2020, http://www.britannica.com/event/Strategic-Arms-Limitation-Talks.

25. "Strategic Arms Limitations Talks/Treaty (SALT) I and II," Office of the Historian, US Department of State, https://history.state.gov/milestones/1969-1976/salt, accessed August 8, 2022.

26. "Strategic Arms Limitation Talks," *Encyclopedia Britannica.*

27. Avis T. Bohlen, "Arms Control in the Cold War," Foreign Policy Research Institute, May 15, 2009, https://www.fpri.org/article/2009/05/arms-control-in-the-cold-war/.

28. A thoughtful and wide-ranging exploration of the potentialities of cooperation across severe rivalries can be found in Gabriella Blum's *Islands of Agreement: Managing Enduring Armed Rivalries* (Cambridge, MA: Harvard University Press, 2007).

Chapter Nine: Four Bridges to a Cold Peace

1. Bjorn Lomborg has asserted that climate effects are swamped by the effects of economic growth in reducing death through malnutrition, leaving aside that eliminating those 85,000 additional deaths in 2050 from climate-induced malnutrition might well be achieved without reducing economic growth; furthermore, the total of 250,000 deaths per year attributable to climate change in general would certainly be worth reducing. Bjorn Lomborg, "Climate Change Barely Affects Poverty," *Wall Street Journal,* October 7, 2021, https://www.wsj.com/articles/climate-change-malnutrition -regulation-economic-growth-glasgow-conference-11633551187.

2. Anthony Costello, Mustafa Abbas, Adriana Allen, et al., "Managing the Health Effects of Climate Change," *The Lancet* 373, no. 9676 (May 2009): 1693–1733.

3. Uta Steinwehr, "Fact Check: Is China the Main Climate Change Culprit?" Deutsche Welle, June 30, 2021, https://www.dw.com/en/fact-check-is-china-the-main -climate-change-culprit/a-57777113.

4. Frank Ackerman and Elizabeth A. Stanton, *The Cost of Climate Change* (New York: National Resources Defense Council, 2000), vi, https://www.nrdc.org/sites/default/files/cost.pdf.

5. Ryan Nunn, *Ten Facts About the Economics of Climate Change and Climate Policy* (The Hamilton Project and the Stanford Institute for Economic Policy Research, 2019), 7, https://www.brookings.edu/wp-content/uploads/2019/10/Environmental-Facts_WEB.pdf.

6. Office of the Spokesperson, "U.S.-China Joint Statement Addressing the Climate Crisis," US Department of State, April 17, 2021, https://www.state.gov/u-s-china -joint-statement-addressing-the-climate-crisis/.

7. Lily Kuo and Brady Dennis, "Kerry Calls on China to Do More to Tackle

Climate Change Crisis as China Warns U.S. Pressure Will Derail Cooperation," *Washington Post*, September 2, 2021, https://www.washingtonpost.com/world/asia _pacific/climate-change-kerry-china/2021/09/02/65291fde-0b93-11ec-a7c8-61bb7 b3bf628_story.html.

8. UN General Assembly Resolution 3314 and the ICCPR both highlight self-determination of peoples. Famously, the Quebecois were told in the *Quebec Case* before the Canadian Supreme Court that short of extreme oppression, the Quebecois had to seek their future in democratic Canada.

9. David D. Laitin, *Identity in Formation: The Russian-Speaking Populations in the Near Abroad* (Ithaca, NY: Cornell University Press, 1998).

10. Steven Lee Myers and Ellen Barry, "Putin Reclaims Crimea for Russia and Bitterly Denounces the West," *New York Times*, March 18, 2014, https://www.nytimes .com/2014/03/19/world/europe/ukraine.html?login=email&auth=login-email; John J. Mearsheimer, "Why the Ukraine Crisis Is the West's Fault: The Liberal Delusions That Provoked Putin," *Foreign Affairs* 93, no. 5 (September/October 2014): 2, 5, https://www .jstor.org/stable/24483306.

11. Daniel Treisman, "Why Putin Took Crimea: The Gambler in the Kremlin," *Foreign Affairs* 95, no. 3 (May/June 2016): 4, 6, www.jstor.org/stable/43946857. Also see Michael McFaul, Stephen Sestanovich, and John Mearsheimer, "Faulty Powers: Who Started the Ukraine Crisis?," *Foreign Affairs* 93, no. 6 (November/December 2014): 167–178, www .jstor.org/stable/24483933.

12. N.S., "What Are the Minsk Agreements?" *The Economist*, September 14, 2016, www .economist.com/the-economist-explains/2016/09/13/what-are-the-minsk-agreements.

13. See Alexandra Ma, "Russia Says Its Goal in Ukraine Is to Conquer the Country's Eastern and Southern Regions," *Business Insider Africa*, April 22, 2022, https://africa.businessinsider.com/military-and-defense/russia-says-its-goal -in-ukraine-is-to-conquer-the-countrys-eastern-and-southern/jz4rby1; and John Beyer and Stefan Wolff, "Linkage and Leverage Effects on Moldova's Transnistria Problem." *East European Politics* 32, no. 3 (July 2016): 335–354, https://doi.org/10.1080/21599165 .2015.1124092.

14. Irina Ivanova, "Western Sanctions Are Pummeling Russia's Economy," *CBS News Moneywatch*, April 6, 2022, https://www.cbsnews.com/news/sanctions-russia-economy-effect/.

15. Holly Elyatt, "Washington Hits Back at 'Desperate' Putin," CNBC, September 8, 2022.

16. Fareed Zakaria, "The Only Plausible Path to Keep the Pressure on Russia," *Washington Post*, April 21, 2022, https://www.washingtonpost.com/opinions/2022/04/21/ russia-ukraine-oil-production-saudi-arabia-uae-gulf-states-security/. Zakaria refers to a new study by Steven Cook and Martin Indyk for the Council on Foreign Relations that describes the compromises needed with Saudi Arabia.

17. "Unrest in Eastern Ukraine Risks 'Seriously Destabilizing' Entire Country— UN Rights Official," *UN News*, April 16, 2014, https://news.un.org/en/story/2014/ 04/466392-unrest-eastern-ukraine-risks-seriously-destabilizing-entire-country-un -rights#.U1Ar56x8SNB.

18. Even though the specifics differ, these and the following compromises accord with the spirit of the argument made by Thomas Graham and Joseph Haberman in "The Price of Peace in the Donbas: Ukraine Can't Keep Both Territory and Sovereignty," *Foreign Affairs*, February 25, 2020, https://www.foreignaffairs.com/articles/united-states/2020-02-25/price-peace-donbas.

19. For a study of the ambiguities in the Minsk Protocols, see Duncan Allen, *The Minsk Conundrum: Western Policy and Russia's War in Eastern Ukraine* (London: Chatham House Research Paper, May 22, 2020).

20. Clara Ferreira Marques, "Crimea's Water Crisis Is an Impossible Problem for Putin," Bloomberg, March 19, 2021, www.bloomberg.com/opinion/articles/2021-03-19/russia-vs-ukraine-crimea-s-water-crisis-is-an-impossible-problem-for-putin.

21. "U.S. Energy Information Administration - EIA - Independent Statistics and Analysis," International, U.S. Energy Information Administration (EIA), January 2017, www.eia.gov/international/analysis/country/UKR.

22. Donghui Park and Michael Walstrom, "Cyberattack on Critical Infrastructure: Russia and the Ukrainian Power Grid Attacks," The Henry M. Jackson School of International Studies, October 11, 2017, https://jsis.washington.edu/news/cyberattack-critical-infrastructure-russia-ukrainian-power-grid-attacks/; Kim Zetter, "Inside the Cunning, Unprecedented Hack of Ukraine's Power Grid," *Wired*, March 3, 2016, www.wired.com/2016/03/inside-cunning-unprecedented-hack-ukraines-power-grid/.

23. For a good outline of this start on START, see Michael McFaul, "How Biden Should Deal with Putin: Summits Are Good, but Containment Is Better," *Foreign Affairs*, June 14, 2021, www.foreignaffairs.com/articles/russia-fsu/2021-06-14/how-biden-should-deal-putin.

24. Michael O'Hanlon makes the important observation that the NATO Article 5 guarantee of collective defense does not presuppose an automatic declaration of war if a member is attacked. Instead, it requires consultations to implement a common and "as deemed necessary" response to an armed attack. These consultations could lead to economic sanctions rather than an armed response, making the Article 5 guarantee that much more credible in the event of an attack on an Eastern European member. Even with this qualified understanding, NATO should not be extended further into Eastern Europe unless NATO is prepared to actually act in protection (presumably, therefore, to protect a stable democracy that adds net security to the alliance). See Michael O'Hanlon, *The Art of War in an Age of Peace* (New Haven, CT: Yale University Press, 2021), 72.

25. O'Hanlon, *Art of War in an Age of Peace*, 77. Also see Anton Troianovski, who reports on Dmitri Trenin's (of the Carnegie Moscow Center) analysis of Putin's ambitions in "On Putin's Strategic Chessboard, a Series of Destabilizing Moves," *New York Times*, November 19, 2021, https://www.nytimes.com/2021/11/19/world/europe/russia-putin-belarus-ukraine.html.

26. James Dobbins, Howard J. Shatz, and Ali Wyne, *Russia Is a Rogue, Not a Peer; China Is*

a Peer, Not a Rogue: Different Challenges, Different Responses (Santa Monica, CA: RAND Corporation, 2019), https://www.rand.org/pubs/perspectives/PE310.html. They note that Russia has invaded neighbors Georgia and Ukraine, intervened in Syria, and assassinated domestic political rivals. China has heretofore resisted a nuclear arms competition, but China is capable of reshaping the international order in ways adverse to the United States and its democratic allies, while Russia is not.

27. Randall G. Schriver, "Memo to the Next President: The Inheritance in the Indo-Pacific and the Challenges and Opportunities for Your Presidency," Project 2049 Institute, December 1, 2020, https://project2049.net/2020/12/01/memo-to-the-next-president-the-inheritance-in-the-indo-pacific-and-the-challenges-and-opportunities-for-your-presidency/.

28. Xi announced: "The country must be unified, and it will be unified." For information on Taiwan relations, see Hanns W. Maull, "Dire Straits: Taiwan's Fragile Status Quo," *The Diplomat*, July 3, 2021, https://thediplomat.com/2021/07/dire-straits-taiwans-fragile-status-quo/; and Thomas Wright, "Taiwan Stands Up to Xi," *The Atlantic*, January 15, 2020, https://www.theatlantic.com/ideas/archive/2020/01/taiwans-new-president-is-no-friend-of-beijing/605020/.

29. Robert D. Blackwill and Philip Zelikow, *The United States, China, and Taiwan: A Strategy to Prevent War* (New York: Council on Foreign Relations, 2021).

30. Both sides are currently inserting naval assets in the Taiwan Strait: "U.S. Warship Transits Taiwan Strait after Chinese Assault Drills," Reuters, August 27, 2021, https://www.reuters.com/world/us-warship-transits-taiwan-strait-after-chinese-assault-drills-2021-08-27/.

31. Drawing on a "porcupine" strategy advocated by retired Admiral Stavridis, Robert C. O'Brien and Alexander B. Gray, "How to Deter China from Invading Taiwan," *Wall Street Journal*, September 15, 2021, https://www.wsj.com/articles/china-invade-taiwan-strait-pla-missile-mines-counterinsurgency-biden-xi-tsai-ing-wen-11631721031. A related metaphor describes the strategy.

32. Chris Dougherty, Jennie Matuschak, and Ripley Hunter, *The Poison Frog Strategy: Preventing a Chinese Fait Accompli Against Taiwanese Islands* (Washington, DC: Center for a New American Security, 2021), 8, https://www.cnas.org/publications/reports/the-poison-frog-strategy. A distinctive feature of the poison frog strategy is that one advertises its condition, as the frog does with bright colors.

33. Ishaan Tharoor, "China Shifts the Military Status Quo on Taiwan After Pelosi Visit," *Washington Post*, August 9, 2022.

34. Dipanjan Roy Chaudhury, "India-US-Japan-Australia Quadrilateral Initiative Explores Partnership with EU," *Economic Times*, March 15, 2021, https://economictimes.indiatimes.com/news/politics-and-nation/india-us-japan-australia-quadrilateral-initiative-explores-partnership-with-eu/articleshow/81504113.cms?from=mdr.

35. Charles A. Kupchan, "The Right Way to Split China and Russia: Washington Should Help Moscow Leave a Bad Marriage," *Foreign Affairs*, August 4, 2021,

https://www.foreignaffairs.com/articles/united-states/2021-08-04/right-way-split
-china-and-russia.

36. This section has benefited from the research assistance of Hannah Houpt.

37. Paul R. Kolbe, "With Hacking, the United States Needs to Stop Playing the Victim,"
New York Times, December 23, 2020, https://www.nytimes.com/2020/12/23/opinion/
russia-united-states-hack.html?referringSource=articleShare.

38. See David E. Sanger, David D. Kirkpatrick, and Nicole Perlroth, "The World Once
Laughed at North Korean Cyberpower. No More," *New York Times*, October 15, 2017,
https://www.nytimes.com/2017/10/15/world/asia/north-korea-hacking-cyber
-sony.html; and David E. Sanger and Nicole Perlroth, "Iran Is Raising Sophistica-
tion and Frequency of Cyberattacks, Study Says," *New York Times*, April 15, 2015,
https://www.nytimes.com/2015/04/16/world/middleeast/iran-is-raising-sophisti
cation-and-frequency-of-cyberattacks-study-says.html.

39. "Cyber Incidents Since 2006," Center for Strategic and International Studies, https://
csis-website-prod.s3.amazonaws.com/s3fs-public/210604_Significant_Cyber_Events
.pdf?Ig0rKRzJ9Bc2WS95MJVt1pkZll5eJLE7, accessed August 8, 2022.

40. The NATO Cooperative Cyber Defence Centre of Excellence, *Tallinn Manual on the International Law Applicable to Cyber Warfare*, ed. Michael N. Schmitt (Cambridge, UK: Cambridge University Press, 2013), http://csef.ru/media/articles/3990/3990.pdf.

41. "Paris Call for Trust and Security in Cyberspace: Six Working Groups Launched
to Advance Global Cybersecurity," Cybersecurity Tech Accord, March 1, 2021,
https://cybertechaccord.org/paris-call-for-trust-and-security-in-cyberspace-six
-working-groups-launched-to-advance-global-cybersecurity/; Page Stout-
land, "The Paris Call: A Step Toward Greater Global Cybersecurity," Nuclear
Threat Initiative, January 31, 2019, https://www.nti.org/analysis/atomic-pulse/
paris-call-step-toward-greater-global-cybersecurity/. Also see ongoing processes within
the United Nations to develop an agreement around the application of international law
to cybersecurity and norms to prevent conflict: a background paper for the UN Open-
Ended Working Group states that the 2014–2015 GGE and the corresponding A/70/174
Report agreed that international law applies to cyberspace: "International Law in the
Consensus Reports of the United Nations Groups of Governmental Experts," United
Nations Office for Disarmament Affairs, pp. 2–4, https://unoda-web.s3.amazonaws
.com/wp-content/uploads/2020/01/background-paper-on-international-law-in
-the-gges.pdf.

42. Adam Segal, "The U.S.-China Cyber Espionage Deal One Year Later," Council On Foreign Relations, September 28, 2016, https://www.cfr.org/blog/
us-china-cyber-espionage-deal-one-year-later. NATO condemned China's recent activity in cyberspace: "Statement by the North Atlantic Council in Solidarity with Those
Affected by Recent Malicious Cyber Activities Including the Microsoft Exchange Server
Compromise," NATO, press release issued July 19, 2021, https://www.nato.int/cps/en/
natohq/news_185863.htm; and Astead Herndon, interview with David Sanger, The

Daily, podcast audio, July 21, 2021, https://www.nytimes.com/2021/07/21/podcasts/
the-daily/chinese-microsoft-hack.html?showTranscript=1.

43. Maggie Miller, "Top FBI Official Says There Is 'No Indication' Russia Has Taken
Action Against Hackers," *The Hill*, September 14, 2021, https://thehill.com/policy/
cybersecurity/572184-top-fbi-official-says-there-is-no-indication-russia-has-taken
-action/.

44. Shannon Pettypiece, "Biden-Putin Summit: Key Takeaways from an 'all Business' Meeting
in Geneva," *NBC News*, June 16, 2021, https://www.nbcnews.com/politics/white-house/
biden-putin-summit-key-takeaways-all-business-meeting-geneva-n1271042.

45. Zachary Cohen and Alex Marquardt, "White House Cyber Official Says 'Commitment'
by Ransomware Gang Suggests Biden's Warnings Are Working," CNN, August 4, 2021,
https://www.cnn.com/2021/08/04/politics/neuberger-ransomware-blackmatter/index
.html.

46. Ellen Nakashima and Joseph Marks, "Russia, U.S. and Other Countries Reach
New Agreement Against Cyber Hacking, Even as Attacks Continue," *Washington
Post*, June 12, 2021, https://www.washingtonpost.com/national-security/russia-us-un
-cyber-norms/2021/06/12/9b608cd4-866b-11eb-bfdf-4d36dab83a6d_story.html. Also
see Erica D. Borghard and Shawn W. Lonergan. "Confidence Building Measures for the
Cyber Domain," *Strategic Studies Quarterly* 12, no. 3 (Fall 2018): 10–49.

47. President Biden presented President Putin with a list of prohibited targets at their
Geneva Summit in 2021. See Richard J. Harknett and Joseph S. Nye, "Is Deterrence
Possible in Cyberspace?," *International Security* 42, no. 2 (November 2017): 196–199,
https://doi.org/10.1162/ISEC_c_00290. These attacks involve significant commitments; therefore, if they are fulfilled, state commitments may address the problem; see
Rebecca Slayton, "What Is the Cyber Offense-Defense Balance? Conceptions, Causes,
and Assessment," *International Security* 41, no. 3 (January 2017): 72–109, https://doi
.org/10.1162/ISEC_a_00267.

48. Ellen Barry, "How Russian Trolls Helped Keep the Women's March Out of Lock Step,"
New York Times, Sept. 18, 2022.

49. As has been suggested by Michael Walzer in a thoughtful essay, "The Reform of the
International System," in *Studies of War and Peace*, ed. Øyvind Østerud (Oslo: Norwegian
University Press, 1986), 227–250.

50. Justin Sink, "Biden to Ditch 'America First' in Appeal for Partnership," Bloomberg,
February 19, 2021, https://www.bloomberg.com/news/articles/2021-02-19/
biden-to-ditch-america-first-in-appeal-for-global-partnership.

51. For a good example of how this can work, see Christodoulos Kaoutzanis, *The UN Security Council and International Criminal Tribunals: Procedure Matters* (Cham, Switzerland:
Springer Nature, January 2020).

52. "In Hindsight: Getting Across the Line on Syria's Cross-Border Mechanism,"
Security Council Reports, July 30, 2021, https://www.securitycouncilreport
.org/monthly-forecast/2021-08/getting-across-the-line-reaching-an-agreement-on
-syrias-cross-border-mechanism.php#:~:text=30%20July%202021-,In%20

Hindsight%3A%20Getting%20Across%20the%20Line%20on%20Syria's%20
Cross%2DBorder,humanitarian%20assistance%20into%20Syria's%20northwest.
"Ambiguity Is the Mother of Consensus" is a frequent UN rhetorical tactic, employed
for example in the resolution (UN Security Council Resolution 1441) that authorized
the inspection regime for Iraq.

53. Henry Farrell and Abraham L. Newman, "The Janus Face of the Liberal International Information Order: When Global Institutions Are Self-Undermining," *International Organization* 75, no. 2 (February 2021): 333–358, https://doi.org/10.1017/
S0020818320000302; Sarah Kreps, *Social Media and International Relations*, Elements
in International Relations (Cambridge, UK: Cambridge University Press, July 2020);
and Editorial Board, "The Internet Became Less Free This Year — Again," *Washington
Post*, September 27, 2021, https://www.washingtonpost.com/opinions/2021/09/27/
internet-freedom-decreases-again/.

54. Jan-Werner Müller, *Democracy Rules* (New York: Farrar, Strauss and Giroux, 2021). And
for an excellent overview of the experience of democracy in Europe, Sheri Berman's
Democracy and Dictatorship in Europe: From the Ancien Régime to the Present Day (Oxford:
Oxford University Press, 2019).

55. Sarah Repucci and Amy Slipowitz, *Freedom in the World 2021: Democracy Under
Siege* (Washington, DC: Freedom House, 2021), https://freedomhouse.org/report/
freedom-world/2021/democracy-under-siege.

56. France made this a central theme in its groundbreaking study of cyber interference in
the European 2017 elections. For the seminal study, see Jean-Baptiste Jeangène Vilmer,
A. Escorcia, M. Guillaume, and J. Herrera, *Information Manipulation: A Challenge for our
Democracies* (Paris: Policy Planning Staff [CAPS] of the Ministry for Europe and Foreign
Affairs and the Institute for Strategic Research [IRSEM] of the Ministry for the Armed
Forces, 2018), https://www.diplomatie.gouv.fr/IMG/pdf/information_manipulation_
rvb_cle838736.pdf.

57. David Petraeus and Sheldon Whitehouse, "Putin and Other Authoritarians'
Corruption Is a Weapon—and a Weakness," *Washington Post*, March 8, 2019, https://
www.washingtonpost.com/opinions/2019/03/08/putin-other-authoritarians
-corruption-is-weapon-weakness/.

58. For the People Act of 2021, H.R. 1, 117th Cong. (2021), https://www.congress.gov/
bill/117th-congress/house-bill/1?r=30.

59. Juana Summers, "The House Has Passed a Bill to Restore the Voting Rights Act,"
NPR, August 24, 2021, https://www.npr.org/2021/08/24/1030746011/house
-passes-john-lewis-voting-rights-act. Both bills have passed the House and await a Senate vote.

60. Amy Gutmann, *Liberal Equality* (Cambridge, UK: Cambridge University Press, 1980).

61. For a valuable case for the importance of domestic democratic reform, see Robin Nib-
lett and Leslie Vinjamuri, "The Liberal Order Begins at Home: How Democratic Revival
Can Reboot the International System," in the excellent collection edited by Charles A.
Kupchan and Leslie Vinjamuri, *Anchoring the World: International Order in the Twenty-first*

Century, Essays from the Lloyd George Study Group on World Order (New York: Council on Foreign Relations, 2021), 10–23.

62. Lilliana Mason, Julie Wronski, and John V. Kane, "Activating Animus: The Uniquely Social Roots of Trump Support," *American Political Science Review* 115, no. 4 (November 2021), 1–9, https://doi.org/10.1017/S0003055421000563.

63. Paul Krugman, "The Gentrification of Blue America," *New York Times*, August 27, 2021, https://www.nytimes.com/2021/08/27/opinion/California-housing-price-economy .html.

64. M. T. Anderson, "In Medieval Europe, a Pandemic Changed Work Forever. Can It Happen Again?" *New York Times*, February 16, 2022, https://www.nytimes.com/2022/02/16/ opinion/sunday/covid-plague-work-labor.html.

65. Richard Reeves, "Inequality Built the Trump Coalition, Even if He Won't Solve It," *Las Vegas Sun*, September 19, 2016, https://lasvegassun.com/news/2016/sep/19/ inequality-built-the-trump-coalition-even-if-he-wo/.

66. David Leonhardt, "Our Broken Economy, in One Simple Chart," *New York Times*, August 7, 2017, https://www.nytimes.com/interactive/2017/08/07/opinion/leonhardt-income -inequality.html. Leonhardt is drawing on the seminal work of Thomas Piketty and Raj Chetty. For a deep diagnosis of the dangers of a growing "precariat" of uncertainty and what to do about it, see Michael Graetz and Ian Shapiro, *The Wolf at the Door* (Cambridge, MA: Harvard University Press, 2020); and Kathleen Thelen, "The American Precariat: US Capitalism in Comparative Perspective," *Perspectives on Politics* 17, no. 1 (March 2019): 5–27.

67. Eric Levitz, "Will 'the Great Wealth Transfer' Trigger a Millennial Civil War?," *New York Magazine*, July 18, 2021, https://nymag.com/intelligencer/2021/07/will-the -great-wealth-transfer-spark-a-millennial-civil-war.html.

68. Eric Liu, *Become America: Civic Sermons on Love, Responsibility, and Democracy* (Seattle: Sasquatch Books, 2019), 204. For another insightful take on the challenge of rebuilding the social foundations of democracy, this time from a European observer, see Vittorio Emanuele Parsi, *The Wrecking of the Liberal World Order*, trans. Malvina Parsi (London: Palgrave Macmillan, 2021).

69. Emily Cochrane, "Senate Passes $1 Trillion Infrastructure Bill, Handing Biden a Bipartisan Win," *New York Times*, August 10, 2021, https://www.nytimes.com/2021/08/10/us/ politics/infrastructure-bill-passes.html.

70. Tami Luhby and Katie Lobosco, "What the Democrats' Sweeping Social Spending Plan Might Include," CNN, November 19, 2021, https://www.cnn.com/2021/09/12/politics/ house-reconciliation-package-explainer/index.html. The bill dropped Medicare expansion and free community college. Unfortunately, the bill faced opposition from Democratic senator Joe Manchin from coal state West Virginia, whose vote was essential for Senate passage.

71. Allison Pecorin and Trish Turner, "Universal Pre-K, Free Community College Tuition: What's in $3.5T Budget Bill," *ABC News*, August 9, 2021, https://abcnews.go.com/ Politics/universal-pre-free-community-college-tuition-35t-budget/story?id=79361478.

72. Kevin Rudd, "Short of War: How to Keep U.S.-Chinese Confrontation from Ending in Calamity," *Foreign Affairs*, March/April 2021, https://www.foreignaffairs.com/articles/united-states/2021-02-05/kevin-rudd-usa-chinese-confrontation-short-of-war.

Afterword and Acknowledgments

1. I published a version of this as "An International Liberal Community," in Graham Allison and Gregory Treverton, eds., *Rethinking America's Security* (New York: Council on Foreign Relations/Norton, 1992), 307–333.

2. I sent this op-ed to the *New York Times*, but the staff had no interest in it.

"EUROPE'S OAS" by Michael W. Doyle, June 1, 1990, KINGSTON, NEW JERSEY

What we, the Russians, and the Europeans need now is an Organization of European States—Europe's own version of an Organization of American States. Not the OAS that sometimes served in the 1950s and 1960s as a front organization for US hegemony in Latin America, but (as any Europe-wide organization would have to be) an organization of near equals committed to preserving the peace, fostering economic cooperation, and advancing the cause of universal human values.

An organization of regional "collective security" established like the OAS under Article 52 of the United Nations Charter differs from a "collective defense" organization under Article 51, an alliance such as NATO or the Warsaw Pact, in that it faces as much inward as outward. It is designed to preserve a local peace and foster local cooperation as much as to unite against a common external enemy. Unlike NATO, which a united Germany seems about to join, an OES would include the Soviet Union and the members of the Warsaw Pact. Unlike the Warsaw Pact, an OES would include NATO.

All other alternatives are less acceptable. Having a united Germany join NATO, however unaggressive that body now seems, signals to the Soviet historical consciousness a dangerous shift in the correlation of forces. If the achievements of the Gorbachev era somehow unraveled, it would place the Soviet Union in the isolated geostrategic position it confronted in the 1930s. Having a united Germany join the Warsaw Pact (inconceivable as that seems) would raise for the West an equivalent specter of the dreadful era of the Molotov-Ribbentrop Pact of 1939–1941. A neutral Germany leaves too large a hole in the political space of a Europe that is bound to face difficult tasks of economic cooperation and political upheaval in the years ahead and desperately needs German cooperation and resources. A German member of both NATO and the Warsaw Pact leaves too large and too independent a Bismarckian role for a state that twice before has sought to dominate the continent.

An OES would include a united Germany at its center but also include both the US, an extra-continental power with vital European interests, and the USSR, a great continental power with vital Asian interests. In the long-awaited European peace treaty, the members would establish a pan-European guarantee of collective security and peaceful change. Military forces would both be significantly reduced and then assigned to the OES. Headquartered in a great central European city such as Vienna, an OES could soon become a focus of European diplomacy and social and economic cooperation helping the EEC expand into the new areas of Eastern Europe.

A challenging transition would lie ahead. NATO and the Warsaw Pact would phase out over two or three five-year periods, withdrawing first from the inter-German border and reducing overall troop levels. Germany's membership in NATO would be a temporary measure, one that had to be respected by all as a German choice, but one whose significance should for the Soviets greatly lessen because of its temporary nature and because of the simultaneous beginnings of the OES in which common European interests could soon overshadow the alliances. The spread of democratic forms of legitimacy and market-based methods of economic organization will go a long way toward reducing regional tensions and supporting the regional solidarity a collective security organization needs. Here at last a balance of interests rather than a balance of power would begin to shape the construction and consciousness of the new Europe.

An OES involves risks, of course. Like all attempts to organize international collective security it requires a strong sense of interdependence and common purpose, leadership and diplomatic skill. For lack of such attributes the League of Nations failed and the United Nations soon became stalemated. The alternative to an OES, however, lies in the increasing tensions of the European status quo. And nothing in the attempt to create an OES precludes our return to where we now are. Sometimes failing to move forward is the equivalent of slipping back; sometimes the only course of prudence is innovation. We live in those times today.

Index